Written by two talented school leaders who have truly walked the walk in their own thriving specialist setting, this incredibly practical handbook will ease your path forward like a trusted friend. Through case studies, thinking points and first-person accounts, this book is an invaluable one-stop shop in how to offer exceptional school leadership in the current educational landscape.

Dean Beadle, Autistic Advocate and Speaker

SEN-SATIONAL LEADERSHIP

SEN-sational Leadership is the essential guide to transformative leadership in special education. Tailored for both new and experienced leaders, it offers practical guidance and strategies to both enhance the quality of education and successfully grow specialist provisions.

Covering key topics such as the curriculum, culture, parental engagement, and personal development, the book provides a thorough overview of leading specialist settings. Drawing upon the authors' own rich experiences and conversations with specialist colleagues, chapters include inspiring real-life examples, practical strategies, and prompts to help the reader develop their own leadership and provision. It provides a framework for improving and growing sustainable specialist settings, underpinned by empathetic, collaborative, and innovative leadership, which can be adapted to different educational contexts.

Written by current special school senior leaders, the book brings credible and authentic perspectives on what it means to lead and grow a successful specialist provision. It will be essential reading for all those looking to become a sensational system leader of SEND.

Nicola Brooks is an established leader within specialist education with experience of whole trust leadership. She has been teaching for 20 years in both mainstream and special schools. Nicola is passionate about developing people and culture, with a particular focus on staff and leadership development.

Nicola Whitcombe is an experienced SEND Headteacher, Trust Regional Director, and School Improvement Advisor. As a former SENCO, she is driven by a passion to ensure pupils with additional needs thrive and achieve their potential through high aspirations and exceptional teaching.

SEN-SATIONAL LEADERSHIP

Leading a Successful and Sustainable Specialist Provision

Nicola Brooks and Nicola Whitcombe

Routledge
Taylor & Francis Group
LONDON AND NEW YORK

Designed cover image: © Getty Images

First published 2026
by Routledge
4 Park Square, Milton Park, Abingdon, Oxon OX14 4RN

and by Routledge
605 Third Avenue, New York, NY 10158

Routledge is an imprint of the Taylor & Francis Group, an informa business

British Library Cataloguing-in-Publication Data
A catalogue record for this book is available from the British Library

ISBN: 978-1-032-98919-8 (hbk)
ISBN: 978-1-032-98917-4 (pbk)
ISBN: 978-1-003-60138-8 (ebk)

DOI: 10.4324/9781003601388

Typeset in Interstate
by Apex CoVantage, LLC

CONTENTS

ACKNOWLEDGEMENTS

From Nicola Brooks

Radley – The First Friend. I'm sorry you never got to sniff this book. I miss you.

Tessa – Every word you type, I'll be watching you. My shadow and constant companion. Yes, that was a lot of writing, now we can play fetch!

Otis – My Future Friend. I look forward to meeting you.

Although dogs are my favourite people, I quite like these ones – for Doll and Paul, the best teachers.

From Nicola Whitcombe

To Cadence and Caleb, you inspire me on my journey to make sure I see everything through the lens of a child.

Lee, thank you for your unwavering support and encouragement to further my career. I will be forever grateful. Thank you for picking me up when I've been down.

To Ronnie, thank you for the cuddles.

From both of us

Thank you to Clare Ashworth at Routledge for encouraging us to submit the proposal for this book.

Thank you to Molly Kavanagh at Routledge for your support and answering our questions.

Thank you to Alison Jones for being a fantastic and supportive editor.

Thank you to Dean Beadle for providing the humorous and authentic foreword we wanted.

Thank you to the exceptional Springfields and Reach South Academy Trust team (past and present) and everyone who has been on this journey of school improvement with us.

In particular thanks to the team we couldn't do it without - Sam, Connie, Lee, Liz, Claire, Iian, Darren, and Max - Upper Crust is on us!

Finally, we feel incredibly privileged to have the opportunity to write a book. Everything we do is for our learners, our school, and its community. We received no payment to write this book and have requested that any royalties be paid to our school. Thank you for purchasing this book and supporting our young people.

OUR CONTRIBUTORS

We are indebted to our contributors. You have been central to writing this book and we couldn't have done it without your voice and experience – to paraphrase Issac Newton, we stand shoulder to shoulder with giants.[1] We were keen to speak with leaders from a range of provisions across the country and it has been a humbling experience to hear about the fantastic work taking place in (and beyond) their settings. We're grateful for the generosity with which everyone shared their time and expertise. It is safe to say that the specialist and alternative sector contains a multitude of passionate, dedicated leaders who are driven by a moral purpose to make a difference.

We're also committed to being ambassadors for the SEND community – we wanted to amplify their voices and provide them with a platform to share their lived experiences. After all, the best advice on how to lead a specialist provision comes from those who can best understand and think like our learners.

Alex Tomkins, Headteacher at Greenside School

Alex went to university, not knowing what to do, and studied for a degree in Environmental Studies. He lost interest and failed his dissertation, gaining only a basic degree. Alex's mum worked in the office of a residential special school, and, as he didn't have any job prospects, he applied to be an Assistant Houseparent. In this role he worked with autistic children with complex needs and it inspired him to train to become a teacher. Alex attended another special school for experience, and after five schools became the Headteacher of a local-authority-maintained special school.

Alex is now Headteacher of Greenside School in Stevenage – a large, complex special school with 140 staff supporting the needs of 200 children with Severe Learning Difficulties. Alex has written articles for the Chartered College of Teaching's *Impact* journal and is pursuing a Doctorate of Education.

1 Original wording: "If I have seen further, it is by standing on the shoulders of giants". Isaac Newton (1675). Letter to Robert Hooke. Original can be seen at https://digitallibrary.hsp.org/index.php/Detail/objects/9792

Andrew Poole, Director of School Improvement at The People's Learning Trust

Andrew is a highly experienced school leader with a strong track record of driving improvement and raising attainment. Currently serving as Director of School Improvement at The People's Learning Trust, he has held senior roles including Assistant Head, SENCO, and project coordinator for the DfE's Alternative Provision Specialist Taskforce.

At Everton Free School, Andrew transformed literacy provision, expanded EHCP support from two to almost thirty students, and oversaw significant improvements in GCSE outcomes. His leadership contributed to the school being graded 'Outstanding' in every category by Ofsted in 2024.

Andrew has also successfully led school improvement beyond his own setting and his expertise has been sought nationally, with contributions to local authorities, the Government of Jersey, and the Ministry of Justice.

Recognised as NASEN Leader of the Year in 2023, Andrew is passionate about ensuring that *nothing but the best is good enough* for students, staff, and schools across the People's Learning Trust.

Angela O'Rourke, Headteacher at Southfield SEN School, Hatfield

Angela has been a teacher for nearly 40 years. She has a track record of excellence in leading, managing, and stabilising schools in difficulty and in challenging circumstances. She demonstrates high levels of accountability in strategic and operational management in supporting rapid growth and in getting schools back on track.

Southfield is a primary school for 103 pupils with Learning Difficulties, which include, Autism, Speech Language and Communication Needs, Global Developmental Delay, and other conditions.

Ashley McCormick, SENCO and Senior Leader at Archers Brook School

Ashley started out as a teaching assistant in a special primary school. He then became a teacher and he is now a full time SENCO and senior leader at Archers Brook School, a SEMH provision in Chester. He describes it as a marvellous school with 103 kids all of whom have an EHCP and every day is different!

Bridget Young, Headteacher at The Holmewood School in London

Bridget has been part of The Holmewood School community for more than 12 years, gradually working her way up to becoming Headteacher. Bridget describes it as being her 'life's work'. Bridget is currently completing the National Professional Qualification for Headship. She believes in the importance of trying to learn more about yourself and recommends putting yourself forward for leadership opportunities. Bridget is neurodivergent and was recently diagnosed with ADHD.

The Holmewood School is an independent day school for neurodivergent children and young people aged from 7 to 19 who have a primary diagnosis of autism. All the school's 100 pupils present differently. The school forms part of the Cavendish Group, a group of specialist schools.

Charlotte Barton, Managing Director of Progress Schools

Progress Schools is a collective of 12 independent schools across 13 sites that provide alternative provision (AP). Students are predominantly those who have been permanently excluded, many of whom have an EHCP or undiagnosed SEND.

Charlotte is an experienced leader in AP, serving as an Executive Head. She is also a qualified teacher and SENCO with a Master's Degree in Educational Leadership. Charlotte regularly writes for Schools Week.

Danielle Cooper, BEM, Behavioral and Attendance Lead at Everton Free School

You can read about Danielle's story from TA to teacher in Chapter 6.

Dean Beadle, autistic speaker and trainer

Dean has spent 20 years publicly sharing his experiences of being autistic. Alongside delivering conference keynotes across Europe, Dean has completed four seminar tours of Australia and New Zealand. All in all, he has delivered over a thousand keynotes, INSET sessions, talks, and webinars worldwide, and has become known for his engaging delivery style, which is both humorous and thought-provoking in equal measure.

Devoting his career to being a change-maker, Dean has used his own experiences to increase understanding and challenge the negative attitudes that autistic people come up against in society. Only once society better understands the autistic experience will it be able to better meet needs and create spaces that are both accessible to and empowering for autistic people.

Dean holds honorary roles at three autism related UK charities. He is president of AP Cymru, an autistic led charity which has created an empowering community for autistic people and their families in Wales. He is also patron for OneToOne Enfield, a charity that supports LD and autistic adults in North London and SPACE, a parent-led organisation in Hertfordshire. Dean also has a class named after him at The Springfields Academy.

Emma Twell, Safeguarding and SEND Specialist and autistic adult

Emma is a Safeguarding and SEND Specialist, Ex-Headteacher, Education Consultant, and School Governor with lived experience of Autism and ADHD. Emma has experience of leading specialist provisions as well as whole trust leadership experience.

Gemma James and Melissa Taylor, Lead Teachers, Ellesmere College

Ellesmere College in Leicester is a large, all-through special school for 439 students with a range of special educational needs.

Gemma was an Early Years Foundation Stage (EYFS) teacher in a mainstream primary. She worked in Year 1, where she observed learners starting the curriculum despite not being developmentally ready for it. She was always interested in SEND and became a SENCO. She enjoyed working with children with additional needs and seeing the small steps progress they made. Gemma decided to make the move into specialist settings and got a job at Ellesmere. On arrival she job shared with Melissa and they are still job sharing 6 years later!

Melissa completed her teacher training in a special school. She grew up alongside a family member who is autistic and this sparked her desire to be a SEND teacher. She started in EYFS with autistic children and children with Profound and Multiple Learning Difficulties (PMLD). When she moved to Ellesmere she was paired with Gemma as a job share and the rest, as they say, is history! They have worked and researched together to establish the EYFS provision at Ellesmere.

Helen Parry, Head of Foundation Curriculum/Mental Health and Wellbeing Lead at Three Towers Alternative Provision Academy

I first discovered my passion for SEN settings when I took a role as art lead teacher in a boys' SEMH school. Three years later I moved to a large AP in Wigan and became Head of Foundation Curriculum. As an art practitioner I have had an interest in mental health and wellbeing for as long as I can remember and am a big advocate of the benefits of participating in the arts. I enjoy the role as I believe in the setting I am in and the positive impact it has for our children and their families. I have gone on to study for the MA Leadership of School Mental Health and Wellbeing and am currently completing my dissertation.

Jo Dennis-Minns, late diagnosed neurodivergent with lived experience of autism, OCD, and situational mutism

Jo has experience of working for local authorities as well as the Autism Education Trust. She is the founder of SLCN Training and is passionate about communication. She is late-diagnosed autistic with OCD and selective/situational mutism.

Julliet Doherty, Head of Adult Services at Ascent Autism Specialist College

Julliet is an experienced specialist leader and has been in education for more than 30 years. She started as a mainstream secondary English teacher before becoming Head of Drama. She was Head of Sixth Form at Ascent Autism College, part of the charity Remarkable Autism Limited, before becoming Head of Adult Services. She says she works in a 'joyous place' and that this is where she will retire. Julliet was a finalist at the TES School Awards 2024 in the Specialist Provision School Leader of the Year Award.

Juliette Baldwin, Headteacher at EOTAS, Swindon

Juliette is an experienced teacher and leader with experience of both mainstream and AP. Juliette's leadership journey has seen her progress from a Head of Maths to Acting Principal of a large mainstream secondary. Juliette joined EOTAS, an AP in Swindon, as Deputy Headteacher in 2019 and she is now Headteacher.

Karen Parker, Head Teacher at Sir Charles Parsons School

Karen trained as a secondary History teacher before taking a job at a specialist provision. She initially moved to Sir Charles Parsons School as a Humanities teacher. She has been at the school for 26 years and has held several roles from middle leadership to her current role as Head Teacher.

Sir Charles Parsons School is a special school for secondary age pupils in Newcastle upon Tyne with around 210 students and 110 staff.

Kelly Deighton, SENCO and Senior Leader at West Exe School

You can learn more about Kelly and how she implemented an alternative curriculum in Chapter 2.

Kimberley Legg, Assistant Headteacher, Addington School

Kimberley was told that she would make a great teacher, but she was initially reluctant to enter the profession because she thought she might get bored in mainstream. She joined a special school as a Learning Support Assistant and worked her way up to an unqualified teacher role before gaining QTS. Kimberley moved to Addington to take on a senior leadership role and has been there for 7 years. She's had different responsibilities during that time, including leading on assessment and Pupil Premium.

Addington School is an Outstanding Special School in Wokingham and a founding member of Ascendancy Partnership Trust. All learners at Addington have an EHCP. They currently have 310 pupils across two sites, aged between 3 and 19 years.

Lauren Smith, autistic adult and postgraduate researcher

Lauren Smith is an autistic author and PhD student. Her research focuses on holistic wellbeing within AP settings. Lauren is the founder of A Different Perspective Community Interest Company, a community group supporting young autistic people and their families.

Lucy Kreczak, Deputy Headteacher at River Tees Hospital School

Lucy has been teaching for more than 15 years. Her background is as a Secondary Art teacher, but she has always been attracted to specialist provisions. Her first job was in a pupil support unit in Scotland for students with SEMH needs - she loved it! She has experience of running nurture rooms as well as mainstream leadership experience as a SENCO. She has worked in a variety of specialist settings, including SEMH, Autism, and PMLD. She says that even when you're experienced at specials schools, a new special setting can feel like a new world!

Lydia Colios, Assistant Headteacher and Designated Safeguarding Lead, Addington School

Lydia's mum was a teacher, which initially put her off! As a teenager, Lydia was a carer for a child with cerebral palsy and this developed her interest in SEND. After gaining her degree in philosophy, Lydia worked as a TA and one day looked at the teacher at the front of the class and said, "I want to do that!".

In her third year of teaching, Lydia joined Addington, a large special needs school in Wokingham. She felt nurtured to develop as a leader and reflects on the potential the previous Headteacher saw in her. As a result, she's been promoted from Head of Department to Associate Assistant Head and she is now Assistant Head and Designated Safeguarding Lead.

Matt Bindon, Trust Lead for Alternative Provision and Specialism at the Ted Wragg Trust

Matt is an experienced teacher, having spent 15 years in mainstream schools in pastoral and SEND, middle, and senior leadership roles. He then spent 5 years as a Headteacher of a multi-site AP in the South West and then went onto to lead a special measures all-through SEMH school. Matt is now the Trust Lead for Alternative Provision and Specialism at the Ted Wragg Trust. The Ted Wragg Trust is a mainstream trust of 18 schools, consisting of primary, secondary, and all through provisions.

Miranda, late diagnosed autistic adult and parent to an autistic child

Miranda's reflections on her time at school have been invaluable. She says that, "the most helpful part of secondary school was being allowed to be a student librarian. I found this such a sanctuary where I could put books in order, make recommendations, and support younger pupils with homework. I was part of a quirky little group who all had additional pastoral support from the chief librarian who would check in with us. I also found that none of those who bullied me ever came to the library, so I was safe".

Natalia Pragnell, Senior Leader for Equity in Education, IAP Lead, and Teacher of History at West Exe School

You can learn more about Natalia and how she implemented an alternative curriculum in Chapter 2.

Remie Colledge, Neurodivergent Speaker, Trainer, and Writer

Remie is a freelance neurodivergent Speaker, Trainer, and Writer. She has particular insight into eating disorder recovery and is an advocate for reducing health and employment inequalities. Remie is passionate about working together to create a more neuro-inclusive world to live, work, and belong.

Robert Bell, Headteacher at Consilium Evolve

Robert has been a leader and educator for nearly 20 years. Starting out as a Physical Education teacher in a traditional secondary setting (he prefers to use the terms 'traditional' and 'non-traditional' settings as opposed to 'mainstream' and 'specialist'), he quickly developed a passion for teaching and learning. Robert progressed from Head of Department to Assistant Head and then Deputy Head. However, he felt that the curriculum in some traditional settings was too narrow and did not suit all learners.

Consequently, Robert took the opportunity to work in an AP for permanently excluded children that had been rated 'requires improvement'. Robert's commitment to making a difference there was so strong that he commuted from Leeds to Essex for two and a half years! Alongside his staff team, they improved the provision and secured 'Good'.

Consilium Evolve is a specialist AP Academy supporting secondary age students who experience emotionally based school avoidance. Evolve fosters each student's growth, empowering them to find their place in the world regardless of the challenges they've faced.

Sarah Cullip, Behaviour Lead at Greenside School

Sarah is Behaviour Lead at Greenside School in Stevenage; a large, complex special school supporting the needs of 200 children with severe learning difficulties. Sarah supports their 140 staff to develop a therapeutic thinking approach.

Zoe, autistic teenager

Zoe is currently studying for her A-Levels and has a place waiting for her at university to study Marketing and Advertising. When she is older, she hopes to travel to Japan or Korea. This is not surprising, given that going on trips, escaping school, and having fun with her friends is what she enjoys most about education.

FOREWORD

Okay, so I'll address the elephant in the room straight away. I'm writing the foreword to a book on how to be a specialist school leader, but I'm not a school leader. There, I've said it. I've never been a headteacher nor am I ever likely to be. If, by some unfathomable twist of fate, I was handed a headship, the curriculum in my school would be taught exclusively through the prism of the life and times of Kylie Minogue. History lessons would involve researching the year Kylie first appeared in *Neighbours*. Maths would consist of adding up how many 'La-la-las' were uttered in the seminal *Can't Get You Out of My Head*. And PE? Interpretive dance to *I Should Be So Lucky*. Ofsted would combust.

So, I'm the first to admit that I'm far from an expert on school leadership, and on the surface of it should not be writing this foreword. However, as an autistic child who initially struggled to get my needs met in education due to poor leadership, I know only too well the power headteachers hold. And as an inset trainer who has delivered sessions in hundreds of schools over the past 20 years, I have seen first-hand the difference good leadership makes to the culture of a setting.

If you're reading this book, then it's probable that you have just started in a new specialist headship or are considering making that career move. Congratulations, you are in a position to make such a huge positive difference.

As a progressive headteacher, it is you that will drive the core values of your setting. You'll be setting the tone. Many of your students will have negative past experiences in education. A number of them will have experienced trauma. Some may have previously attended settings that exposed them to harmful behaviourist approaches that stamped all over their autonomy. It is you as the school leader who ensures that those learners get a better deal in your setting. How? By guiding staff to ensure that their practice is neuroaffirming. By guaranteeing that learners' boundaries are always validated and respected. By showing learners that they are safe in your care.

Now if that sounds like a daunting task, then fear not because this book has got you covered. Written by two talented school leaders who have truly walked the walk in their own thriving specialist setting, this incredibly practical handbook will ease your path forward like a trusted friend. Through case studies, thinking points and first-person accounts, this book is an invaluable one-stop shop in how to offer exceptional school leadership in the current educational landscape.

I was particularly delighted to see the book turn its focus to creating inclusive workspaces for neurodivergent staff. This is an often under-discussed topic in other literature but it's powerfully covered here. As the authors say towards the end of the book: "Seeing adults with additional needs and disabilities in our settings matters. Representation shapes culture and shows staff and learners what's possible. When educators with SEND are visible in classrooms, leadership teams, and educational communities, they become role models, inspiring confidence and helping create organisations that value difference". I couldn't agree more.

Another highlight of the book is how it prioritises student wellbeing. As it says in Chapter 6: "For many learners with SEND, progress in literacy, numeracy, and other areas can only take place if they feel safe . . .". That for me highlights the brilliance of this book. Whilst it looks in detail at every logistical aspect of school leadership, it does so through the continual lens of student safety.

Now, it's almost time for me to stop rabbiting on and let you get on with reading the book, but first I'd like to take a brief moment to tell you about a school leader who had a huge impact on my life.

Let's go back through the mists of time to 1999. Britney Spears was finding fame, Peggy still ran the Vic in EastEnders and me? I was a nine-year old at a crossroads. Half-way through year 5, my school placement had completely broken down. I'd been suspended more times than you can count and our family trust in the headteacher to meet my needs had evaporated. When we looked for alternative placements in other local primaries, they all refused me. It seemed I was the 'naughty boy' they wouldn't take a risk on.

Mrs Lyons bucked the trend. Pauline Lyons was the headteacher of a local primary school and she believed in me. She ignored the ableist rumour mill and behaviourist nonsense. Her only concern was how to successfully meet my needs. What can we do to smooth this nine-year old's transition to us? What can we do to make him feel safe?

I will never forget during my induction interview, she asked me if I had any questions for her. What would I like to know about my new school? My instinctive answer was: "I'd like to see what the toilets are like". Instead of dismissing me or invalidating my request, she sprung to her feet and personally took me on a guided tour of the loos. It seems like a small trivial gesture, but for me as a nine-year old, it was enormous. Knowing what the toilets were like was clearly important to me and she respected that. She showed me that my needs mattered. I walked away thinking that I might be okay at this new school after all. Maybe I'd be safe with Mrs Lyons. And I absolutely was.

And that's the crux of it. It's easy to think that being a headteacher is just juggling budgets, fixing roofs and sitting through interminable Teams meetings. But it's so much more than that. It's sitting with a child in distress and co-regulating with them. Those positive interactions in the corridor that makes a learner feel seen. Those times when you guide staff to truly get it right for their young people.

It's taking a moment to give that nervous nine-year old a guided tour of the toilets during his induction interview. Devoting that time to showing him that he matters. That he belongs. And maybe, just maybe, it's advocating for a personalised curriculum via the prism of Kylie Minogue because that's what a particular learner needs in order to thrive. Your learners need you to be *their* Mrs Lyons, championing their needs, safety and sense of belonging. And if you're looking for trusted practical guidance on how to do just that, then this book is definitely the best place to start.

Dean Beadle
Autistic advocate and speaker

Introduction

This introduction shares the purpose of this book: to inform, inspire, and support those leading, or aspiring to lead, specialist and alternative provisions. As the number of children with special educational needs and disabilities (SEND) continues to rise, the demand increases not only for high-quality specialist education, but for educational leaders to make this possible. Across England, the specialist sector is changing - free schools are opening, existing settings are expanding, and alternative provisions (APs) are increasing. This change reflects not only the complexity of need but also the rapidity with which we, as educators, must respond.

Yet growth, on its own, is not enough. Specialist and alternative settings need leaders who are both compassionate and passionate, able to think strategically while responding operationally, and, most importantly, leaders who stay true to the belief that children and families come first.

Although leadership in any context is demanding, the specialist sector brings unique challenges: acute financial pressures, the rising complexity of pupil need, the widening gap between capacity and demand, the requirement for multi-agency working, and a growing responsibility to support mainstream counterparts.

But within these challenges lies the opportunity to build provisions that are nurturing, innovative, and life-changing for children. This chapter explores the complex and rewarding reality of leading specialist provisions and the expectations placed on leaders as the sector becomes more stretched. We share our own leadership journeys, recognising the lack of leadership guidance that includes specialist voices. It is this gap (and the motivation to change it) that led us to write this book.

Most of all, this introductory chapter is a call to action. Whether you're already a leader in a specialist provision, or someone considering stepping into this role, we hope it helps you feel seen, supported, and excited to lead in specialist and alternative settings.

The urgent case for specialist leaders

The number of children with additional needs is increasing, reflected in a rise in the percentage of pupils with an Education, Health and Care Plan (EHCP) from 3.1% in 2019 to 5.3% in

DOI: 10.4324/9781003601388-1

2025 (Department for Education, 2025). This rise in EHCPs has placed increasing pressure on specialist and alternative settings, which are growing in number yet struggling to keep pace with demand. In 2019, 37 new special free schools were announced by the Government (Department for Education, 2020), with a further 15 announced in the Spring 2024 Budget (Whittaker, 2024). Research by *Schools Week* suggests there are approximately 4,000 more learners enrolled in special schools than their reported capacity (Booth, 2024). This means nearly two-thirds of special schools are operating at or above their intended capacity, compared with just 17% of mainstream primary schools and 23% of secondary schools (Booth, 2024). Government data also show the percentage of pupils in alternative provision (AP) rose by almost 20% between 2022/23 and 2023/24, returning to pre-pandemic levels (Department for Education, 2024).

In response to this growing demand, in March 2025 the Government committed over £700 million to fund another 10,000 specialist places (Department for Education, 2025b). The number of Resource Bases (RBs) or specialist units attached to mainstream settings is also expected to rise significantly. As the sector expands and diversifies, the need for high-quality, passionate leaders (like you!) becomes even more pressing. This book offers insight into leading a specialist provision, providing both existing and aspiring leaders with the support, guidance, and inspiration to meet these demands. When we refer to specialist provisions we include:

- Pupil Referral Units (PRUs)
- Alternative Provisions (APs)
- Nurture Bases
- Internal Alternative Provisions (IAPs)
- Resource Bases (RBs)
- Hospital schools
- Special schools (maintained and non-maintained)

As the sector expands, the role of a specialist leader has never been more demanding or more vital. Over the past decade, schools have become more complex, with rising accountability and the growth of multi-academy trusts (MATs). At the same time, our learners are changing too. Not only are there more children with EHCPs, but there is a notable rise in pupils entering school without being school-ready. This could be due to the long-term effects of the Covid-19 pandemic, the widening disadvantage gap, or the increase in screen time for toddlers. In Reception, more children now require intimate care or targeted support with speech and language development (Powell et al., 2024). Effective specialist leaders must take time to understand these children, their needs, and the staff who support them every single day.

These increasing demands are not without consequence, and being a specialist leader is challenging. Research focusing on specialist provisions is rare, however broader data show that although more than 90% of headteachers under retirement age remain in post each year, the overall retention has fallen since 2012, particularly in secondary schools (Lynch et al., 2017). Reversing this trend is crucial, given that headteachers become more effective, and have greater influence, the longer they stay in the same school, with a window of 3-7 years being particularly impactful (Zuccollo et al., 2023). If the guidance in this book supports headteachers to remain in post and to lead schools where children feel safe, seen, and able to grow, then for us it would have been successful.

Despite the pressures, leading a specialist provision remains one of the most exciting and meaningful roles in education. For those who step into it, the opportunity to transform lives is immense. We view leading a specialist provision as a privilege - a notion that also radiates from our case study contributors. Leading a specialist provision requires astute financial management, deep knowledge of SEND legislation, awareness of therapeutic interventions, and the ability to collaborate effectively with external agencies. Increasingly, specialist leaders are also expected to extend their influence beyond their own settings, supporting mainstream schools through outreach and partnerships. We hope this book supports you to meet these challenges with confidence, providing the guidance, inspiration, and insight for you to thrive as a specialist leader and make a lasting difference for your learners. The thinking points below encourage you to reflect on your motivations as a leader and the principles that shape your practice.

Thinking points

- What motivates you to be a leader in a specialist or alternative setting?
- How do your personal values shape the way you lead and make decisions?
- What do you view as your personal and professional strengths? How might these help you meet the unique challenges of leading a specialist provision?
- Which parts of your practice could benefit from reflection or development over the next year?
- What are you hoping to gain by reading this book?

Writing the book we needed

Nicola W and I always wanted to become teachers and we went straight from university into teacher training. Collectively, we've been in education for more than 35 years, with 20 of those in specialist provisions. Neither of us ever thought we'd be authors. Yet, as Toni Morrison, the Pulitzer and Nobel Prize winning author suggests, if the publication you wished existed isn't on the shelf, then it's up to you to bring it to life (Morrison, 1981, as cited in Quote Investigator®, 2018). The book we wanted was a guide for leaders in specialist education that was practical, relevant, and rooted in the day-to-day realities of supporting children with additional needs.

In January 2017, we found ourselves part of a leadership team at a special school deemed as 'Requiring Improvement'. Not only did we need to improve the quality of education for learners rapidly, we also needed to grow the provision to remain financially viable. Unfortunately, with very few leadership publications referencing specialist settings, there was little guidance on how to do this.

We therefore wrote this book because we needed it ourselves. Our conversations with other specialist colleagues suggest that existing leadership development programmes don't prepare people fully for the unique challenges of specialist settings. As Julliet Doherty, Head of Adult Services at Ascent Autism Specialist College, explains:

> *There aren't any relevant qualifications for specialist leaders. The National Professional Qualification for Headship is quite a mainstream qualification – it's not the job that we do. In a big mainstream secondary you can sometimes have little connection with the young people. You follow the bell and everyone is rushing. One of my colleagues in mainstream thinks their school is working well when it's quiet and everyone's in class. I think my provision is working well when I hear laughter and people are directly connected to the students.*

This book is our attempt to fill the gap left by current leadership development programmes and the available qualifications, and provide guidance, strategies, and insights relevant to the realities of leading a specialist provision. It is designed not only for those in specialist settings, but, given the increasing need for *all* settings to be more inclusive, for colleagues in mainstream schools who are looking for strategies that transfer. You may be curious to find out what leading a specialist provision is like or perhaps you're looking to understand how you can be a supportive and collaborative ally. Perhaps you're a governor or trustee of an AP looking for ways to support your leadership team. Maybe you're a leader in commerce who wants a fresh perspective on leadership from a different context. Maybe you're leading inclusion across a MAT. Either way, this book is a celebration of what makes the specialist sector, well special, and we hope it confirms to you that it's a great place to be a leader. We hope it goes some small way to helping you feel inspired, confident, and part of a growing network of specialist provisions. If our case study contributors have shown us anything, it is that those who work in specialist settings are happy to help and support each other, so do reach out to anyone who inspires or resonates with you.

One leader doesn't suit all

A phrase often-heard in specialist provisions is that 'one size *doesn't* fit all' and the same could be said of leaders. Ask 100 people who the most effective Prime Minster was during the last 20 years and you'll probably get eight different answers (that's how many Prime Minsters there have been from 2005 to May 2026). Everyone has an opinion on what makes an effective leader and the type of leader they wish to follow. Therefore, we understand we won't have been effective leaders for everyone we've worked with. As John C. Maxwell (2014) suggests, a leader knows the path and shows the way, but ultimately, they can't make everyone follow them. Part of leadership is accepting that while you lead everyone, not everyone will want to be led by you.

Neither of us are perfect leaders - we both have our flaws and areas for development. Likewise, this book doesn't have all the answers; to paraphrase Professor Dylan Wiliam (2018), a leadership approach can be effective in some contexts, but no single leadership approach or leader is universally effective. What this book *will* give you, however, is a broad insight into leading a specialist provision and signpost you to the incredibly supportive network of specialist leaders who are out there to help you. As current leaders in a specialist provision, we understand the complexities and possibilities of the sector. As we write this in June 2026, we are no longer 'Requires Improvement' but a thriving, innovative, and successful specialist provision for 275 young people between the ages of 4-19 - a growth in pupil numbers of over 160% in 8 years. From our conversations with colleagues across the sector, it's clear that every setting faces their own challenges and opportunities and that no single approach works universally. What makes leadership effective is a willingness to learn, reflect, and collaborate. By sharing our experience, along with the insights of those we've spoken to, we hope to help you navigate your own path as a specialist leader.

How to read this book

In his essay, *The Death of the Author*, the French literary theorist, Roland Barthes (1977), proposed that once a work is written, it belongs not only to its creator but its readers. How you read this publication (and what you take from it) will be shaped by you, your experiences, interests, and context. Although each chapter stands alone, meaning if you wish, you can start with the chapter most meaningful to you, the book moves from looking inward to looking outward. Most chapters include:

- **thinking points** to help you reflect on your own practice
- a **leadership scenario** to explore how you might respond in real situations
- a **case study** showing how other specialist leaders have navigated similar challenges
- an **activity** that applies ideas from the chapter
- one or more **learning from lived experiences**, so the perspectives of young people and adults with SEND are valued and inform practice
- real-life **anecdotes** and advice from leaders of specialist settings
- suggestions for **further reading**.

The **Foreword**, written by the autistic speaker and trainer, Dean Beadle, provides a neurodivergent perspective of education and forefronts our commitment to learning from lived experience. This is complemented by this **Introduction**, which establishes our ethos towards leadership and SEND and explains why we've written this book. The rest of the book can be summarized as follows.

- **Chapter 1** focuses on establishing your values and how these underpin your vision as a leader of a specialist provision.
- **Chapters 2-4** focus on the core business of an educational setting, looking at curriculum, pedagogy, and assessment through a specialist lens.

- **Chapter 5**, with its focus on personal development, starts to broaden our perspective, and to think about learners transitioning on from our provision and how this can be supported by enriching experiences and community links.
- **Chapter 6** explores therapeutic approaches and the role of an enabling environment, showing how they underpin effective classroom practice.
- If Chapters 2–6 focus primarily on the children in our settings, **Chapters 7 and 8** focus on another important group of people – the staff team. Here, we explore current issues in recruitment and retention as well as the importance of staff development and wellbeing.
- In **Chapter 9**, we turn our attention to families and the important role they play in knowing and enabling their children.
- **Chapter 10** looks at the challenges and opportunities that come with growing a specialist provision.
- **Chapter 11** looks outward, focusing on partnerships and relationships beyond your setting.
- Finally, after looking outwards, our **Conclusion** looks forwards, anticipating the key issues and opportunities facing specialist provisions in the years ahead.

How will reading this book benefit you?

There are thousands of leadership books, so what makes this one right for you?

- *Relatability* – we know what it's like to lead both in mainstream and specialist settings and to experience the demands and rewards daily.
- *Credibility* – you want to read a book where the authors are actually doing the job they're writing about. We're senior leaders based in a large, all-through special school working with (and learning from) learners, families, and staff each day.
- *Lived experience* – we understand the day-to-day realities of leading a specialist provision and can reflect on our learning and development as leaders.
- *Experience of successfully growing a specialist provision* – we've gone from 104 pupils to 275 pupils in 10 years: an increase of more than 160% in pupil numbers.
- *Experience of school improvement* – we've helped move a school from 'Requires Improvement' to 'Good' and beyond.
- *Practical insights from others* – you want to hear how leaders in specialist settings across the country have achieved success and grown their provisions.
- *Valuing lived experience* – you want to learn from the lived experience of those with additional needs and strive for leadership that reflects the young people you serve.

If this feel familiar or relevant to your leadership role then this book is for you – keep reading!

The school that helped us grow: An introduction to ourselves as authors

I'm Nicola Brooks and I'm pleased to introduce you to my co-author, Nicola Whitcombe. My respect for Nicola W stems from her humility and authenticity – she is simply the most child-centred practitioner I have ever met. Our respect for each other stems from the fact that we are both driven by a strong moral purpose for equity and social justice. We want to make a difference, not just for individual children or our immediate school community, but for the whole of society – in fact, the world. We don't just want children in our school to benefit; we want *all* children in *all* schools to benefit (as well as the wider SEND community), and that's why we're writing this book. Later in this chapter, we'll explore the social model of disability and for us it's about modelling this and actively dismantling barriers and leading change, rather than waiting for change to happen.

Nicola W started her career as a class teacher in a mainstream primary school. Nicola is one of those people born to be a primary teacher, with an infectious energy (she has a degree in Theatre and Performance), expressive hand gestures, and beautiful handwriting. She was a leader from the start, achieving the Rights Respecting School Award early on in her career, showcasing her commitment to equality.

Moving schools to become Inclusion Leader, Nicola followed her continuing interest in SEND with further postgraduate study, achieving a PG Cert in Autism, and the NA SENCO (National Award for Special Educational Needs Coordination). Her humility shines through in the fact that she first and foremost calls herself a SENCO (Special Educational Needs Co-ordinator). Nicola's experience of overseeing a Resource Base helped to develop her strategic leadership skills and provided her with extensive partnership and multi-agency working.

Our paths, though in this case it's probably more fitting to say wires, crossed during a phone call in the autumn of 2017 when Nicola enquired about the position of SENCO at Springfields. I recall being honest about our current situation and the desperate need for things to improve. I spoke about my passion for change and the desire I had to improve not only our provision but also to play a wider part in SEND system leadership. Fortunately, what I said resonated with Nicola and, after a competitive interview process, she joined us as SENCO. Looking back, it was a pivotal moment that shaped both of our careers.

Our organisation has been a different place since Nicola joined. Although she is both knowledgeable and visionary when it comes to SEND provision, she is not a hero leader. She believes in the strength of the team and in developing a distributed leadership model that isn't person dependent. Her experience at all tiers of leadership means that she has true empathy and understanding of leading specialist provisions. Her contribution to bid writing and interviewing as part of the Free School and Alternative Provision bid process demonstrates her understanding of SEND at both the whole trust and regional level. As well as being our Executive Headteacher, she is also a Regional Director for our trust. I am always learning from her and I'm sure that you will too.

I, Nicola B, could not be more different from Nicola W – I certainly don't have nice handwriting and I had no intention of ever teaching in a specialist provision. In fact, if you had told me during my teacher training that I would spend most of my career in the specialist sector I would probably have laughed. I always wanted to be a teacher (I used to line my Playmobil® people up and take a register) and despite seeing the realities of teaching from my mum, I wasn't deterred. Like many secondary teachers, I was driven by the love of my subject (English Literature) and inspiring children to love Shakespeare, poetry, and books as much as my English teachers (Mr Alderson, Mrs Bolwell, and Miss Fleming) inspired me. Writing a book is therefore a dream come true, even if I imagined it would be about dragons or talking dogs.

I was fortunate to secure my first teaching position at a wonderful mainstream secondary school in Wiltshire. Large, leafy green and with school sheep outside my window – it was perfect. I was keen on becoming a Head of English and held different positions within my department. However, during my leadership of GCSE English I became concerned that I was losing sight of children as individuals, instead seeing them as grades. In large year groups of nearly 300 children, I was worried that my attention was focused on a small group of borderline students each year rather than seeing each pupil as an individual.

When the role of Head of English and Whole School Literacy came up at a local special school I went for a look round. I felt that if I was going to leave my current school (which I loved) it needed to be for something completely different. The thought of being able to understand and respond to the needs of individual children appealed to me. It was also completely different. My current timetable reflected my strengths at teaching exam classes, and it was GCSE and A-Level heavy – moving to specialist provision would give me an opportunity to leave my comfort zone. I still remember the unpleasant comments from some of my colleagues when I shared news of my move – the insinuations that I wouldn't cope and would be doing supply before Christmas, and the dramatic declaration that it would end my career as no mainstream school would ever employ me again!

It's lucky then that I've never looked back. I've had some fantastic opportunities across our multi-academy trust (MAT), leading Continuing Professional Development (CPD) across 14 schools in 4 different counties, but I've never quite been able to leave behind the joys and challenges that come with working in the specialist sector. September 2025 marks 20 years since I started my teacher training and what I'd tell my younger self (and you) is to keep an open mind because it is the career path I initially disregarded that has brought me the greatest joy.

Although both our career pathways have been different, Nicola W and I are united by the same ethos:

- We're not the same leaders we were a decade ago (thank goodness!). The best leaders reflect, adapt, and learn from experience, continually evolving their practice.
- Leadership is a set of skills that can be developed and shaped through learning and by experiencing different contexts. The word 'skills' emphasises that leadership capacity is not fixed – it can be practised, refined, and developed.
- Leadership learning is often experiential (and sometimes accidental!), emerging from real-world experience, reflection, and learning on the job.
- Different contexts require different leadership approaches and styles – that's why we've included case studies from a range of leaders in different specialist provisions.

- Part of being a leader is to develop other leaders. As Mary Parker Follett (1940) – the 'mother of modern management' – describes: 'Leadership is not defined by the exercise of power but by the capacity to increase the sense of power among those led. The most essential work of the leader is to create more leaders'.
- Good leaders build a diverse team that complements their strengths and weaknesses. To paraphrase Lin-Manuel Miranda (2015), American singer, songwriter, and all-round genius, you shouldn't be the smartest person in the room.
- You can get smarter, however, by reading lots – leaders should be readers, something former US President Harry S. Truman intimates (Truman Library Institute, n.d.).
- Being a leader is a privilege. We believe in leading ethically and working within the Nolan Principles, or The Seven Principles of Public Life (UK Government, 1995).
- People come to work in specialist settings because they care about children and want to make a difference. McGregor's 'Theory Y' (1960) reminds us that most people are naturally motivated and want to do well. When leaders listen, seek feedback, and act on it, they create the conditions for creating great organisations.
- We're not concerned with titles or status. As American author John C. Maxwell (1998) suggests, leadership isn't defined by hierarchy but about having an impact on people's lives.
- We practise servant leadership: being there for children, staff, and the responsible stewardship of public money.
- We model relational leadership: valuing connections, collaboration, and recognising that the answer often lies outside of us.
- We use democratic leadership approaches to foster inclusivity, shared values, openness, and compassion.

Taken together, these principles and skills offer a glimpse into the principles that guide us as leaders. We don't claim to have all the answers, but we do believe that reflecting on what matters to you, and the kind of leader you want to become, is essential to becoming an authentic and meaningful leader.

Thinking points

We've outlined our principles above, but every leader's values look different. Spend some time exploring yours using the prompts below:

- Which principles sit at the heart of who you are as a leader and where did they come from?
- How would your team describe your leadership ethos? When did you last ask them?
- What non-negotiables ground your approach?
- What kind of leadership culture do you want to grow around you? What behaviours and attitudes will help you model and nurture that culture?

Our SEND ethos - identity-first language and the social model of disability

In specialist settings, leadership principles and SEND principles go hand in hand - how we lead and how we understand our learners are inseparable. Central to our practice is a commitment to the social model of disability, first introduced by disabled academic Professor Mike Oliver in 1983. This concept reminds us that it is our responsibility to remove barriers that might prevent a child from making progress. As Safeguarding and SEND Specialist, and autistic adult, Emma Twell emphasises, creating these conditions is a key part of compassionate leadership:

> *If a child is presenting in a particular way, what are we going to do differently? The emphasis should be on us changing or the provision changing - not the child changing. We need to meet the child where they are and not where we want them to be. We need to really look and understand where they're at.*

As Emma explains, the focus should always be on what we, as professional adults in education, can do differently rather than expecting the child to change. We need to meet children where they are, not where we wish them to be, taking time to understand their needs and experiences.

Likewise, the social model of disability moves the focus from the individual to the ways society can limit their participation. Instead of seeing disability as something that needs to be 'fixed' or 'cured', the model highlights that society is what disables people through barriers such as inaccessible buildings, outdated policies, or negative attitudes. In specialist settings it is our responsibility to remove these obstacles and ensure young people are fully included and supported to achieve their goals.

The voices of those with additional needs and disabilities are therefore paramount: it is only by listening to lived experience that we can understand and respond with empathy. We have interwoven lived experience throughout this book and we are delighted that our foreword, as already mentioned, is written by autistic speaker, trainer, and advocate, Dean Beadle.

We appreciate that all learners, even those who have the same diagnosis, present heterogeneously with different characteristics, needs, strengths, and preferences. We know that a 'one size fits all' approach doesn't work but since we only have 80,000 words here, there are times where we've had to make some generalisations: e.g. using 'Headteacher' to encompass various leadership roles or 'school' as a universal term for educational settings. We know that not every learner in a specialist provision has additional needs or a formal diagnosis, but many of them do and we see this as a difference and not a deficit. We understand the tensions inherent in what Norwich (2009) calls the 'Dilemma of Difference' and the complexity surrounding labelling and the language we use. No two learners are the same: they are all individual, even if they have the same diagnosis. For the purposes of this book the concept of everyone being a unique individual underpins our use of the word 'different'.

A co-research project involving young people with lived experience of disabilities by Maloy et al. (2025) found that many children prefer the term 'additional needs' to 'SEND', with some feeling that 'SEND' didn't represent them accurately. Consequently, we often use the term 'additional needs' to reflect this preference.

Moreover, there is a growing body of research which suggests most autistic adults prefer identity-first language - e.g. autistic adult - rather than the person-first language - e.g. adult with autism (Taboas, Doepke, and Zimmerman, 2023). Autism is a fundamental part of who someone is - it cannot be removed or separated from them. This is humorously illustrated by Jon Adams (2024), autist artist, advocate, and speaker. Jon suggests that autism is not something you live with. Instead, he asserts that he doesn't live with autism, he lives with his wife and cat because he *is* autistic.

In everyday life, it is good practice to ask for individual preference or to copy the language someone uses to describe themselves. However, since it is impossible to ask every reader, we will respect the preference of the majority of the autistic community and use identity-first language predominantly. To recognise and accept that there are different perspectives, we will use person-first language occasionally.

As leaders, understanding the social model of disability challenges us to examine our provision, our policies, and our attitudes. It is a reminder that inclusion starts with us and that it should be visible in every decision and action we take. We want you to know that we see the world this way because it shapes everything in this book. Understanding our ethos helps you understand why we focus on removing barriers and advocate for inclusion in everything that we do.

Chapter summary

- Leading in specialist settings is complex but deeply rewarding.
- The growth of the specialist sector brings new opportunities but also increasing challenges - from rising demand for places to tighter budgets to the need to support mainstream schools.
- Effective leadership in specialist settings requires a commitment to put children at the heart of every decision.
- We are two experienced, serving leaders of specialist provisions. We understand the sector firsthand and know what it's like to lead within it.
- Although this book has been written in the order from looking inwards to looking outwards, you can read it in the order you like.
- The social model of disability underpins our ethos - we understand that we must advocate for change and dismantle actively any barriers that exist within and outside of our provision.
- Learning from lived experience is essential if we want to understand and empathise truly with the young people in our provisions.

References

Adams, J. (2024). *Autistic Creativity: The World in Our Eyes*. Keynote speech delivered at A-Fest 2024, 19 February 2024. [In-person event], Calne, Wiltshire, UK.

Barthes, R. (1977). 'The death of the author'. In: *Image, Music, Text*. London: Fontana Press, pp. 142–148.

Booth, S. (2024, 21 March). 'Two-thirds of special schools full or over capacity, new data shows'. *Schools Week*. Available online at: https://schoolsweek.co.uk/two-thirds-of-special-schools-full-or-over-capacity-new-data-shows/ [accessed 24 May 2025].

Department for Education (2020, 11 March). 'Thousands of places created in new special free schools'. Available online at: https://www.gov.uk/government/news/thousands-of-places-created-in-new-special-free-schools [accessed 1 April 2026].

Department for Education (2024, 6 June). 'Schools, pupils and their characteristics'. Available online at: https://explore-education-statistics.service.gov.uk/find-statistics/school-pupils-and-their-characteristics/2023-24 [accessed 5 May 2025]. Updated 5 June 2025.

Department for Education (2025a, 12 June). 'Special educational needs in England. Academic year 2024/25'. Available online at: https://explore-education-statistics.service.gov.uk/find-statistics/special-educational-needs-in-england/2024-25 [accessed 1 April 2026].

Department for Education (2025b, 27 March). '£740 million allocated for 10,000 new places for pupils with SEND'. Press release. Available at: https://www.gov.uk/government/news/740-million-allocated-for-10000-new-places-for-pupils-with-send [accessed 18 August 2025].

Follett, M. P. (1940). *Dynamic Administration: The Collected Papers of Mary Parker Follett* (H. C. Metcalf and L. Urwick, Eds.). New York: Harper & Brothers.

Lynch, S., Mills, B., Theobald, K., and Worth, J. (2017). *Keeping Your Head: NFER Analysis of Headteacher Retention*. Slough: NFER.

McGregor, D. (1960). *The Human Side of Enterprise*. New York: McGraw-Hill.

Maloy, L., Tolley, J., King, S., Barwell, N., Cross, E., and Brown, A. (2025). *Young Researchers Young Voices: Co-research SEND Project. Final Report*. Available online at: https://www.researchgate.net/profile/Liam-Maloy/publication/394447746_Young_Researchers_Young_Voices_Co-research_SEND_project_Final_Report [accessed 13 August 2025].

Maxwell, J. C. (1998). *The 21 Irrefutable Laws of Leadership: Follow Them and People Will Follow You*. Nashville, TN: Thomas Nelson.

Maxwell, J. C. (2014). *Life Wisdom: Quotes from John Maxwell: Insights on Leadership*. Nashville, TN: B&H Publishing Group. Available at: https://books.google.co.uk/books/about/Life_Wisdom_Quotes_from_John_Maxwell.html?id=sumKAgAAQBAJ&redir_esc=y [accessed 18 August 2025].

Miranda, L. (2015). *Non-stop*. In: *Hamilton: An American Musical*. Atlantic Records, New York.

Morrison, T. (1981). As cited in Quote Investigator®, 2018, 16 July, 'Quote origin: If you find a book you really want to read but it hasn't been written yet, then you must write it'. Available online at: https://quoteinvestigator.com/2018/07/16/unwritten/ [accessed 18 August 2025].

Norwich, B. (2009). 'Dilemmas of difference and the identification of special educational needs/disability: International perspectives'. *British Educational Research Journal*, *35*(3), 447–467.

Oliver, M. (1983). *Social Work with Disabled People*. Basingstoke, UK: Macmillan.

Powell, L., Spencer, S., Clegg, J., Wood, M. L., et al. (2024). *A Country that Works for All Children and Young People: An Evidence-based Approach to Supporting Children in the Preschool Years*. Child of the North and Centre for Young Lives. Available online at: https://www.n8research.org.uk/media/CotN_Preschool_Report_9.pdf [accessed 24 May 2025].

Taboas, A., Doepke, K., and Zimmerman, C. (2023). 'Preferences for identity-first versus person-first language in a US sample of autism stakeholders'. *Autism*, *27*(2), 565–570.

Truman Library Institute (n.d.). 'Truman quotes'. Available online at: https://www.trumanlibraryinstitute.org/truman/truman-quotes/ [accessed 28 September 2025].

UK Government (1995). 'The Seven Principles of Public Life' [Nolan Principles]. Available online at: https://www.gov.uk/government/publications/the-7-principles-of-public-life/the-7-principles-of-public-life-2 [accessed 24 May 2025].

Whittaker, F. (2024, 6 March). 'Budget 2024: £105m for 15 special free schools, and nothing else'. *Schools Week*. Available online at: https://schoolsweek.co.uk/budget-2024-105m-for-15-special-free-schools-and-nothing-else/ [accessed 18 August 2025].

Wiliam, D. (2018). *Creating the Schools Our Children Need: Why What We're Doing Right Now Won't Work and What We Can Do Instead*. Bloomington, IN: Solution Tree Press.

Zuccollo, J., Dias, J. C., Jiménez, E., and Braakmann, N. (2023). *The Influence of Headteachers on their Schools*. London: Education Policy Institute. Available at: https://epi.org.uk/wp-content/uploads/2023/10/The-influence-of-headteachers-on-their-schools-1.pdf [accessed 19 July 2025].

1

What makes you special? Finding your identity as a leader and a provision

Model the behaviour you wish to see. Be the example of professionalism, kindness and determination. Your leadership will set the tone for the entire school community.

Charlotte Barton, Managing Director of Progress Schools

Chapter overview

This chapter looks at creating a vision through the lens of the leadership qualities and expertise needed in specialist provisions. It explores how you can develop a values-based ethos and culture to deliver your vision and how collective efficacy and psychological safety contribute to this. It explores the benefits of being a leader in a specialist provision and the knowledge and skills that existing leaders think you'll need.

See it to be it – why vision matters

Ask most people what defines a leader and they'll likely say, 'having a vision'. We start by focusing on vision for two reasons. First, it channels moral purpose – guiding not only what leaders do, but why they do it. Second, because educational research highlights that the ability to communicate a compelling vision is a hallmark of effective leadership (Leithwood et al., 2019). A vision doesn't just shape your strategy – it gives you purpose, energises your team, and provides the momentum for change.

Although having a strategic plan is important, an inspiring vision – as suggested by the popular sentiment, 'Wherever you go, go with all your heart' – begins not in the head, but with the heart. We begin with the heart because a compelling idea rarely begins with logic, plans, and spreadsheets, but with conviction, compassion, and moral purpose. In specialist provisions, the heart always leads the way, shaping an approach built on empathy, understanding, and values-driven leadership.

Your vision, and the picture you create of the organisation you wish to build, will inspire and motivate not only your immediate team but also your wider school community. Fittingly,

DOI: 10.4324/9781003601388-2

the etymology of the word 'provision' alludes to foresight and planning to anticipate and meet needs (Harper, 2025). This reflects the reality that most educators are driven by moral purpose and a commitment to doing the best for their learners, rather than by financial gain (Kozlowski and Lauen, 2019). Your vision anchors this social responsibility, providing the inspiration for change.

Understanding your values and how they inform your vision is key to leading with purpose. Successful leaders develop a vision for their setting based on their personal and professional values. They articulate this vision at every opportunity and influence staff and other stakeholders to live and share it (Bush and Glover, 2003). Your values will help crystalise what's most important to you. For example:

- Do you value academic outcomes or holistic achievement?
- Do you want children to be happy or financially successful?
- Do you want your learners to have fun at school or be academically challenged?

Of course, these aren't binary propositions and you will probably want to achieve all of them. However, when thinking about your vision, identifying those aspects that really matter to you will provide the authenticity and passion needed to motivate your team. Alex Tomkins, Headteacher at Greenside School, shares his views on values and vision:

> *I always say leading in a special school is all about ideas. There's no book to follow or another school to replicate. Special schools can be difficult places to work, especially with the increasing emphasis on supporting complex children in specialist settings. I suggest prospective leaders think of leading as both management and leadership.*
>
> *Management is a complex task with a large staff team - we have 140 members of staff. Much of a leader's time is spent managing adults and ensuring quality in the classrooms. Leading is usually harder - having a clear purpose, drive and vision must be central to the role. This is where ideas are important. The best special schools go beyond the 'expected' school functionality and have a true purpose or vision.*
>
> *At Greenside I have built a vision for severe learning difficulties education based on my previous leadership experiences. I believe that 'knowing' is key. Every child is different and we don't truly know them, unless we spend as much time as we can understanding the child in all contexts. I believe in this idea so strongly that I'm testing it by pursuing a Doctorate of Education. I'm not suggesting leaders go to these lengths, but you do need evidence behind your ideas. Evidence can come from a range of sources, but your 'why' needs to be something others can buy into.*

Alex suggests that clear ideas and purpose can motivate your entire staff body. When a team has a sense of direction and purpose, it fosters the belonging and motivation needed for 'collective efficacy'. Albert Bandura (1986), the social psychologist who coined the term, defined it as the shared belief that a group can make a difference through collective effort. Bandura (1986) suggests that when a team believes in their collective ability, they're more likely to take action, overcome challenges, and achieve change. Exactly what you want your staff to do!

'The Stonecutters' Principle' provides another perspective on this. In this story, three stonecutters are asked about their role: the first says, 'I cut stone', the second, 'I earn a wage to support my family', and the third, 'I build cathedrals' (adapted from Sawyer, 2003). Each stonecutter is doing similar work, but only the third recognises that their effort contributes to something greater. Imagine what could happen in your setting if everyone thought like the third stonecutter – if every action, however small, was seen as part of building the 'cathedral' of your vision! Every communication you make helps lay another stone in your cathedral, and together, you team can build extraordinary things. Helping staff see the connection between their work and the bigger picture strengthens engagement, fosters collective efficacy, and helps your vision become a lived reality.

In 2015, Professor John Hattie identified collective teacher efficacy as one of the most powerful influences on student achievement. Building on Bandura's concept of collective efficacy, Hattie's work (2015) suggests that when educators share a strong belief in their collective ability to make a difference, children benefit. However, for teams to work successfully, creating an environment of psychological safety is key. First introduced by the psychologist Carl Rogers in 1954, and later developed by Amy Edmondson (1999), the importance of psychological safety is perhaps more clearly understood and appreciated post-pandemic. As educators, we spend a significant amount of time working, well beyond a traditional working week. When a team feels supported, able to take risks, and confident that their work matters (i.e. psychologically safe), they are more likely to invest in your vision.

Collective efficacy may be a relatively recent term, but the concept itself is not new. Aesop, in the sixth century BC, wrote the fable of *The Four Oxen and the Lion* (Aesop, cited in DaBoss, 2013). In this parable, a group of oxen are grazing in a field watched by a hungry lion. When the lion goes to attack the oxen, they stand rear to rear with their horns facing outwards towards the predator. Met with a united front, the lion is unable to find a way in and retreats. Over time, the oxen start to quarrel and gradually drift apart. Now when the lion attacks, the oxen no longer work together in harmony. Instead, the lion faces each ox alone and brings them down individually. Collectively, the oxen had the ability to overcome the lion – their ability to trust and value each other provided them with safety. In 2026, keeping your team safe means creating an environment of trust and mutual support. When your team feels connected, understood, and listened to, they are better able to bring your vision to life. As Eleanor Roosevelt (1960) once said: 'To handle yourself, use your head; to handle others, use your heart'.

Hence, a clear vision and a sense of psychological safety reinforce each other. A compelling vision sets the direction for your provision – it helps people understand their purpose and goals. But developing a vision is just the beginning. Continuing to communicate it during difficult days and long terms is crucial to helping everyone stay engaged and aligned. Yet, for your vision truly to take hold, your team need to feel safe enough to engage with it, challenge it, and contribute to achieving it. Without psychological safety, even the strongest vision can feel detached or imposed - done *to* people rather than *with* them. It is that meeting of head and heart that matters. Consequently, perhaps the saying should be reworded to: '*know* where you're going and go with all your heart'. The questions given below can help you to reflect on your heart and how it might affect your vision.

Thinking points

- What do you want your provision to be known for?
- What are your core values and how do these influence your leadership? You may find it useful to ask friends, family and your work colleagues for their perceptions - do they align with your own?
- What do you want your legacy to be as a leader? What difference do you hope your leadership will make?

Building a culture that reflects your values

With a clear vision in place and a team confident in their collective ability, you can start to shape your ethos and culture. It is widely accepted that you can have a brilliant strategy, but if your culture isn't aligned with it, it simply won't work. Deal and Kennedy (1982) suggest that culture is the established norms and shared practices that define how an organisation functions day to day. This includes the embedded habits, attitudes, and unwritten rules that affect us in the workplace. It's the shared, but often unspoken understanding of what your provision stands for. Everyone can feel the culture of your organisation, but they may struggle to articulate it. Although certain aspects of culture can be invisible, there are some visible aspects such as, for example, the organisational environment or dress code. These aspects of culture can provide a sense of belonging, supporting group identity and wellbeing.

Although there's no formula for creating culture, you can nurture it. Defining your culture and values as a team creates a shared sense of understanding and buy-in. Give staff time to discuss the questions below:

- Why are we here?
- What matters to us?
- What is our aim?
- How do we know we're on track to achieve our goals?
- Who can help us stay on track or get better?
- What one word defines our purpose?

As leaders, our role is to identify and highlight our organisation's core beliefs. It is important, however, to be realistic about what your values are and your commitment to delivering them daily – even when you're tired, it's raining, and it's the last week before Christmas. Therefore, as Charlotte Barton, Managing Director of Progress Schools, explains, it is vital there is congruence between what you *say* your culture is and how you *act*:

> *Model the behaviour you wish to see. Be the example of professionalism, kindness and determination. Your leadership will set the tone for the entire school community.*

Your culture will also be influenced by whether you are establishing the ethos of a new provision or inheriting the culture of an established setting. In a new provision you have the freedom to shape culture intentionally, whereas in an existing setting, you need to understand its heritage and introduce change more thoughtfully. Starting a new provision often feels more straightforward because there are no existing traditions or habits. Instead, every choice can be intentional, from logo to uniform to colour schemes; every decision can be aligned with your vision straight away. In contrast, inheriting a culture requires careful listening, understanding what already exists, and gently guiding change without losing what already works.

Thinking points

- What habits and traditions are important to your organisation?
- Do you speak about 'our pupils', 'our curriculum', 'our responsibility' – is there a shared language?
- What routines or rituals currently strengthen your team's belief in their ability to make a difference?
- Imagine you ask staff to complete the sentence, 'Because of us, our learners . . .'. What do you think they would say? (You might like to try this at your next staff meeting.)

Author anecdote

After careful consideration and consultation with staff, last year we introduced an optional staff uniform. In hindsight, it's been a great decision. It provides a sense of belonging and team identity while serving as a great equaliser. As a school which believes in a distributed hierarchy, a uniform ensures that there is no visible division between leadership and the wider staff group – just one unified team, reinforced by the shared symbol of sweatshirts and hoodies. As one of our colleagues said: 'I love putting on my hoodie and feeling part of a supportive team'.

Activity: Creating culture

Small, everyday actions contribute to your culture. This activity invites you to reflect on the daily behaviours you notice and model. You can complete it individually or with governors or members of your leadership team.

- List three behaviours you see daily that contribute positively towards your organisational culture.
- Are there any daily behaviours that undermine the culture you are trying to create?
- Are any of these undermining behaviours becoming normalised because people are tired or busy?
- How might you begin to notice and challenge these undermining behaviours?
- List three behaviours that you and other leaders model for others.
- How might your behaviour change during moments of pressure? How could you invite or gain feedback on this?

Speaking with purpose

Once your vision is clear and your culture is taking shape, the next step is to share it. To become a reality, a vision must be articulated and shared with others. Speaking with purpose is how you bring your vision and values to life. Every briefing, email, and conversation becomes an opportunity to align stakeholders with your goals, creating a sense of shared responsibility for achieving your aims.

The way you communicate, and how often you do so, determines how well your vision is understood and implemented. Choosing the right methods and maintaining consistency increases the chance that your message will stick. In smaller provisions, a range of daily interactions can happen organically between staff. When colleagues see each other regularly, relationships are quick to form and a shared sense of purpose is established. As your provision grows, however, either across multiple sites or within the current setting, face-to-face interactions become less frequent, making it harder to maintain a sense of closeness. Poulsen et al. (2024) found that teachers in rural schools were more likely to form close relationships with colleagues in the classroom next door. Although this sounds common sense, it has implications for the physical layout and rooming of classrooms and the importance of considering where professional connections could be encouraged to grow. As their provision expands, leaders need to be intentional about nurturing these relationships so that professional closeness and collaboration aren't lost.

As your staffing body grows, maintaining a strong, connected culture becomes increasingly difficult. In a staff group of 100, even just spending five minutes with each individual would take up 8 hours of leadership time every week - a near impossible ask of any leader. This is where effective line management becomes crucial (more on this in Chapter 7). Although regular one-to-ones are important, not every colleague will require this level of contact every week. Whole-staff briefings, whether in person or on demand, can provide an additional layer of connection and communication. An open-door policy can also be useful, as this reassures colleagues that support and time with leaders is available when they need it. To clarify, an open-door policy doesn't mean that you will be available in your office 8 am–4 pm just waiting for staff to pop by. What it means is that if someone requires a conversation, they can indicate that this is needed and a leader will get back to them that day.

Your colleagues won't always come to you with problems – sometimes they'll want to share feedback, offer ideas, or constructively challenge your thinking. Research suggests that a genuine open-door policy supports these kinds of open, direct interactions (Geneen and Moscow, 1985).

A well-structured approach to communication ensures that every staff member feels seen, heard, and valued. Arguably, in a technology-rich age it is easier than ever to create intentional communication channels. Cloud-based systems allow for real time collaboration and centralised information sharing – particularly useful for split site provisions.

The following questions may help you to reflect on how you can structure communication and opportunities for connection to ensure that staff feel engaged and aligned with your vision.

Thinking points

- How will you ensure that every staff member feels connected to your vision?
- How will you ensure that someone from your leadership team checks in with all staff regularly?
- What might be the benefits of an open-door policy in your setting?
- What opportunities can you create to bring staff together?
- In a world that is constantly connected, how will you support staff to switch off and maintain healthy boundaries?

Leadership scenario

You've been Principal of an all-through specialist provision for 2 years. Over that time your organisation has expanded rapidly. When you were appointed, you knew every member of staff personally and could check in regularly. Recently, you employed your 100th member of staff. Some existing team members feel that you and other leaders are less visible and that there are lots of new staff they don't know.

How do you help your team feel connected and aligned without creating an unsustainable workload for the leadership team? You could consider:

- How you will balance visible leadership with leadership capacity.
- What systems or structures might help colleagues feel seen, valued, and heard.
- How you can support staff to build relationships with one another as the team grows.
- How you will support new staff to understand your vision, culture, and ethos and get to know their colleagues.

As your provision grows, visible leadership and the maintenance of relationships take planning as well as presence. Strategies like an open-door policy, team briefings, and digital collaboration tools can help staff feel acknowledged, known, and valued without overloading your leadership team.

What motivates people to lead specialist provisions?

Moral purpose is hugely important to those who work in specialist provisions, and this sustains them when the work is emotionally demanding. Specialist leaders are motivated not just by professional ambition, but by a commitment to creating environments where children can flourish. As progress often comes in small steps, what might seem like small victories in other settings can be significant achievements for our young people. Recognising and celebrating these steps requires relentless positivity, which will sustain morale and reinforce a culture of aspiration and possibility. This commitment often means rethinking what success looks like (more on this in Chapter 3). Lucy Kreczak, Deputy Headteacher at River Tees Hospital School, explains that success may not always be measured in exam results, but in the small steps of progress that equip learners for the future.

> *I like the small steps of progress. They might not all go off to Oxford. They might not all get 8s and 9s at GCSE, but they all will make small steps of progress. For students with medical needs, it's helping them acknowledge what's going on and helping them make small steps towards their future. Social and emotional progress is also important e.g. leaving the house.*

These small steps of progress that Lucy describes don't happen in isolation - they're made possible by the collective skills and contribution of the whole team. In specialist provisions everyone contributes to success. Whether they're educators, therapists, or support staff, a multidisciplinary approach ensures that expertise is harnessed effectively. When everyone understands their role and sees the positive impact of their work, belief in the collective vision grows. As Lucy highlights:

> *I was a mainstream trust leader for SEND. All I did was SEND - quality assurance, annual reviews. Now, in special, I'm doing a bit of everything - Quality of Education,*

managing staff, timetabling. I'm part of everything. It's nice because everyone here has experience of SEND. In mainstream, you're the expert and everyone comes to you. Here, everyone is knowledgeable. It makes the job easier. Everything is linked up and it is easier to communicate. The dialogue is always ongoing about SEND.

This shared expertise forms the foundation of collective efficacy - it's about the team having all the answers, not one person. Effective leaders recognise this concept by building diverse teams and growing staff (more on this in Chapter 7). In doing so, they move from having a vision to building a team to achieve it.

Why be a leader in a specialist provision?

Specialist leadership differs from mainstream leadership in scope and intensity. Complex funding models, multi-agency collaboration, and the relational demands of multi-disciplinary teams create a distinctive leadership landscape. So why do people step into these roles? Unsurprisingly, it often comes back to moral purpose. When speaking with specialist leaders about the rewards of the role, clear themes emerged. One inspirational account comes from Charlotte Barton:

If you are considering stepping into leadership in Alternative Provision, then first and foremost, thank you. The fact that you are even contemplating this path means you care, and care is exactly what our young people need! But let me be honest with you - this will be one of the most challenging, exhausting, yet deeply rewarding journeys you will ever embark upon!

There will be days when the weight of responsibility feels overwhelming - when the stories of trauma, exclusion, and struggle follow you home. You will fight battles you never anticipated: advocating for children the system has long given up on, pushing against policies that don't fit the reality of your students' lives, and carrying the emotional load of young people who see you as their last chance. Some days, it will feel like you're the only one fighting for them.

But then there are the breakthroughs. The moments that remind you why you do this. The student who hasn't spoken in weeks finally opening up. The child who has been written off by everyone else sitting their first GCSE. The young person who tells you, "I never thought I'd have a future, but you made me believe I could." These are not just small wins; they are life-changing victories and they will carry you through the toughest of days.

Leadership in AP isn't about power, policies or ticking boxes. It's about people. It's about seeing potential where others see problems. It's about leading with compassion, resilience and an unshakable belief in the young people you serve. It will test you, stretch you and at times break you - but it will also shape you into a leader who makes a real difference.

So, if you're thinking about stepping into this world, my advice is this: do it, but do it for the right reasons. Do it because you believe in second chances, in untapped potential,

> *in fighting for those who have no one else fighting for them. Do it because you are willing to lead with your heart, not just your head.*
>
> *And on the hardest days, remember – this work matters.* ***You will change lives.*** *And in the process, it just might change yours too.*

Charlotte captures eloquently both the weight and wonder of specialist leadership. She reminds us that central to the role is a belief in young people and the resilience to keep going when days feel tough. In describing how specialist leadership is as much about the heart as it is about the head, Charlotte suggests that it is our emotional connection to our vision and values that sustains us and makes the hard work worthwhile. The questions below can encourage you to consider how you stay true to your vision and the principles that guide you.

Thinking points

- How will you stay connected to your sense of purpose on challenging days?
- How do you lead with the heart as well as the head, balancing compassion with accountability?
- What personal qualities do you see as essential for motivating and sustaining teams?
- How do you cultivate a culture where staff feel seen, supported, and part of something bigger than themselves?
- In specialist settings, success often looks different. What does success mean to you and how do you celebrate it within your community?

Throughout our conversations with leaders, a few recurring themes emerged that highlight the challenges and rewards of specialist leadership – being child-centred, being innovative and creative, and the need to make a difference – which we discuss in a little more detail below.

You are committed to being child-centred

In specialist settings, the starting point for effective leadership is a commitment to understanding each child as an individual. Leaders emphasise that this goes beyond a child's diagnosis – it's about knowing and understanding each learner individually. As Charlotte Barton explains:

> *Understand your context. Take time to learn about students, their needs and the barriers they face. Building deep understanding of their lived experiences will shape your leadership approach.*

Successful specialist leaders enjoy meeting the individual needs of pupils and relentlessly challenge themselves to do so. This is highlighted by Angela O'Rourke, Headteacher of Southfield SEN School:

> *Every child in your school could be your own child. Is it good enough? Ask yourself this as you leave school every day – if it wasn't good enough today, what are we collectively going to do about it?*

Connection with learners comes from interacting with them. Karen Parker, Head Teacher at Sir Charles Parsons School, explains:

> *The most important and enjoyable part of my day is spending time with the students at break, lunch and on arrival. As Deputy I did have a bit of teaching, but I don't have the capacity anymore and I miss it.*

Yet, sometimes, putting children first means stepping back and letting someone else take the lead, as EOTAS Headteacher, Juliette Baldwin, shares:

> *We believe in a change of face. A teaching assistant can dismiss me from the moment if I'm not the right person to work with that child.*

Put simply, leading a specialist provision means keeping the children front and centre.

You are fuelled by innovation and creativity

Our leadership contributors also emphasised the need for innovation, noting that conventional approaches often fall short in specialist settings. Specialist leaders are unwaveringly optimistic about the future, driven by a strong desire for meaningful change. Their curiosity fuels their leadership – they ask insightful questions, challenge assumptions, and seek creative solutions. As Charlotte Barton details, to thrive, leaders must think flexibly and adapt quickly to the evolving demands of the sector:

> *You need to be flexible and creative. Every day can bring unique challenges in AP. Be open to adapting strategies and exploring innovative approaches to meet the diverse needs of your students.*

You want to make a difference

Many people work in education because they want to make a difference (Kozlowski and Lauen, 2019). Leaders in specialist provisions are often driven by social justice or the notion that the most vulnerable in our society deserve the best education. This is the view of Bridget Young, Headteacher at The Holmewood School:

What I would say to somebody considering working in the specialist sector is that you see more progress here and there's more positives from the progress. You're changing lives doing this work.

Many specialist leaders, such as Julliet Doherty, Head of Adult Services at Ascent Autism Specialist College, felt frustrated working in mainstream provisions and saw the move to specialist education as an opportunity to enact change:

I was always given the 'naughty' classes. They were predominantly full of boys and predominantly difficult. Back then in the 90s nobody had any understanding of SEND and I loved to see the difference that I could make with them. However, I was frustrated at the lack of resources, the lack of creative of thinking around them and the lack of flexibility in the curriculum.

I decided to go and work in a college and I worked in the Foundation Department and I just felt like I had found my thing. It was far more flexible and far more understanding. In some of the mainstream colleges the kids wouldn't last the day and that was really sad. They would find the lights too bright, or the kitchen/dining areas too overwhelming. I really loved working in the college, there was a good leader with a good culture and understanding. I came here 15 years ago - I started on supply and now I'm Head of Adult Services.

Julliet highlights that specialist leadership is about seeing potential where others see challenge. It can be emotionally intensive work, but the impact you can have is extraordinary.

The key skills and qualities necessary for specialist leadership

Effective leadership in any setting requires good communication and interpersonal skills, but specialist settings bring their own unique demands. Below we explore what leaders identify as the skills and traits needed to lead a specialist provision.

Resilience

Successful leaders in specialist settings understand the realities of the role but remain positive and resilient because of their commitment to the children and their determination to secure the very best for them. Juliette Baldwin explains:

Leaders need to be resilient. In AP you can work with children and you might have vicarious trauma. You have to have your own moral purpose and resilience as you will find it challenging at times. You need to sit back and see the long game. I was in mainstream education for 29 years. In mainstream you get affirmation on a daily basis. In AP you're dealing with children who've been permanently excluded, who've experienced rejection. By the time they get to us they've been failing in education for

> *a long time. You need to take that step back - today I might not notice a difference, but in six weeks I will. The positive feedback comes later, but it's worth so much more.*

Complementing this, Julliet Doherty emphasises that resilience alone isn't enough - leaders also need passion and a commitment to change:

> *Leaders in specialist provisions need passion and they have to want to do it. It can be a tiring, draining job and it's important that you can see beyond those immediate difficult days. You need to really want to follow that dream of change. You need to truly believe that the world can be a better place and our job is to model and inspire. You need to be a system leader, you need to say, 'I'm going to shape this'. You have to look beyond, 'I'm doing it for Ofsted' and you're certainly not doing it for the money. You're doing it because you have that dream of change. You want to be a voice for the most vulnerable in our society. Quite often you're not told of all the success and the amazement and the joy and the wonder in this job.*

This commitment to being an advocate for the wider SEND system is echoed by Karen Parker:

> *My role is really positive. I enjoy being a voice and being an advocate for the students. You think about what you'd want for your child or your niece or nephew. It's important that the children have the right to access what everyone else does.*

The sentiments of these leaders echo President John F. Kennedy's 1962 moon speech (cited in Bizony, 2019). In this famous address, Kennedy sets out America's ambition to fly to the moon. Kennedy suggests that humankind chooses to take on great endeavours precisely because they are challenging. Like many specialist leaders, Kennedy recognises that aspirational goals demand resilience and courage. We take on these challenges not for public accolades, but because we believe in transforming children's futures.

Embracing change

Leaders of specialist provisions don't just respond to change - they embrace it. They are professionally curious, willing to ask questions, and committed to continuous learning. Lydia Colios, Assistant Headteacher at Addington School, suggests:

> *It's absolutely important to walk the walk and have that SEND knowledge, but you also have to appreciate that you don't know everything. One of the key issues is that our cohort is getting more complex and as leaders we need to carry on learning to meet their needs. I challenge upwards to other leaders and I challenge down to staff where needed. I believe in radical candour. Let's challenge this idea we're thinking about.*

Lydia's reflection reminds us that specialist leadership requires a mindset that welcomes challenge, curiosity and growth.

Leading with compassion

In specialist settings, the emotional demands on learners and staff can be significant. Being an effective leader in these settings requires emotional intelligence and empathy. Charlotte Barton emphasises:

> *Empathy is key in AP settings. Approach decisions with compassion for students recognising the challenges they encounter daily.*

Compassion is equally as vital as your staff team start work every day committed to doing their best. Lydia Colios reflects on the importance of being personable and approachable:

> *It's really important to be personable when you've got a large cohort of staff at all levels. Support staff vastly outweigh all other groups of staff and it's a hard role and it needs a high level of skill for what isn't a super high paid job. It helps that I've been in that role as I understand what it's like to walk in their shoes.*
>
> *Being genuine and approachable is important. There are some days when you're the Human Resources person and there's days when you're doing coaching and mentoring as the level of complexity coming through is really starting to stretch staff. Learn to give good attention and make meaningful relationships that will see you through. Give an individual who needs it two minutes of good attention rather than 10 minutes of poor attention. People want to feel understood and listened to. The issue doesn't always need solving. Sometimes they just need to feel heard.*

Lydia suggests that sometimes simply listening and being present is more valuable than trying to solve a problem. Lydia's reflection, and those shared by other leaders, suggest a common thread – specialist leadership requires a combination of resilience, curiosity, and compassion. The following questions invite you to reflect on these insights and your own leadership qualities.

Thinking points

- Which of these qualities do you already demonstrate consistently and where could you grow?
- Is your tendency to listen deeply or to step in and solve the problem?
- How does modelling empathy and compassion for staff translate into better outcomes for students?
- What leadership qualities would you add to resilience, curiosity, and compassion?
- How do you stay curious?

Case study: Introducing a culture of Critical Friends

In this chapter, we've explored the qualities and attributes that specialist leaders require. A recurring theme has been the importance of collaborative learning and reflection. Angela O'Rourke, Headteacher of Southfield SEN School, illustrates this in practice through their culture of Critical Friends. It's a lived example of how the values, vision, and principles we've discussed come together in action.

☆

Not everyone can make it working in a SEN school. For many, it is 'too difficult'. Working in a SEN school requires tenacity, thinking outside the box, investment in your own professional development, teamwork, patience and determination for success.

I often remind my colleagues at Southfield that they 'are the chosen ones'. They are 'the minority of the population' and have qualities that not many people have in digging deep every day, especially when it's hard.

A Critical Friends culture is one where all stakeholders believe in their value and work hard to improve the lives of children every day - this is our expectation of each other. We talk about 'safeguarding being everyone's responsibility' - a Critical Friends culture is also 'everyone's responsibility'. It is not about 'knowing best or knowing better', but about us all having high standards for which we hold ourselves to account and therefore we hold others accountable to our own high standards too.

Critical Friends:

- *Act as professional sounding boards - this does not involve gossiping about colleagues but is the ability to listen to peers with empathy*
- *Ask curious questions*
- *Stimulate thinking and provide new ideas*
- *Provide positive challenge*

A Critical Friend:

- *Has a license to help*
- *Is external to the situation*
- *Builds and maintains a relationship of trust*
- *Brings relevant knowledge and experience*
- *Establishes and adheres to clear foci and boundaries*

- *Balances friendship and critique*
- *Is facilitative rather than directive*
- *Understands the complexities of change*
- *Is an advocate for the success of work*
- *Is concerned for the outcome and effectiveness of the work*
- *Enables friends to become more self-sufficient*
- *Can be viewed as an educational connoisseur and critic*

Hierarchy doesn't play a part in this culture. It stems from all staff upholding the same standards we expect of others, creating a culture of shared responsibility and accountability. For example, the expectation is that if the Headteacher is supporting a young person in crisis and a staff member feels that they could support the young person better, they will say 'change of face' and the staff member will take over supporting the young person. A conversation will take place after helping the Headteacher reflect as to how their practice with this young person could have been better or what they might not have known at the time. We can all learn from each other, no matter what stage we are at in our careers.

At Southfield, all members of the leadership team have an 'open door' policy. This means that leaders are there to facilitate others being able to undertake their role to the best of their ability. If staff need resources, guidance, or support, leaders step in to make it available. There is no reason for our pupils not to experience the very best teaching and learning every day. Leaders at Southfield are 'never too busy' for pupils and staff.

Teamwork is also strong in class teams. This means that each team is striving to be the best they can be and provide the best possible education for their pupils. Teams will be 'critical friends' to each other without anyone taking offence. We are all at different points on our career pathways and this means that it is imperative that staff are supported by each other. A Critical Friends culture is about openness, clear processes and shared aspiration. It's a commitment to continually improving so we can provide the very best support for our pupils.

Critical Friends:

- *See your strengths*
- *Want to help you move forwards*
- *Encourage you to think differently*
- *Shape and frame our reflection*

The model we use is pictured in Figure 1.1

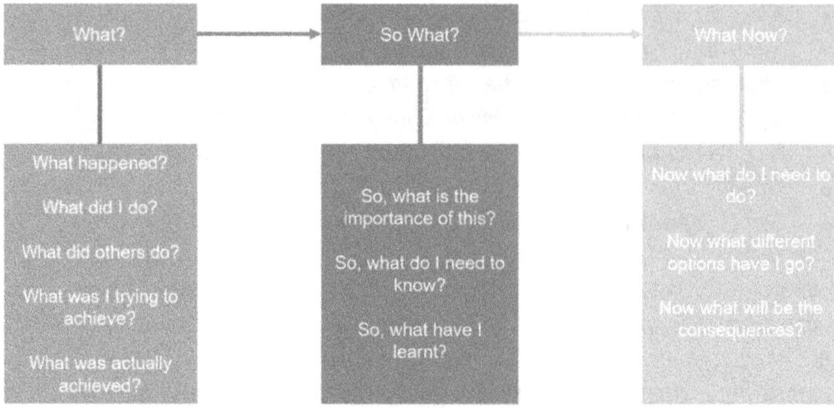

Figure 1.1 The Critical Friends Model used at Southfield SEN School, Hatfield

☆

At Southfield, developing a Critical Friends culture is about mindset – being open, curious, and committed to getting better together. Leaders give feedback, but importantly, actively seek it out. Not only does this sharpen their own practice, but it enables their team to support young people better. The questions below invite you to consider how you can foster a Critical Friends culture in your own setting.

Thinking points

- How could introducing a Critical Friends model build collaboration, accountability, and professional growth in your setting?
- How comfortable are you with giving honest, constructive feedback and receiving it in return?
- What practices could help make feedback a regular, positive part of your team's routine?
- How could you make space for reflection, learning, and discussion during a busy school day?

Learning from lived experience

Everything we do in specialist settings should be influenced by those with lived experience. These perspectives can help us better understand what makes a positive culture. Lauren Smith, autistic adult and postgraduate researcher, shares how attending an alternative provision (AP) positively shaped her school experience:

I share the following values, which draw on the work of the author Brené Brown, which I feel should underpin specialist education. All learners should be valued for who they are – there should be a foundation of care and love. Both learners and staff should feel a sense of psychological safety; only when learners are feeling calm and connected, can they learn. There should be an emphasis on friendship within specialist education since there are higher levels of loneliness amongst those with additional support needs and there are limited opportunities for social connection. Learners should be encouraged to be curious. Additionally, a growth mindset should be modelled, enabling a sense of growth and optimism.

I began attending a medical tuition centre, which sits under the umbrella of alternative provision. At first, I was apprehensive since I fear change and had established friendships in my mainstream school. However, the anxiety quickly subsided and I began to flourish. For a while, I only attended in the mornings, then gradually increased my time there. There was individual teaching, reduced pressure and small groups. I was given the opportunity to develop positive relationships since there were only three other students in my class and eleven people in the entire school. The staff were always available to talk about whatever I needed. They listened to me and nurtured my strengths.

I gradually gained confidence and was able to articulate my emotions about my educational experience into a collection of poetry which was later published. The AP was my lifeline. Thanks to my transformational experience there, I am now undertaking a doctorate focusing on autism and AP with the goal of one day setting up a similar provision.

Lauren Smith, autistic adult and postgraduate researcher

Lauren's experience shows the impact that specialist provisions can have. Miranda, a late-diagnosed autistic adult, echoes the importance of staff in specialist settings working collaboratively in a child-centred manner:

I think 'aspirational' and 'empowering' should underpin specialist education, particularly developing a strong community of belonging. My observations of strong specialist education is where there is a strong community, where children are celebrated and valued and the whole community works together. High expectations and care is important – staff must respond to children's expressed needs rather than what they infer. There is a lot of making assumptions about what individuals need rather than asking them.

Miranda, late diagnosed autistic adult and parent to an autistic child

Miranda's warning against making assumptions reminds us that listening to lived experience is crucial. The thinking points below invite you to reflect on how lived experience can affect your own leadership and practice.

Thinking points

- How do you ensure every learner is recognised and valued for who they are?
- How might you notice when learners and staff feel psychologically safe?
- How do you listen actively to your learners and avoid making assumptions about their needs?
- How do you develop a sense of community in your setting?

Chapter summary

This chapter explores what it takes to lead a specialist provision, highlighting the vision, values, and personal qualities that underpin effective leadership in these settings.

- Leadership in specialist provision is challenging and emotionally demanding but deeply rewarding.
- Leaders in specialist provisions start with a clear, child-centred vision that energises their team and supports meaningful change.
- Specialist leaders focus on the child, ensuring every decision considers, 'Is this good enough for this child?'
- Collective efficacy and psychological safety are essential in building a culture where everyone can thrive.
- Open-door policies are a common feature in specialist settings - they foster openness, connection, and feedback.
- Specialist leadership requires a blend of creativity, resilience, and adaptability to meet learners' highly individualised needs.
- Leaders of specialist provisions are child-centred, placing great emphasis on knowing the child.
- Leaders of specialist settings are resilient - they can see beyond the immediate and emotionally draining occasions to the long-term impact they have.
- Specialist leaders are advocates for social justice, embracing change and leading with compassion.
- Lived experience highlights the importance of valuing individuality, fostering belonging, and creating environments of psychological safety.

Further reading

- To find out more about introducing a culture of Critical Friends you may like to read 'Through the lens of a Critical Friend' by Costa and Kallick (1993).

References

Bandura, A. (1986). *Social Foundations of Thought and Action*. Englewood Cliffs, NJ: Prentice Hall.

Bizony, P. (2019). '"We choose to go to the Moon": Read JFK's Moon speech in full'. *BBC Science Focus Magazine*. Available online at: https://www.sciencefocus.com/space/we-choose-to-go-to-the-moon-read-jfks-moon-speech-in-full [accessed 14 August 2025].

Bush, T., and Glover, D. (2003). *School Leadership: Concepts and Evidence*. A review of literature carried out for National College for School Leadership, Nottingham. Available online at: https://dera.ioe.ac.uk/id/eprint/5119/14/dok217-eng-School_Leadership_Concepts_and_Evidence_Redacted.pdf [accessed 1 April 2026].

Costa, A., and Kallick B. (1993). 'Through the lens of a Critical Friend'. *Educational Leadership*, *51*(2), 49–51.

DaBoss (2013). 'The Four Oxen and the Lion'. Fables of Aesop. Available online at: https://fablesofaesop.com/the-four-oxen-and-the-lion.html [accessed 20 August 2025].

Deal, T. E., and Kennedy, A. A. (1982). *Corporate Cultures: The Rites and Rituals of Corporate Life*. Reading, MA: Addison-Wesley.

Edmondson, A. C. (1999). 'Psychological safety and learning behavior in work teams'. *Administrative Science Quarterly*, *44*(2), 350–383.

Geneen, H., and Moscow, A. (1985). *Managing*. New York: Doubleday.

Harper, D. (2025). 'Provision'. In: *Online Etymology Dictionary*. Available online at: https://www.etymonline.com/word/provision [accessed 28 September 2025].

Hattie, J. (2015). 'The applicability of visible learning to higher education'. *Scholarship of Teaching and Learning in Psychology*, *1*, 79–91.

Kozlowski, K. P., and Lauen, D. L. (2019). *Understanding Teacher Pay for Performance: Flawed Assumptions and Disappointing Results*. Available online at: https://dlauen.web.unc.edu/wp-content/uploads/sites/3060/2019/02/Kozlowski-Lauen-Performance_Pay_Flawed_Assumptions_TCR.pdf [accessed 19 August 2025].

Leithwood, K., Harris, A., and Hopkins, D. (2019). 'Seven strong claims about successful school leadership revisited'. *School Leadership & Management*, *40*, 1–18.

Poulsen, T., Leary, H., Whiting, E. F., and Sansom, R. (2024). 'Social network analysis of educators in rural schools: A literature review'. *Educational Research: Theory and Practice*, *35*(4), 30–48.

Rogers, C. (1954). 'Towards a theory of creativity'. In: Vernon, P. E. (1970). *Creativity: Selected Readings*. Harmondsworth, UK: Penguin, pp.137–152.

Roosevelt, E. (1960). *You Learn by Living*. New York: Harper & Brothers.

Sawyer, R. K. (2003). *Explaining Creativity: The Science of Human Innovation*. Oxford: Oxford University Press.

2

From vision to impact: Developing curriculum in specialist settings

Is the curriculum having impact?! This is the key question! Be mindful a child does not have 'The Hungry Caterpillar' each year. A curriculum should be as broad as the world around the child, not just limited to their attainment steps.

Alex Tomkins, Headteacher, Greenside School

Chapter overview

With your ethos and values established, it's now time to bring your vision to life and define what learners need to know, experience, and remember. This chapter will look at the three tenets of curriculum (intention, implementation, and impact) through a specialist lens. We will consider what an aspirational curriculum looks like in specialist settings, illustrated through two real-world examples – the introduction of a play-based curriculum at Ellesmere College, Leicester and the rollout of an internal alternative curriculum at West Exe School in Devon.

The national picture

A national curriculum review, led by Professor Becky Francis CBE, was commissioned in July 2024. The final report, published in November 2025, concludes that the current curriculum and assessment system does not work well for all children, particularly disadvantaged learners and/or those with SEND (Department for Education, 2025). The review emphasises the need to build a more coherent, inclusive, and ambitious curriculum that secures high standards for all learners. It highlights that:

- The curriculum and assessment system needs to be more inclusive, flexible, and equitable.
- Learners need to be prepared for social and technological change e.g. learning about digital skills or climate change.
- Learners need to be supported better through key transitions, particularly moving into post-16 pathways, with better alignment between curriculum, qualifications, and future destinations.

DOI: 10.4324/9781003601388-3

Thinking points

- What implications do these findings have for curriculum design in your setting?
- How can your curriculum prepare learners better for key transitions e.g. primary to secondary or post-16?
- How can we integrate contemporary concerns, such as digital skills and global citizenship, into a curriculum that is meaningful and relevant for learners with additional needs or disabilities?

Curriculum intent: Principles and purpose in action

The aim of a curriculum is its intention. When well-designed, curriculum intent ensures learners acquire the knowledge, skills, and experiences to progress. Effective curriculum design begins by clarifying your intent – the 'why' that shapes the principles and priorities of your provision. You may already have a curriculum – in which case you may be looking to review this in anticipation of a changing pupil cohort. Alternatively, you may be establishing a new provision and starting with a blank page. We will explore different curriculum principles and how to develop a guiding philosophy for your curriculum.

A good starting point is to ask: What do you want your curriculum to achieve?

- A good Progress 8 score?
- Fabulous academic achievements?
- Outstanding progress towards EHCP outcomes?
- Effective transition into post-16 provision or employment?
- Happy and fulfilled learners who can live safely and independently?

You most likely want to achieve all these things, but clarifying your priorities will help you design a curriculum that meets your aims. In doing so, consider Tomkins' (2019) challenge: What type of curriculum will give your learners the best chance of progress? Since most specialist provisions think holistically about a child's development, they will often design a curriculum that emphasises skills such as independence, resilience, functionality, and safety. Some specialist provisions have a 'golden thread' running through their curriculum on aspects such as communication, independence, or life skills.

Specialist provisions support learners with a wide range of needs and often have diverse pupil populations. Tomkins (2019) emphasises designing and delivering a curriculum that truly fits your cohort, recognising that mainstream provision hasn't always provided the right environment or learning opportunities for them. This echoes Wiliam's (2013) suggestion that every educational setting should have a different curriculum tailored to meeting the needs of their learners.

Consequently, specialist settings often require multiple curriculum pathways to meet each learner's developmental stage and needs fully e.g. formal, semi-formal, preparation for adulthood, or functional skills. Tomkins (2019) used the four areas within the SEND Code of Practice (Department for Education, 2014) to structure his school's curriculum. Although each provision's curriculum intent will be different, all curricula should be carefully sequenced to ensure learners build knowledge, skills, and understanding progressively.

Author anecdote: our curriculum principles

We use the principles of Professor Dylan Wiliam to underpin our curriculum (Wiliam, 2013):

- Balanced - we have a broad and balanced curriculum that teaches the key knowledge and skills our learners require.
- Rigorous - we use a spiral curriculum that revisits learning on a cyclical programme, providing overlearning and the opportunity to build on and deepen knowledge.
- Coherent - we ensure connections are made between stages and subjects, building on previous learning.
- Sequenced - we ensure content, knowledge, and skills are revisited but not repeated.
- Appropriate - we ensure the curriculum matches each learner's level of maturity and understanding but still provides the aspiration to achieve at each individual's level of challenge.
- Focused - we provide the content, knowledge, and skills that our learners need the most.
- Relevance - we help our learners understand how their learning can support them in everyday life.

Aspirational curricula in specialist provisions

We asked leaders of specialist and alternative provisions, as well as adults with additional needs, to share their views on what makes an aspirational curriculum.

> *For me, an aspirational curriculum is one that nurtures the whole child. It creates a safe environment for every young person to learn and for their skills and strengths to grow. Like a diverse garden, an aspirational curriculum recognises that each learner needs different soil, light and water, but with the right care, every seed can flourish in its own way.*
>
> *It is a curriculum rooted in safety and trust, with trauma-informed and validating practices that removes barriers. It's working to find a balance within neuro-affirmative*

practice of how we can celebrate and embrace difference, without minimising individual needs and the day-to-day challenges we might face as neurodivergent people. It supports young people to recognise, believe in and strive towards a future that fits them.

Remie Colledge, Neurodivergent Speaker, Trainer, and Writer

We have an aspirational statement of desired outcomes of education. These are dependent on a pupil's ability. They're about enjoying learning – if you enjoy learning, then you enable learning to happen. If learning happens then you enable pupils to achieve. The important thing is to focus on what the children can do, not what they can't do. We have seven aspirational pathways which follow a rainbow. On the red pathway pupils might go into independent living, they might access social and community activities, they need to learn to manage their home budget and this is built into their curriculum.

Karen Parker, Head Teacher, Sir Charles Parsons School

All curriculums should be 'aspirational.' From my viewpoint, this means supporting the individual's goals and ambitions that they set for themselves. Providing an array of opportunity and a combination of classroom learning and exploration in the wider community can help prepare learners for adulthood, which for some, may be considered the goal of education. To further aid this preparation, providing work experience in a supported environment with a mentor may be beneficial.

Additionally, it is imperative for there to be wellbeing support for learners; teaching them to communicate their needs, self-regulate and learn about how their needs or disability affects them can support learners when preparing for adulthood.

Lauren Smith, autistic adult and postgraduate researcher

You need to ensure that your curriculum is academically challenging. Our learners might not be very well, but they can still do well. We work with lots of different agencies to balance the medical needs with the educational needs.

One of the main misconceptions is – do they do GCSEs? Of course they do! People think there's no level of challenge just because they're unwell and in a special school. They've worked their socks off – they can go to uni or get a job. Some teachers put a glass ceiling on them just because they're unwell. There is a misconception that they're too poorly to learn. Our job is to adapt the teaching to the child.

Lucy Kreczak, Deputy Headteacher, River Tees Hospital School

We can't just do the traditional things with the children – that approach has failed them. We must change what we are doing. We shape the curriculum to meet the needs of our learners. The traditional set-up of arriving at 8.45am, having form time and then doing 5 lessons – does that work? Does that system meet the needs of the children or the adults? We do a lot of things in education for the adults.

Robert Bell, Headteacher, Consilium Evolve

Collectively, these voices suggest that an aspirational curriculum is about ambition, holistic development, and personalisation. Consider your approach to curriculum design using the questions below.

Thinking points

- How do these perspectives shape your understanding of what an 'aspirational curriculum' looks like?
- Is your curriculum designed around learners' needs and strengths?
- How can you be ambitious for learners whilst being creative in the ways you help them reach their goals?
- How do you involve pupils in shaping their learning pathways?

Implementation - from intent to action

Implementation is the bridge between curriculum design and classroom practice, ensuring that the planned learning is delivered consistently and meaningfully across subjects and settings. Many specialist and alternative provisions follow the National Curriculum and this is often referred to as the 'core offer'. However, as discussed above, additional pathways may be required, particularly if you have learners working towards the National Curriculum. Key principles for implementing the curriculum in specialist settings include:

- Practical learning - developing skills and understanding through hands-on tasks or activities.
- Experiential learning - reflecting on and making meaning from learning experiences.
- Concrete to abstract progression - moving from the concrete to abstract or from tangible experiences to conceptual thinking.
- Making meaningful connections - linking learning to the individual's sphere of understanding, connecting new knowledge to what is meaningful and familiar to the learner.
- Repetition and overlearning - ensuring concepts are reinforced through spaced practice to support retention.
- Social and emotional integration - embedding opportunities for social communication, emotional regulation, and wellbeing within learning experiences.
- Choice and agency - giving learners opportunities to make decisions and influence their learning.

Learners are likely to follow a range of timetables that implement the curriculum, including individual, flexible, and structured timetables. Some specialist provisions, such as Hospital Schools, require curriculum flexibilities since timetables can alter daily to accommodate medical or therapeutic interventions.

The staffing structure of your provision will also shape the learning opportunities you can offer. For example, your range of Key Stage 4 options may be influenced by the expertise and number of staff available to deliver them. Although this is a practical consideration, it also offers an opportunity to review how you deploy staff, combine expertise, and collaborate across departments or settings to provide access to different subject areas.

Consequently, since it is shaped by the needs of learners, the size and expertise of the staff body, and the resources available, implementation looks different in every setting. The examples below show how specialist provisions implement their curriculum pathways.

> *We have a unique afternoon curriculum. We have pastoral time in pastoral classes which are mixed ability in Years seven and eight. Learners access a therapeutic sensory curriculum, for example TACPAC, hydrotherapy, Rebound Therapy or sensory circuits. It's a personalised learning curriculum. There's also emotional support, for example Thrive, Forest School, social and emotional assisted learning. We also have an occupational therapist, community nurse, a physiotherapist and speech and language therapists working with students daily.*
>
> Karen Parker, Head Teacher, Sir Charles Parsons School

> *We're working on transforming our PE curriculum. In particular, our autistic girls are struggling with a traditional PE curriculum of football and rugby. We're creating a Health and Wellbeing Curriculum instead. We're incorporating elements of PSHE, Mindfulness and Preparation for Adulthood. We're developing the social side and developing social skills alongside the academic.*
>
> Lucy Kreczak, Deputy Headteacher, River Tees Hospital School

> *Our cohort is changing and our learners are becoming more complex. As our learners with complex needs began moving towards sixth form, I could see they needed a different curriculum pathway, which we now call the High Needs Pathway. These are children who are likely to need a residential or specialist placement once they leave us. These children need a curriculum that can be transferred across settings. Though independence is important, this curriculum is about generalising learning so that our young people will be safe once they leave us. It also provides a high level of therapeutic support to enable pupils to engage in learning opportunities.*
>
> *For younger pupils, we've written an Access to Learning Curriculum which looks at growing independence and supporting learners to regulate and communicate their needs. We use the acronym REC, which stands for Regulation, Engagement and Communication. We've seen the impact of this curriculum already as it gives pupils extra time to become ready to learn and consolidates those learning to learn behaviours.*
>
> Kimberley Legg, Assistant Headteacher, Addington School

> *I think there is very little space or time for neurodivergent learners to pause and reflect. I feel that when I was at school we had much more self-driven projects and activities which we could tailor to our interests. We had lots of times where teachers would respond to current events, or even the weather, and we were all able to go*

outside and play in the snow. I used to make snow sculptures whilst others would have snowball fights or sledge on snowy days. I sometimes feel there is so much rush and so much crammed in, that having time to move a little slower and manage transitions is harder.

Miranda, late diagnosed autistic adult and parent to an autistic child

These perspectives remind us that successful implementation comes from understanding our learners and shaping provision around them. The thinking points below invite you to reflect on what implementation looks like in your own setting and how you meet learners' needs.

Thinking points

- What commonalities are there between these different approaches to curriculum design and implementation?
- How do you know your curriculum is fit for purpose? What are the indicators that a new pathway is needed?
- Could aspects of your timetable (e.g. afternoons) be redesigned to enable more therapeutic or pastoral activities?
- Tomkins (2019) suggests visiting other specialist provisions to understand their approach. How could this help your setting?

Activity: Curriculum redesign

Imagine you could redesign your curriculum.

- What would it look like if money and staffing were no issue? How close is your current curriculum to that vision?
- What different curriculum pathways would you implement?
- How would you structure the school day?
- How many hours would you give to each subject?
- What would staff need to feel confident delivering this curriculum?
- What resources would you require?
- What would be the first step to achieving this vision?

Impact - measuring the impact of the curriculum in specialist settings

Tomkins (2019) suggests that it is difficult to measure the impact of a curriculum. In specialist and alternative provisions, impact likely encompasses how well the curriculum supports every learner to fulfil their potential - academically, socially, and emotionally. You will need to consider how you will look beyond academic measures to capture holistic progress. Common impact measures include:

- Progress data and outcomes, including national benchmarks
- Feedback from children, staff, and families

- Pupil engagement and attendance data
- Progress towards EHCP outcomes
- Learning walks and book looks
- Inspections from School Improvement Partners or Ofsted
- Pupil destinations, which may be broader than in mainstream settings including supported employment, independent living skills, and community participation

Leadership scenario

You are Headteacher of an all-through specialist provision. At your most recent governors' meeting, a new governor questions why your provision's academic results are below the national average. They suggest that raising exam outcomes should be your top priority and that your curriculum should be reviewed to achieve this.
How do you respond? You could consider:

- How your curriculum is intentionally designed to meet the diverse starting points, needs, and aspirations of your learners.
- How data are presented so that they capture all aspects of progress, including personal development, communication, independence, and wellbeing.
- How governors and other strategic partners can be supported to understand progress in your context.
- How you could use case studies, destination data, and lived experience to show the impact of your curriculum.

This task encourages you to articulate a curriculum narrative that connects intent, implementation, and impact. In specialist provisions, a meaningful curriculum begins with the learner, and a powerful measure of success is the difference it makes to their lived experience. The following case study illustrates what this looks like in practice through the introduction of a play-based curriculum to meet learners' developmental needs.

Case study: Implementing a play-based curriculum

In this case study, Lead Teachers Gemma James and Melissa Taylor outline the introduction of a play-based curriculum at Ellesmere College, a large all-through special school in Leicester.

Together, Gemma and Melissa established the Early Learning Pathway, one of four curriculum pathways at Ellesmere. The Early Learning Pathway supports learners aged 4 to 7 through a lively, thoughtfully designed curriculum that lays strong foundations in communication and language; personal, social, and emotional development; and physical development. Learners on this pathway are typically at the early stages of communication and need tailored strategies to support them e.g. Makaton or Picture Exchange Communication Systems.

☆

The Early Learning Pathway uses a continuous provision approach known as 'Busy Time'. During these sessions, learners are free to explore their environment and engage with different areas of the curriculum. Learning is led and initiated by the child, with adults on hand to support and extend the learning. The continuous provision model means that money isn't only taught in Maths and reading doesn't just happen during reading time – learners use these skills naturally in areas like the Home Corner of the classroom. Themed activities change fortnightly, with immersive environments created to engage and inspire learners.

The success of the play-based curriculum in the Early Years Foundation Stage prompted senior leaders to explore whether a similar approach could be introduced in Key Stage 2, where it would be developmentally appropriate for some pupils. Additionally, in Key Stage 3 (KS3), teachers with learners with moderate or severe learning difficulties were struggling to plan an engaging curriculum as the resources and materials weren't developmentally appropriate. Developmentally, the children needed early learning and hands on, practical activities. The introduction of a play-based curriculum has enabled learners progressing into KS3 to engage purposefully in role play that blends core skills with meaningful, everyday scenarios. For example, learners may write shopping lists, read and interpret medicine labels, calculate timings or manage money – important activities that prepare them for an independent life.

Ellesmere understands that a play-based curriculum pathway is appropriate because it:

- *Is flexible and responsive – adults are continuously refining the learning experience for children.*
- *Provides continuous learning which meets learners at their level of challenge.*
- *Is child-led, which facilitates the child to be independent and develop autonomy.*
- *Enables learners to practise key skills in a safe setting, experiencing different outcomes before testing them out in real life.*
- *Builds valuable life skills by mimicking real life through role play.*
- *Is incremental, building progress in small steps.*
- *Is hands-on and practical, providing sensory input, feedback and play.*

The approach has been successful across different provisions at Ellesmere because it enables teachers to carefully consider the needs of each child. Every individual is different and a play-based approach enables staff to prioritise communication, physical development and self-regulation to suit each learner. Although academic outcomes are important, independence is key and the curriculum places strong emphasis on developing real-world skills in small, manageable steps.

As with any new initiative, there were some challenges and myths that needed to be addressed, particularly that teenagers shouldn't be playing. Gemma and Melissa argue that the key to this is rethinking what play means. Play doesn't always mean cuddling soft toys. Play is important at any age – adults still play and many buy toys, such as Lego®, for themselves! We need to think about what we mean by play. You can substitute toys with real life items. Play-based learning doesn't have a ceiling and it doesn't stop children from learning more challenging concepts when they're ready. Learners on the play-based curriculum may be able to write, but they still benefit from tactile experiences and having their sensory needs met.

Gemma and Melissa acknowledge that the introduction of a play-based curriculum was initially daunting for some staff. To support, they encouraged colleagues to come on good practice visits; completed learning walks; and provided training on using Tuff Trays and sensory learning. They identified that Key Stage 4 (KS4) teachers coming from a mainstream secondary background needed more support, so as part of their trial phase they placed a primary trained colleague in KS4 to help. Some staff needed more support to understand what a play-based approach looked like in their context. To help, Gemma and Melissa carried out observations, provided feedback, and shared detailed curriculum plans to provide a clear structure. Gemma and Melissa used their whole school bulletin to share a 'Tuff Tray of the Week', which helped create a culture of collaboration and good practice. A play-based approach encourages creativity and adaptive teaching as staff focus on how to make it work for their learners.

☆

Gemma and Melissa's passion and enthusiasm for play-based learning have been integral to its success. Their commitment to reflective practice and continuous improvement is evident. They openly acknowledge that whilst the play-based curriculum has made a successful start, it is not yet perfect and there remain many areas for development. They remain committed to meeting the needs of all their learners through designing and implementing a curriculum that meets young people at their level of challenge.

Thinking points

- How does this case study challenge the idea that play is 'just for young children'? What examples here show that play is relevant at all ages?
- What might 'play' look like for a 4-year-old compared with a 14-year-old?
- How did Gemma and Melissa help staff buy into the approach and share good practice?
- List the types of play-based learning already happening in your setting. How could play be integrated more purposefully across different subjects or year groups?

Leadership scenario

You are Assistant Headteacher with responsibility for curriculum at an all-through specialist provision. After visiting Ellesmere College and seeing their play-based approach in action, several of your teachers are excited about trialling it in their own classrooms. Some staff are fully on board, but others are sceptical, particularly those in KS3 and KS4 who worry that 'play' isn't age-appropriate and could reduce time spent on academic outcomes. Governors are interested in the approach but want to see clear evidence of impact before committing funding for training or resources.

Consider how you would:

- Determine whether a play-based approach is appropriate for your setting.
- Reframe 'play' so that it feels appropriate and purposeful for learners in KS3 and KS4.
- Gather and present evidence of impact to stakeholders who want proof before progressing the idea.
- Provide professional development or peer learning opportunities to help staff develop their skills and confidence.

Case study: Creating a curriculum for an internal alternative provision by The Ted Wragg Trust

Our next case study also focuses on the implementation of a new curriculum pathway. This time the establishment of internal alternative curriculum at West Exe School, a large mainstream secondary school in Exeter serving over 1,200 learners.

The Ted Wragg Trust is an ambitious and inclusive trust of schools where our aim is to transform lives, strengthen communities and make the world a better place. We're a family of 18 schools, comprising a number of primary, secondary and all-through settings across Plymouth, Exeter and East Devon.

West Exe School, part of The Ted Wragg Trust, are at the start of their journey with implementing an Alternative Curriculum. The case study below focuses on our set-up and learning from our first year of implementation. During subsequent years we expect the provision to grow and evolve as we learn from experience and as our cohort of children change and grow.

Rising levels of SEND pupils in mainstream schools has led some organisations to establish their own internal specialist provisions. One innovative and successful story comes from West Exe School in Exeter which has created its own alternative curriculum and internal alternative provision (IAP).

Key staff in establishing this provision are:

- *Matt Bindon, Trust Leader for Alternative Provision and Specialism*
- *Kelly Dighton, SENDCo and Senior Leader at West Exe School*
- *Natalia Pragnell, Senior Leader for Equity in Education, IAP Lead and Teacher of History at West Exe School*

West Exe School began their journey to establishing an IAP by identifying a gap. They recognised the importance of addressing their pupils' increasing needs in a new and innovative manner. They set up Alternative Curriculum 2 (AC2), which is led by Kelly Dighton. This is an intervention programme with targeted catch-up. It is an alternative curriculum that draws on a traditional model.

West Exe also runs another internal curriculum adaptation called 'The Quay', led by Natalia Pragnell, which supports pupils with regulating their behaviour. It currently focuses on transition and supporting the transition from primary to secondary. Year 7 pupils attend The Quay for 2 days a week, whilst Year 8 and 9 pupils attend for 3 days a week. The provision works on a traditional 12-week block. Pupils receive two separate mentoring sessions a day in which they reflect on their previous day's successes and challenges and create personalised targets. The AC provides a softer start to secondary school that prioritises relationships and feeling a sense of belonging. The Quay houses small groups of 6 students, supported by subject specialist teachers to deliver a range of subjects across the curriculum. They also benefit from a full-time teaching assistant to support learners' needs. The aim is to phase pupils back, after the 12 week programme, to a full timetable within the mainstream provision. The curriculum in The Quay models, where possible, the breadth of subjects that pupils would be following in the mainstream classroom.

The children can practise learning engagement and work towards specific targets. The training and rehearsal element of the provision is key – the children have a safe space in which to practise positive learning behaviours ready for when they need them in the mainstream environment.

Since implementing The Quay in September 2024, the staff at West Exe have seen an increased sense of belonging for the students. They've also seen a reduction in poor behaviour, a reduction of high-cost external alternative provision, a reduction in the number of pupils being removed from lessons, but also an improvement in students' ability to communicate more positively with staff and peers and an increased sense of self-confidence and self-worth. Importantly, the pupils have been extremely positive about The Quay and their want to improve their engagement and behaviour. The pupils articulate that The Quay does really help them. In particular, they like being in smaller groups and the reasonable adjustments that staff make to include them. As well as benefitting children, The Quay programme has helped develop teachers' pedagogical craft and behaviour management skills. It provides a good training environment for staff, enabling them to practise making reasonable adjustments. It's a safe space for both pupils and staff to rehearse self-regulation, relational practice and positive communication.

Smaller class sizes have enabled the team to adopt a primary style communication model. This approach enables a more frequent communication schedule, similar to what parents encounter in primary settings. Parents don't always receive brilliant news about their children, so frequent communication helps build positive relationships. In The Quay, stickers are given to learners to celebrate success, which the learners really enjoy. Parents have also noticed increased confidence in their child.

Reflecting on the skills needed to lead an IAP, the team at West Exe emphasise the need to make decisions quickly and provide a rapid response to new developments. They also stress the importance of communication, particularly around the purpose of the provision. A key element has been supporting staff through CPD to help develop a more specialist skillset. This is one of things the team would like to develop, in particular ensuring that the West Exe coaching strategy for staff is supported in both The Quay and the AC2 programme.

The team ruminates that the provision is never finished as things are changing all the time. This means there will always be tweaks to make, particularly since every cohort is different. They emphasise the balance between needing to be responsive, but not growing and changing so quickly that you don't give things a chance to bed in. Good teamwork and on-going reflection are also crucial.

Good teachers in specialist provisions, like The Quay, need to prioritise building relationships. They need to have effective trauma-informed practice, understand child development, and be flexible and creative. They need to be brave when making decisions. They will sometimes think, 'I'm not going to make it through this content' and make the decision to do something different if things aren't working. The team highlight that in The Quay, curriculum isn't the sole driver on the design of the provision – it's bigger than that. They reflect on the need to balance expectations, be receptive to advice, and be super reflective.

Reflecting on their top tip, the team prioritised getting great people in great spaces. They describe a phrase they like to use – 'think fast, act slow'. Leaders in specialist provisions need to process lots of information quickly but then make a considered decision. They need good attention to detail. Planning is really important and you need to make sure you're adapting to your cohort. It needs real conscientious thought. Of course, good relationships (with staff and students) are also necessary.

One barrier to expanding their current curriculum adaptations is having limited physical space. Without a dedicated classroom on hand, a space needed to be found. The team emphasised the importance of belonging, seeing calm and safety as underpinning the provision. They set out to make the space feel warm and homely to support the self-regulation of students. Wherever possible, they also give pupils ownership of the space.

One element that makes the AC programmes unique is the utilisation of technology. West Exe runs live lessons where the teachers wear microphones and use visualisers – any children not in class are able to log on virtually so they're not missing out. Children can log into lessons from the ACs, which means they don't need to leave a space where they feel safe and emotionally regulated. Live lessons are particularly valuable at GCSE as they ensure that pupils retain access to specialist teachers and specialist content.

When asked about what drives them, the team stress that their values permeate everything they do. They describe the Ted Wragg Trust as 'relentlessly positive collaborators'. One important factor in developing the curriculum adaptations has been their links with the national education charity 'The Difference'. They reflect that they've 'realised that there's no rubric, no book, we therefore have to be outward facing'. Being collaborative is part of the Trust's values and they are committed to working with others at a national level and working with other trust leaders to change things for the better. This is a powerful example of SEND system leadership, driven by civic responsibility and moral purpose.

☆

The team at West Exe emphasise the importance of staffing, relationships, and environment in implementing a curriculum that meets learners' needs. Leaders must be responsive, reflective, and guided by clear values, ensuring that every decision supports meaningful learning and development.

Thinking points

- Matthew, Natalia, and Kelly describe the opportunity to create safe spaces for the rehearsal of learning behaviours. What might this look like in your setting?
- If you were to set up an IAP, who are your "great people in great spaces"?
- The team at West Exe discuss the balance between innovation and stability. How do you decide when to innovate and when to focus on embedding practice?
- One of the key elements of the IAP is the use of live streaming and hybrid learning. This keeps vulnerable pupils connected to specialist teaching without compromising their safe space. How could you implement this in your setting?

Activity: Design your Quay

What does a 12-week internal alternative provision model look like in your context?

Consider:

- Space and environment - what will it look, sound, and smell like?
- Core values and principles - what will underpin practice, relationships, and the overall environment?
- Staff qualities and skills - what knowledge, values, and behaviours will staff need to be successful in the provision?
- Curriculum - what kind of learning happens here?
- Training needs - what do staff need to be successful?
- Parental engagement - how will learners and families know that they've arrived somewhere safe and compassionate?
- The re-integration strategy to the core offer - how will you know when pupils are ready to transition?
- Impact - how will you measure success?

West Exe's story reminds us that a curriculum is never a finished product, but a responsive journey that adapts to the needs of the learners in front of us. It requires innovation, reflection, and the courage to change things for the benefit of young people. We must also listen to our learners, to their families, and to the communities we serve because those who live our curriculum each day are our truest evaluators and our most powerful co-designers. There's no single pathway to success in specialist settings, but what unites us is the aim to create a curriculum that helps every child learn, belong, and move towards a joyful future.

Chapter summary

This chapter explores what learners need to experience, know, and remember to bring your vision to life.

- Curriculum design in specialist provisions must respond to the diverse and complex needs of learners, requiring an adaptive and personalised approach.
- Curriculum intent starts with clarity of purpose, vision, and values, helping you define what your learners need to know, experience, and remember.
- Specialist provisions often design multiple curriculum pathways to meet their learners' needs. However, each framework should be flexible, allowing learners to move between pathways as their interests, needs, and abilities change.
- Curriculum design works best when it reflects the lived experiences and perspectives of learners, making learning relevant and engaging.
- Successful curriculum implementation is underpinned by practical planning, ensuring the right staff, resources, and environment are in place to bring the curriculum to life for every child.
- Measuring the impact of a specialist curriculum goes beyond academic outcomes, to consider social, emotional, and life skill development.
- Leaders should reflect and adapt the curriculum continuously to respond to changing learner profiles, local need, and best practice.

Further reading

- You can read more about Gemma and Melissa's play-based curriculum in their article for the Chartered College of Teaching's *Impact* journal (James and Taylor, 2025).
- You can read Alex Tomkins' (2019) article on introducing a new curriculum within a specialist setting through the Chartered College of Teaching's *Impact* journal.
- For more information on establishing an internal alternative provision, read 'What works: Four tenets of effective internal alternative provision' by the educational charity, The Difference (Simpson and O'Brien, 2025).

References

Department for Education (2014). *Special Educational Needs and Disability Code of Practice: 0 to 25 years*. Available online at: https://www.gov.uk/government/publications/send-code-of-practice-0-to-25 [accessed 12 August 2025].

Department for Education (2025). *Curriculum and Assessment Review: Building a World-Class Curriculum for All*. Available online at: https://assets.publishing.service.gov.uk/media/690b96bbc22e4ed8b051854d/Curriculum_and_Assessment_Review_final_report_-_Building_a_world-class_curriculum_for_all.pdf [accessed 8 November 2025].

James, G., and Taylor, M. (2025, 19 May). '"All they do is play": The importance of play for all ages and stages of learning'. *Impact*. Part of My College, Chartered College of Teaching. Available online at: https://my.chartered.college/impact_article/all-they-do-is-play-the-importance-of-play-for-all-ages-and-stages-of-learning/ [accessed 5 July 2025].

Simpson, E., and O'Brien, C. (2025). 'What works: Four tenets of effective internal alternative provision', The Difference. Available online at: https://the-difference.com/wp-content/uploads/2025/06/What-Works-Four-Tenets-of-Effective-Internal-Alternative-Provision.pdf [accessed 20 September 2025].

Tomkins, A. (2019, 16 May). 'Designing a curriculum: The challenge faced by many specialist settings'. *Impact*. Part of My College, Chartered College of Teaching. Available online at: https://my.chartered.college/impact_article/designing-a-curriculum-the-challenge-faced-by-many-specialist-settings/ [accessed 11 August 2025].

Wiliam, D. (2013). *Principled Curriculum Design*. SSAT (The Schools Network). Available online at: https://webcontent.ssatuk.co.uk/wp-content/uploads/2020/03/20105155/Redesigning-Schooling-3-Principled-curriculum-design-Dylan-Wiliam.pdf [accessed 4 October 2025].

3

Pedagogy: Teaching every learner

Alternative Provision needs staff with integrity and character. Anyone can step in and offer a cup of tea, but what AP truly needs is the strongest, most rigorous and detail-focused teachers – because these are the children who need them the most.

Robert Bell, Headteacher of Consilium Evolve

Chapter overview

Having defined what our learners should know and remember, the next step is to consider how we'll teach the curriculum. In education, effective leaders influence learning continuously, establishing the conditions that enable teachers to be effective. In Chapter 1 we described aspects of transformational leadership – an approach which prioritises relationships and organisational culture by providing a compelling vision of the future. In this chapter we turn our attention to instructional leadership – considering how teaching, learning, and organisational culture come together to achieve effective outcomes for students.

The power of pedagogy

At its heart, pedagogy is about how we teach so that learning is meaningful, engaging, and accessible for every child. Pedagogy is important because high-quality teaching remains a key factor in increasing pupils' success and learning outcomes (Education Endowment Foundation, 2020b). However, it is particularly vital in specialist settings given that learners with SEND continue to experience significantly lower educational outcomes at the end of Key Stage 4 compared with learners without SEND (Department for Education, 2025).

If you're reading this, you are likely a competent and experienced teacher. Instructional leadership utilises this expertise by placing teaching and learning at the heart of leadership practice. It emphasises a leader's role in strengthening classroom practice, developing staff, and establishing the conditions that enable learners to thrive (Hallinger, 2005). Significantly, educational leadership research suggests that an instructional leadership approach can significantly enhance pupil progress. The more leaders are involved in the day-to-day activities of teaching and learning, the more they can influence pupil outcomes

DOI: 10.4324/9781003601388-4

positively (Robinson, Hohepa, and Lloyd, 2019). This is further reinforced by Leithwood et al. (2019), who assert that a fundamental purpose of all educational leaders is to establish a culture of high-quality teaching with a clear focus on learner achievement.

This chapter explores what helps children with additional needs learn, recognising that the strategies that work best for children with SEND form an effective approach for all learners (Education Endowment Foundation, 2020a). We will explore practical classroom strategies and explain what high-quality teaching looks like in our setting, including our a whole-school approach to pedagogy. We will explore how to balance autonomy and consistency as a staffing team grows, ensuring flexibility while maintaining a shared approach.

High-quality teaching in specialist settings

Teaching in specialist settings isn't just about delivering subject knowledge - it's about knowing the children and adapting learning to their needs, a principle emphasised in the *SEND Code of Practice: 0 to 25 Years* (2015, p. 25):

> *High quality teaching that is differentiated and personalised will meet the individual needs of the majority of children and young people [. . .] Special educational provision is underpinned by high quality teaching and is compromised by anything less.*

Despite this guidance, research into the effectiveness of specific pedagogical approaches for learners with additional needs remains limited. As a result, most specialist provisions develop their own lesson frameworks, designing strategies that respond to their cohort. At the heart of this approach is knowing your learners. SENCO and Senior Leader Ashley McCormick at Archers Brook School explains:

> *You need to know your children's needs, you need to know their favourite things, you need to know the names of their pets and the middle names of their pets.*

For many learners in specialist settings, working memory difficulties mean that new knowledge must be introduced in small steps and revisited regularly. Learning is often non-linear, requiring flexibility, patience, and creativity from teachers. The strategies below represent some of the approaches used to support meaningful learning:

- Introducing new learning in small chunks to reduce the risk of cognitive overload
- Making links with prior learning to help pupils connect ideas and deepen thinking
- Use of visuals to support comprehension and provide permanence
- Working walls to provide a visual reference of key concepts and prior learning
- Word mats to support the development of vocabulary
- Manipulatives and concrete resources to support the teaching of abstract concepts
- Teacher modelling to demonstrate expert thinking

- Presenting content in multiple ways to enable overlearning, multiple repetitions, and different ways to grasp a subject
- Provision of different methods for learners to engage so that all can succeed

Consequently, high-quality teaching in specialist settings requires knowing each learner and designing learning that is engaging, accessible, and at their level of challenge. Leaders must create the conditions for this to occur, from shaping pedagogy to providing opportunities for staff development. The thinking points below invite you to reflect on pedagogy in your own setting.

Thinking points

- What does high-quality teaching look like in your setting? How often do you discuss what high-quality teaching looks like?
- How do you stay connected to the core business of teaching and learning while managing the operational and strategic demands of being a leader?
- How do you ensure staff understand each learner's strengths, needs, and interests, and use these to personalise learning effectively?
- How can you create the conditions for your team to develop continuously their pedagogical practice?

Connecting learning to children's lives

When we design learning experiences that connect with what matters to our children, we create the conditions for meaningful engagement and understanding. Robert Bell, Headteacher of Consilium Evolve, outlines their approach to pedagogy:

> *We start lessons with a guided question - something that relates to their lives. We want to spark the curiosity that leads into learning. The question is a stimulus that is instantly relatable, something that learners will have a strong connection to e.g. Do I weigh pizza in slices? This leads into a Maths lesson on weights and measures and then into Food Technology where they make and cook the pizzas. Those cross-curricular links and borrowing experiences from other lessons are important. It's not just about getting the children excited - when staff get excited then children get excited too.*

Robert describes how meaningful links are created for learners between Maths and Food Technology, with the learning building and deepening across the school day. This approach supports engagement for pupils in specialist provisions, as when learning is connected to their interests or lived experience, their engagement often increases. Another powerful way to engage learners is to draw on their special interests. Many neurodivergent learners, especially autistic ones, will often have intense interests. These interests can create a monotropic way of thinking which enables deep focus, akin to a flow state (Murray, Lesser, and Lawson, 2005). It is potentially a similar concept to the hyperfocus which characterises Attention Deficit Hyperactivity Disorder (ADHD) (Dwyer et al., 2024). Monotropism and hyperfocus can help explain why neurodivergent individuals may find it difficult to switch tasks (or in school, subjects) when fully immersed in an activity (Murray, Lesser, and Lawson, 2005).Yet, many specialist settings still run traditional mainstream timetables, particularly in secondary provisions where learners may change topic every 50 minutes. Embedding cross-curricular links and building on learning throughout the day through a consistent topic can support smoother transitions between activities.

Recognising and working with intense interests reframes them not as obsessions or distractions, but as a gateway to learning and engagement. Research by Wood (2019) suggests that embracing a learner's special interests can provide them with a range of educational, social, and emotional benefits. They can support positive interactions between students and staff, reducing the need for prompts, lessening task repetition, and allowing for more attuned support (Wood, 2019). Murray, Lesser, and Lawson (2005) suggest for learning to be effective, learners need to:

- understand what the task is and why it matters
- feel motivated to do it
- know exactly what's being asked
- feel confident in how to complete the task

This type of information can be shared with learners via a task card. However, for monotropic individuals, completing the activity can still be challenging. If the task doesn't align with their current focus or interest, then it still may not be meaningful for them. Linking a task to a learner's current interests or strengths, or relating the purpose of the task to something that's important to them, can help overcome this. When we see learning through the eyes of our pupils, we can design experiences that truly engage them (think about the Kylie Minogue curriculum Dean Beadle mentions in the Foreword). The thinking points below encourage you to think about how you can make learning meaningful for your pupils.

Thinking points

- Robert Bell emphasises the importance of starting with what matters to your learners. How is this reflected in your pedagogical approach?
- What flexibility is there to allow pupils to engage in learning through their own interests?
- How do you encourage staff to understand and appreciate monotropism as a cognitive difference and not a behavioural issue? How could teachers in your setting harness the strengths of hyperfocus or monotropic thinking?
- Robert Bell highlights links between Maths and Food Technology. How do you develop cross-curricular connections in your setting?

Leadership scenario

During a learning walk, you notice that one learner is not engaging with a written task, despite repeated prompting from the teacher. The task is open-ended and based on a theme the learner doesn't appear excited by. The learner continues to draw in their notebook, something their One Page Profile says they do when anxious or disinterested. After the lesson, the teacher expresses frustration, saying the pupil is 'refusing to participate' and 'needs to learn to follow instructions'.

How do you respond? Consider the points below.

- How do you support the teacher to consider this behaviour through the lens of monotropism rather than defiance?
- How might you support the teacher to introduce tasks that harness intrinsic motivation?
- To what extent do you challenge the assumption that the learner must complete the same task in the same way as everyone else?
- Could this be an opportunity to introduce or revisit the concept of monotropism and its practical classroom implications during staff training?

When we connect learning to what matters to our pupils, we nurture engagement. Understanding the way each learner thinks and what captures their curiosity helps us see engagement and focus through a more compassionate lens. The next step is to respond flexibly, adapting our teaching so that each individual can access, engage with, and succeed in learning that feels meaningful to them.

Adaptive teaching

Adaptive teaching is essential to ensure all learners can access the purposefully sequenced curriculum we discussed in Chapter 2. Although SEND can be a useful umbrella term, it doesn't capture the complexity or individuality of every learner. Learners with additional needs are not one homogenous group and you will need to adapt your pedagogical approach to meet their differing and individual profiles. In fact, Maloy et al. (2025) found that when they asked learners with additional needs what support was most beneficial to them, the top answer was 'individualised learning'. This highlights that equity, not equality, is key and this means providing each learner with what they need to succeed. Good adaptive teaching is underpinned by knowing your learners and their differing needs both across and within subjects. As Dr Kevin Maxwell (n.d., cited in: Aungst, G. n.d.) suggests, it's our responsibility to educate the pupils in front of us – not the students we'd like to have, not the ones we've enjoyed teaching before, but the learners we have today.

Adaptive teaching is often construed as teaching one topic to the whole class and supporting everyone to achieve the learning intentions. We view adaptive teaching as the responsive adjustments a teacher makes during a lesson to meet each learner's needs. When planning, we focus on individual enablement strategies for each learner, such as tailored prompts or visuals, to help each child engage effectively. The smaller class sizes in specialist provisions enable staff to design learning prior to implementation in a way that works for each individual, rather than just adjusting learning when someone finds it difficult. In many specialist provisions, educators teach across multiple year groups in a single class, either due to a mix of chronological ages or ability. In these instances, differentiated, rather than adapted, resources are often necessary to ensure that each learner works toward an appropriate end goal. As discussed in Chapter 2, many specialist provisions have multiple curriculum pathways and each pathway may require a different pedagogical approach.

It is important to ensure that where Teaching Assistants (TAs) are supporting learning, they have a good understanding of the classroom routines and pedagogical approach so that they can support these. Reinforcing shared expectations helps to build collective efficacy within the classroom, ensuring every learner feels supported and included. TAs bring valuable insights into a learner's needs, so it is worth considering how you provide time for teachers and TAs to collaborate. As leaders, it's important to create a culture where the expertise of TAs is valued, actively integrated into classroom decision-making, and continually developed through professional growth.

Springfields Case Study: The 8 Steps to Lesson Success

At Springfields, we know that structure and predictability are crucial for our autistic learners. Our 8 Steps to Lesson Success (see Figure 3.1) offers a practical framework to support understanding, independence, and achievement. It can be adapted for different curriculum pathways (for example, our semi-formal classes may only have one retrieval and recap question) to enable more time for teacher modelling and independent practice.

☆

1. *Retrieve – retrieval practice*
   Starting a lesson with retrieval practice, which recalls learning from previous terms or topics, helps learners activate prior knowledge and creates firm and fluent long-term memories.
2. *Recap – review previous learning*
   The recap stage recalls learning from the previous lesson. It allows the teacher to ensure that the knowledge has been retained in the short-term and that learners are ready to move on. If the recap suggests that learners do not have a secure grasp of recent, prior learning, then this should be retaught before introducing new concepts.

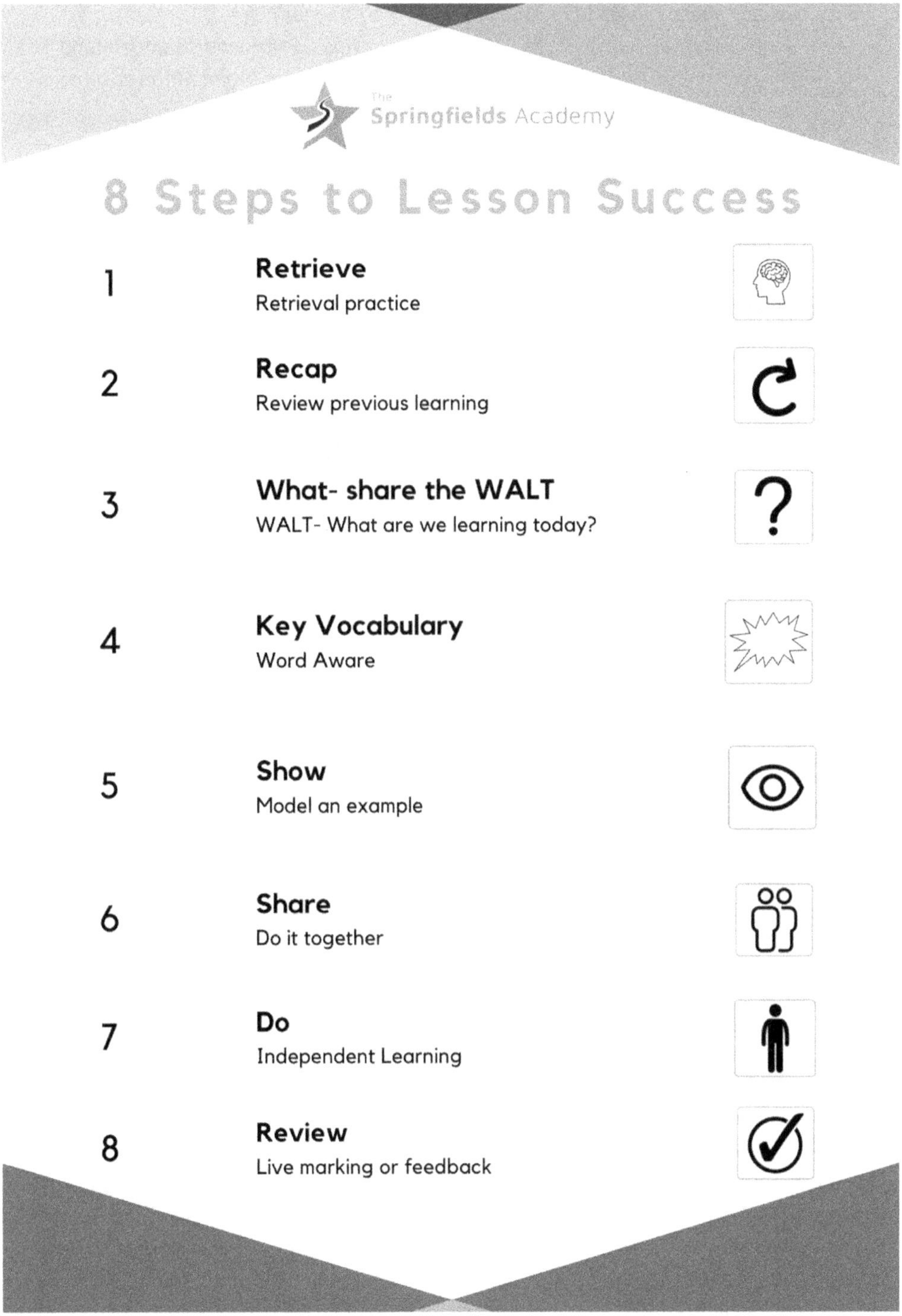

Figure 3.1 The 8 Steps to Lesson Success used at The Springfields Academy

3. *What – share the WALT – What are we learning today?*
   As explored above, children identified as having SEND need to understand the relevance of what they're learning. Sharing the learning intention ensures learners know what they're working towards and why it matters.
4. *Key vocabulary*
   All our learners have communication and interaction needs, so we teach and develop vocabulary explicitly. We use Word Aware strategies to help pupils learn new vocabulary, supporting their comprehension and understanding.
5. *Show – model an example (the teacher models an example)*
   Teacher modelling demonstrates what success looks like and enables learners to hear the thoughts of an expert. It helps pupils understand what's expected and provides a scaffold that can be referred to during independent work.
6. *Share – do it together (guided group example)*
   Working through examples together allows learners to practise skills with support and build confidence. The teacher can also look out for misconceptions and address these as they arise.
7. *Do – independent learning*
   Learners apply their knowledge independently, reinforcing understanding and building autonomy. Teachers observe learners' levels of independence, enabling them to identify whether more prompts are needed or whether scaffolds can be slowly withdrawn.
8. *Review – live marking or feedback*
   Reflection and feedback consolidate learning and the small class sizes mean this can occur instantly. For staff, this step informs future planning, creating a responsive, cyclical classroom culture.

☆

The 8 Steps are more than a checklist for teachers to work through. They embody a philosophy of teaching that supports independence whilst building confidence; provide a framework for staff to respond flexibly to learners' needs as well as offering a shared language to discuss teaching and learning; and, as learners know what to expect within and across lessons, help learners feel secure by enabling routine and predictability. Importantly, teachers have the autonomy to use their professional judgement to adapt the steps to tailor learning in the moment and those teaching within our different curriculum pathways adapt them to meet the needs of their learners – it is not expected that every lesson contains all 8 Steps.

This balance between consistency and individual professional judgement is central to adaptive teaching and something we explore in the next section.

How do you solve a problem like consistency?

As a leader, you'll want to establish consistency within your teaching team. You'll need to be confident that every lesson is well-planned and taught so that all learners receive high-quality teaching. Growing a provision requires consistency, ensuring that both individuals and groups of learners experience a well-sequenced curriculum and effective teaching across all classrooms. However, if leaders are too prescriptive, teachers may feel their professionalism is constrained, which can limit creativity and reduce autonomy. Yet, it can be tricky to find the right blend between shared expectations and frameworks, and to give teachers the space to adapt their practice and bring their own personality to the classroom. When leaders get this right, it builds trust and accountability, whilst ensuring consistency doesn't come at the expense of professional respect or innovation.

However, the need for uniformity can sit uneasily with some teachers, who may question why a consistent approach is required when specialist education is about meeting individual needs. This tension highlights the importance of creating a shared framework that guides practice without dictating it. Leaders can achieve this by:

- Co-constructing frameworks with staff, so that expectations are shared and co-created rather than imposed.
- Using collaborative moderation or planning sessions to define and share what high-quality teaching looks like in your setting.
- Encouraging teachers to adapt agreed principles to their class context, ensuring that personalisation sits within an overarching shared framework.

The following questions can help you reflect on your own approach and how to apply these principles in your setting.

Thinking points

- How do you define 'high-quality teaching' in your setting and how is this communicated with stakeholders?
- In what ways can shared frameworks, such as the 8 Steps, support consistency without limiting teacher creativity?
- How do you ensure that teacher autonomy is respected while maintaining accountability for pupil outcomes?
- What opportunities do teachers have to contribute to shaping shared frameworks and defining what effective practice looks like in your setting?

Activity: Building a consistent pupil experience

In specialist settings, consistency offers learners stability and safety, whilst reassuring leaders that pupils' experiences are equitable. You may wish to complete this activity individually or with members of your leadership team.

- List three pedagogical strategies that are central to effective teaching and learning in your setting.
- How consistently do learners experience these approaches as they move between classes, subjects, or teachers?
- What is one action you could take to increase consistency for learners?
- How close are leaders to the teaching and learning they are responsible for shaping?
- What aspects of pedagogy do leaders see regularly and which are largely inferred through data, reports, or conversations?
- How do you ensure that what leaders believe about classroom practice aligns with what learners actually experience?

Leadership scenario

You are Assistant Head of a pupil referral unit for 11–16-year-olds. You've recently introduced a shared teaching and learning framework designed to help bring consistency across the provision while still allowing for professional autonomy. Most staff have engaged well, but one experienced teacher, Tim, has shared with his line manager that his creativity as a professional is being stifled. His planning doesn't align with the shared framework and his lessons don't follow the agreed structure. This means the quality of learning is variable and learners are increasingly becoming dysregulated. He's well-liked and respected, but other teachers are concerned that the team isn't working together.

How will you support Tim to follow the shared framework without shutting down his creativity? You could consider:

- What data, observations, or feedback you might gather before meeting with Tim
- How you will frame the purpose of the conversation so it feels supportive
- What questions could help you understand *why* Tim is diverging from the shared approach? How might you uncover any barriers, beliefs, or misunderstandings?
- How you will communicate the rationale behind the shared framework
- How you identify which elements of the shared approach are non-negotiable, and those elements where autonomy is appropriate
- What kind of support might help Tim re-align?
- What will you look for in the coming weeks to gauge impact?

This scenario encourages you to explore how leaders can promote consistency while respecting teacher autonomy. It reminds us that frameworks alone don't create consistency - people do.

The success of our pedagogical approach depends on teachers who can interpret it thoughtfully, adapt it responsibly, and respond to what each child needs. This takes us into the next section - what makes an effective specialist teacher?

What makes a good teacher in specialist settings?

Legend has it that in ancient Phrygia (modern-day Turkey), a prophecy foretold that the next person to enter the city in an oxcart would become king. One day, a poor farmer named Gordias entered the city with his oxcart. True to their word, the people honoured the prophecy and made him king.

Gordias marked his good fortune by tying his oxcart to a wooden post at the city gates with a tightly woven knot made of bark. Over time, the complex knot itself became legendary and was known throughout the land as the Gordian Knot. A new prophecy emerged declaring that whoever could untie the Gordian Knot would go on to rule all of Asia. Each day, Phrygians would come to marvel at the knot. Though many tried to untie it, none succeeded. Years passed, yet the Gordian Knot remained as tangled and complex as ever.

Finally, a young man entered the city. He spent a long time surveying the knot and feeling its intricate construction with his hands. No one in Phrygia paid him much attention - he was just another traveller staring at the knot in defeat. Yet this man was not defeated, he was thinking. Twisting around, the traveller drew his sword, grasped the knot and with a single deft swing, severed it in two. The traveller's ability to (literally) cut through the problem in a bold and unconventional way brought him the success the prophecy promised. The traveller who took a novel approach to untying the Gordian Knot is better known today as Alexander the Great - the man who conquered the Persian Empire.

Leaders of specialist provisions often seek teachers who embody the same inventive mindset and lateral thinking that Alexander the Great demonstrated when confronted with the Gordian Knot. The ability of teachers in specialist settings to reflect and problem-solve, both in the moment and retrospectively, is highly valued by leaders. This is highlighted by Charlotte Barton, Managing Director of Progress Schools:

> *Working in Alternative Provision (AP) can be unpredictable - be patient and flexible. Every day brings unique challenges, so patience, adaptability and creative thinking are essential.*

Within the framework of our '8 Steps to Lesson Success', our teachers use the recap stage to assess whether learners are ready to progress. This demands flexibility, responsiveness, and a willingness to adapt the planned lesson if previous content hasn't been fully grasped. Specialist teachers must be prepared to re-teach material in different and creative ways using concrete or multi-sensory resources, as Lucy Kreczak, Deputy Headteacher at River Tees Hospital School, explains:

> *Lots of adaptive teaching is needed. You need the confidence to think 'this isn't working' and be able to adapt this on the spot. Being able to do that dynamic risk assessment is crucial. In mainstream you'd feel scrutiny - you've not covered your content. In specialist contexts you're making your decisions based on the needs of the children in front of you. You need someone who will think differently and is able to do that.*

Headteacher Robert Bell explains why the word 'innovation' is so important to his provision:

> *AP is the corner of education that people often don't want much to do with. We often still call them 'units'. Terminology matters. How would you like it if your child went to a 'unit'? That name instantly suppresses someone's confidence. We use the term 'intervention'. That word implies that I need to intervene to support you. It's a doing process. We have innovation sessions instead of interventions as the intention is that the teacher needs to do something better or different. To help this child be successful, something different or something else is needed and I have to innovate to provide that. It should always be about the adult doing something differently. When you're in AP, you've got to think of different mechanisms - you can't just do the same things over and over. You've got to think differently.*

Finally, Jo Dennis-Minns, late-diagnosed neurodivergent with lived experience of autism, OCD, and situational mutism, provides a valuable perspective on teacher qualities:

> *I had one teacher in primary school, my English teacher, Mrs Walker, she was kind, supportive, gave me (and all the class) time to process questions and adapted her room into different areas for learning. I wish my schools, both primary and secondary, had the experience and knowledge to support all learners with different needs. Many teachers were just harsh and gave little time for small, quiet children to learn or be understood.*

These insights illustrate that great teaching in specialist settings is as much about mindset as it is about method. Creativity, reflection, kindness, and patience underpin successful teaching. For leaders, the challenge lies in recognising and nurturing these qualities within their teams - both when recruiting new staff and supporting existing teachers to grow. The following questions can help you reflect on how you identify, develop, and sustain these qualities within your provision.

Thinking points

- How do you encourage teachers to think creatively when faced with complex challenges in the classroom?
- How can you recognise and celebrate examples of innovative practice that improve learning outcomes?
- What qualities do you look for in your teachers and how do you identify these during the recruitment process?
- Research by Maloy et al. (2025) suggests that young people feel that it is the trusting relationships and everyday interactions with staff that make a difference to their lives. How might this affect your recruitment process?

Leadership scenario

You are the Headteacher of an alternative provision for learners aged 11–16 years. You have recently advertised for a classroom teacher and have received a pleasing response. Many applicants demonstrate strong subject knowledge and classroom experience, yet few reflect on the personal qualities that underpin successful teaching in your context. You want to ensure your recruitment process identifies not only who can teach well, but who can connect well with your learners.

What action do you take? Consider the points below.

- How will you strike the balance between teaching competence and personal qualities when shortlisting and interviewing candidates?
- What interview questions, scenarios, or activities could help you assess personal qualities such as empathy and resilience?
- How might involving learners, families, or other staff in the recruitment process help you identify the personal attributes that matter most in your setting?
- How will you balance the need to fill vacancies with the longer-term goal of building a values-led, emotionally intelligent teaching team?

Learning from lived experience

Our contributors with lived experience offer insights that can guide us toward more inclusive and supportive approaches to teaching and learning. Their accounts can be difficult to read, but they highlight both the barriers and enablers that help individuals with additional needs to flourish in the classroom.

I prefer independent tasks and working on self-directed projects, however most learning in my mainstream school consisted of group work, presentations and rote learning on topics which were not necessarily useful to me. The expectation of communicating with peers in a group meant that I was often too anxious to process and retain any information. Despite English being my favourite subject, I often avoided attending due to the fear of being called upon to answer in front of my peers. Team games in PE were also a source of extreme stress.

I believe neurodivergent learners should be given greater autonomy in schools; they should be given opportunities to participate in self-directed projects and have opportunities to speak up about matters that affect them. I think it's important for neurodivergent learners to have access to educational approaches that work for them; remote studying could be incorporated if necessary. I believe in the importance of having access to learning around life skills, communication, self-regulation and neurodivergent friendly relationships and sex education. To enable neurodivergent learners to be effectively supported, I propose that teacher training include in-depth ideas around trauma, neuroscience and wellbeing.

Lauren Smith, autistic adult and postgraduate researcher

I learn best in shorter periods, with certainty and predictability, when I'm given processing time rather than being 'put on the spot', with opportunities to move about and use fidget aids, and with minimal sensory distractions. This is very different from my school experiences. I recall both my sensory sensitivities and my internal hyperactivity and racing mind. The push-pull between desperately wanting to move around yet not wanting to stand out and break the rules. I ended up regularly having to sit on my hands in assemblies and lessons. I remember the internal pain and tension of trying to keep myself still in an attempt to fit in with people around me. In all the effort to do this, it reduced my ability to focus on what I was learning. Yet, on the surface, I was perceived as a well-behaved student so received minimal support so the pressure was immense.

Remie Colledge, Neurodivergent Speaker, Trainer, and Writer

Another important part of school was my teachers. They praised me for work that I did well and nurtured my ability to question and understand the less literal. One RE teacher would gently challenge me on some of my black and white thinking. Knowing that I was safe and supported, even that there were boundaries so that I would not get hurt by others was really important to me. Despite having to walk a long time to get to school, in retrospect, that long walk helped me to process what had happened during the day before I got home and walk off some of the adrenaline in the mornings. Generally, I enjoyed school. I loved learning in most subjects. I have always struggled with coordination, so I found practical subjects and especially PE very challenging.

Miranda, late diagnosed autistic adult and parent to an autistic child

I need to have a friend with me and interact with them about the work but sometimes a friend who finds it more difficult because explaining it to them helps me to learn it better. I find it hard to learn when I am worried, so if I am by myself or if I think the teacher might cold-call me, I will be focusing on the cold-calling and not the lesson.

Zoe, autistic teenager

I'm very much a visual learner. I learn and still learn best by being shown and modelled something. My time at school was very much learning by textbook or copying from a chalkboard. I did ok, I copied a lot, in fact most of my time was spent copying my friend in the classroom and playground. I now realise I used echolalia all the time. I had few friends, I didn't feel I needed friendships, nor did my peers understand me.

My downfall was in tests and exams. I spent hours and hours revising and struggled a lot to both learn, remember and execute pen to paper. My mental health, now I look back, was overwhelmed and anxious until I left school.

Jo Dennis-Minns, late-diagnosed neurodivergent
with lived experience of autism, OCD, and situational mutism

These accounts highlight the importance of emotional safety. They suggest that, to ensure learners feel safe, understood, and able to focus on learning rather than masking, teachers in specialist provisions need to be supportive and emotionally intelligent as well as adaptable and attuned. Use the questions below to reflect on what resonated with you from these experiences.

Thinking points

- What commonalities are there between these accounts? What are the implications for teaching and learning?
- How do you create opportunities for students to share their experiences of teaching and learning in your setting?
- How well do you listen to and act on requests for reasonable adjustments from learners and families? What procedures are in place to ensure this happens?
- How much choice and autonomy do you currently give learners in shaping their goals and learning experiences?

Chapter summary

This chapter explores the importance of pedagogy, as research indicates that instructional leadership can positively influence learner achievement.

- Learners with SEND often underperform compared to their peers - this means high-quality teaching is vital in specialist settings.
- Intense interests can support motivation and task relevance for learners.
- It's important to help learners understand a task, feel motivated to do it, and be confident to complete it.
- Research suggests that learners with additional needs value individualised learning strategies.
- Teaching Assistants play an important role in teaching and learning in specialist provisions and must be supported and developed appropriately.
- Leaders face the challenging task of maintaining a consistent approach to teaching and learning while supporting the professional autonomy that underpins teacher wellbeing.
- Teachers in specialist settings must be able to analyse situations reflectively and creatively. Their ability to reflect, problem-solve, and adapt will enable them to support all learners to make progress.
- Lived experience suggests that conventional teaching methods do not always match learners' preferred ways of learning. Specialist teachers therefore require a creative, patient, and child-centred approach that responds to the needs of each learner.

Further reading

- For further reading on inclusive classroom strategies, you may wish to explore 'The shift to adaptive teaching: A research-informed guide' by Mark Leswell, Research Lead at Swale Academies Trust (2023).
- An overview on the Word Aware approach can be accessed at: https://www.structural-learning.com/post/word-aware-complete-guide-star-approach

References

Department for Education (2015, January). *SEND Code of Practice: 0 to 25 years*. Available online at: https://assets.publishing.service.gov.uk/media/5a7dcb85ed915d2ac884d995/SEND_Code_of_Practice_January_2015.pdf [accessed 2 January 2025].

Department for Education (2025). *Key Stage 4 Performance: Academic Year 2023/24*. Available online at: https://explore-education-statistics.service.gov.uk/find-statistics/key-stage-4-performance/2023-24 [accessed 7 June 2025].

Dwyer, P., Williams, Z. J., Lawson, W. B., and Rivera, S. M. (2024). 'A trans-diagnostic investigation of attention, hyper-focus, and monotropism in autism, attention dysregulation hyperactivity development, and the general population'. *Neurodiversity, 2*.

Education Endowment Foundation (2020a). *Special Educational Needs in Mainstream Schools Guidance Report*. Available online at: https://educationendowmentfoundation.org.uk/education-evidence/guidance-reports/send [accessed 8 November 2025].

Education Endowment Foundation (2020b). 'High-quality teaching'. Available online at: https://educationendowmentfoundation.org.uk/support-for-schools/school-planning-support/1-high-quality-teaching [accessed 2 January 2025].

Hallinger, P. (2005). 'Instructional leadership and the school principal: A passing fancy that refuses to fade away'. *Leadership and Policy in Schools, 4*(3), pp. 221–239.

Leithwood, K., Harris, A., and Hopkins, D. (2019). 'Seven strong claims about successful school leadership revisited'. *School Leadership & Management, 40*, pp. 1–18.

Leswell, M. (2023,19 May). 'The shift to adaptive teaching: A research-informed guide'. *Impact*. Part of My College, Chartered College of Teaching. Available online at: https://my.chartered.college/impact_article/the-shift-to-adaptive-teaching-a-research-informed-guide/ [accessed 28 July 2025].

Maloy, L., Tolley, J., King, S., Barwell, N., Cross, E., and Brown, A. (2025). *Young Researchers Young Voices: Co-research SEND Project. Final Report*. Available online at: https://www.researchgate.net/profile/Liam-Maloy/publication/394447746_Young_Researchers_Young_Voices_Co-research_SEND_project_Final_Report [accessed 13 August 2025].

Maxwell, K. (n.d.). *"Our job is to teach the students we have. Not the ones we would like to have. Not the ones we used to have. Those we have right now. All of them."* Cited at: https://www.literacytoday.ca/home/differentiation/key-principles [accessed 1 April 2026].

Murray, D., Lesser, M., and Lawson, W. (2005). 'Attention, monotropism and the diagnostic criteria for autism'. *Autism: The International Journal of Research and Practice, 9*(2), 139–156.

Robinson, V., Hohepa, M., and Lloyd, C. (2009). *School Leadership and Student Outcomes: Identifying What Works and Why Best Evidence Synthesis Iteration (BES)*. Available online at: https://www.researchgate.net/publication/242493851_School_Leadership_and_Student_Outcomes_Identifying_What_Works_and_Why_Best_Evidence_Synthesis_Iteration_BES

Wood, R. (2019). 'Autism, intense interests and support in school: From wasted efforts to shared understandings'. *Educational Review, 73*(1), 34–54.

4

Assessment: Small steps, big success

Celebrate progress, big and small. Success in Alternative Provisions often looks different than in mainstream settings. Recognise and celebrate every step forward, whether it's an improvement in a student's attendance or a staff member's creative solution.

Charlotte Barton, Managing Director of Progress Schools

Chapter overview

Assessment is a fundamental component of teaching and learning, directly informing and shaping the curriculum pathway each learner follows. Once we're clear about the knowledge and skills we want learners to develop and the approaches we'll use to teach them, we must then ask: How will we know it's having an impact? This chapter explores what formative and summative assessment looks like in the specialist sector; thinks holistically about different progress measures; and considers social and emotional progress alongside academic attainment. It discusses how leaders can quality-assure assessment judgements and ensure that progress is occurring in settings where national measures may hold less relevance. We'll look at how assessment can reduce staff workload and offer important insight into the pupil experience. Finally, we'll explore the ways that specialist provisions gain pupil voice and introduce the HEARD principle.

Assessment in specialist provisions

Specialist provisions must often define what 'progress' means for their learners given their diverse and wide-ranging needs. The accountability system within English schools often seems to prioritise specific types of progress, particularly English and Maths. However, many learners in specialist education need support with regulation and engagement, meaning their cognitive potential is not always evident through standard assessment methods. Consequently, specialist settings use a variety of measures, including areas of the *SEND Code of Practice* (Department for Education and Department of Health, 2014), to assess their learners beyond the traditional taught curriculum. These include:

- Communication and Interaction – e.g. how a young person's speech and language is progressing and the development of functional communication skills.

DOI: 10.4324/9781003601388-5

- Physical and Sensory – e.g. gross and fine motor skills, sensory awareness, and processing.
- Cognition and Learning – e.g. working memory and attention.
- Social and Emotional – e.g. self-regulation, self-esteem, and working with others.

Many specialist settings will assess progress laterally. This is because it is important to recognise that a child's development may not follow a linear or age-expected trajectory and that significant development and progress may be occurring for the individual. For learners with complex needs, lateral assessment can help highlight achievement, particularly when it falls outside of common progress markers. This approach enables provisions to capture an individual's breadth of learning; how independence and engagement is increasing; and how skills are being applied in or transferred to different contexts. This provides a more holistic measure of progress, reduces the use of deficit language around a learner's need to 'catch up', and supports the celebration of small-step, personalised progress. Some approaches for the assessment of lateral progress include:

- Specialist frameworks – e.g. SCERTA, MAPP, or the Engagement Model.
- Evidence portfolios – e.g. photos, videos, and observation notes.
- Narrative assessment – e.g. teacher commentary and reflection.
- Personalised learning plans.

Success often looks different across settings. It can be difficult to compare performance within and between specialist settings meaningfully when learners' needs can be so different and numbers, grades, or percentages rarely capture the full picture. As Headteacher at Greenside School, Alex Tomkins, explains:

> *In special schools, assessment can be open, unique and interesting. But in some ways that can be a challenge. How do you know your system is right? When planning an assessment system, as well as thinking about what is right for the learners, it is wise to think about the stakeholders of the information you collect. Governors and parents will want to know certain things. An evidence-rich system can enable greater understanding of the children, but it can make summarising this for Governors tricky. The key thing is that assessment needs to focus on what the child needs, be destination-focused and more about progress than attainment.*

Alex's reflection reminds us that assessment is about more than raw data. It must capture the individual learning journey of each learner whilst also producing information that stakeholders can understand. In specialist settings, assessment helps us understand each learner's progress and experience, showing whether our curriculum is having the desired impact. When used effectively, it supports early intervention and ensures that support is responsive and targeted. Assessment also helps leaders by:

- Enabling evidence-based decisions with regard to the allocation of time, support, and resources.

- Highlighting areas of good practice and areas where additional support may be needed.
- Shaping professional development priorities.

In specialist provisions, it's essential to track progress towards Education, Health and Care Plan (EHCP) outcomes. This often involves 12-week cycles following an 'assess, plan, do, review' model. Leaders should also consider how the impact of therapeutic interventions is captured and analysed. The following questions invite you to reflect on the assessment principles in your provision.

Thinking points

- What does 'good' progress look like for learners in your setting?
- What different aspects do you assess to get a holistic understanding of progress and how do you do this?
- How do you present detailed information in a way that stakeholders, including Governors and families, can understand quickly?
- How are staff supported to interpret and use assessment data meaningfully to inform pedagogy?
- How do you ensure consistent and rigorous moderation of judgements across your provision, especially if operating across multiple sites?

Understanding progress at a whole-school level is essential for leaders, but teachers also need strategies to track and respond to learning in the moment. Formative assessment helps guide daily teaching decisions and forms the focus of our next section.

Using formative assessment to inform teaching

Effective formative assessment, which involves observing learners' responses and providing real-time feedback, underpins the adaptive teaching strategies discussed in Chapter 3. Formative assessment shows whether key concepts have been understood or if re-teaching is needed. As the word itself suggests, formative feedback is intended to inform teaching and learning practices, shaping learning to meet each pupil's needs. Yan et al. (2021) describe formative assessment as:

> *an instructional strategy, embedded in daily classroom activities and conversations, which can identify the learning needs of special education students, so that modifications of instruction can be made and more support can be provided.*

Continuous monitoring of progress is embedded in most specialist settings because traditional, standardised tests can lack relevance. Formative assessment, however, enables teachers to be more nuanced in how they assess. Useful strategies can be:

- Red, amber, and green finished trays for learners to self-assess and place completed work.
- Hinge questions, and questioning more broadly, to check understanding before moving on.
- Teacher and pupil conferencing, whether live or asynchronous through technology such as QR codes.
- Pupil observation - this is key particularly for non-speaking learners.
- Multi-modal responses - e.g. using tablets as well as pen and paper, or using the learner's preferred method of communication.

Many specialist provisions use online systems such as Earwig to record formative assessment. These systems often have prepared frameworks, but most specialist provisions design their own to ensure that the small-step progress points effectively match their own context and curriculum.

Leadership scenario

You are Deputy Head of an all-through specialist provision with responsibility for curriculum and assessment. A newly appointed teacher is struggling to navigate and apply your provision's assessment framework, finding it time-consuming and complex. In a recent pupil progress meeting, it was clear that most pupils are making incremental progress, but this is not being recognised.

What action do you take? You could consider:

- How you will support the teacher to understand and use your assessment framework effectively.
- What strategies or training you could implement to ensure that staff consistently capture and celebrate small steps of progress.
- How families are informed and involved in assessment processes.
- How technology could help reduce teacher workload.

Looking beyond the numbers - summative assessment in specialist provisions

Formative assessment is essential for adapting teaching and responding to learners' needs. However, leaders need a clear picture of progress over time. Summative assessment provides this overview, showing what learners have achieved and how effectively the curriculum is supporting their development. It evaluates learning at key points, helping to inform future planning and strategic decisions. Your assessment policy and school calendar will outline your assessment cycle, which is likely to include baseline assessments, end of unit/term assessments, and 12 Week Outcome cycles for progress towards EHCP outcomes.

Baseline assessments are particularly important in specialist provisions as establishing learners' starting points with confidence can be challenging. This can be because:

- Learners may have experienced disrupted learning or reduced learning time, particularly if they have moved between, or been temporarily away from, educational settings.
- Children identified as having SEND may progress at different rates to learners without additional needs.
- Individuals with SEND may not excel at traditional assessments due to anxiety or difficulty concentrating for extended periods.
- Learners joining a new provision may not show their true potential until they feel settled and have built safe, trusting relationships with peers and adults.
- Although hyperlexic students may read at an advanced level, this can make it harder to identify their broader strengths and needs accurately.

Children identified as having SEND can have highly individual learning profiles. The psychologist Francesca Happé (1994) suggests that autistic learners can have uneven cognitive profiles, excelling in some areas whilst needing more support in others. Although all learners have strengths and areas for development, this can be more pronounced in neurodivergent learners. This demonstrates why curriculum pathways must be flexible (as discussed in Chapter 2) and why it's important not to make generalisations about a learner's wider abilities based on a single assessment point or type. To capture a more complete picture, it's essential to provide a range of methods for learners to demonstrate their understanding and skills.

The Uncertainty Principle, proposed by the German physicist Werner Heisenberg in 1927 (cited in *Encyclopaedia Britannica*, 2025), suggests that by trying to measure one aspect of a particle, we inherently limit what else we can know about it. Similarly, in specialist provisions, measurement via summative assessment tends to capture only one aspect of a learner's progress and attainment, thus potentially limiting our understanding of the child. Consequently, assessment shouldn't be treated as a complete or fixed truth, but rather as a snapshot in time.

Assessment in specialist settings also needs to include social and emotional development. Charlotte Barton, Managing Director of Progress Schools, suggests specialist settings should:

> *Assess the 'softer' areas first (engagement, social and emotional development, relationships, and resilience) and hold them in the same esteem as academic subjects. These are key to addressing the barriers that have prevented engagement in mainstream education. These are the data sets that help you to create a different experience for the child.*

As Charlotte points out, assessment data should help learners and families recognise their strength and talents beyond the academic.

As specialist leaders, we need to approach assessment with flexibility and creativity, using a range of methods at different times to build a holistic picture of our learners. This includes considering the accessibility of assessments and how assistive technology can help remove barriers for learners. Individuals who face specific challenges in communicating expressively, for example learners with Developmental Language Disorder, may need support to convey what they know and understand through spoken or written tasks. Their challenges with expressive communication can also affect how their learning is interpreted by educators as their understanding may be harder to assess through conventional methods.

Some specialist provisions use ipsative assessment. This approach measures a learner's current performance by comparing it with their past achievements rather than with external benchmarks or the performance of their peers. Ipsative assessment provides a more personalised measure of progress since it considers how an individual has developed over time compared with personal benchmark. This method acknowledges and values individual progress, particularly where it doesn't align with standardised measures or age-related expectations.

It's also important to consider how assessment outcomes are communicated to learners and their families. Clear, strengths-focused language that is sensitive to individual needs ensures that everyone can understand what progress has occurred and what the next steps are. In this way, assessment creates useful dialogue about each learner's journey both with them and their family. Assessment data should also instigate meaningful conversations with other stakeholders, promoting accountability and supporting strategic planning. Educational settings often collect large amounts of data and it's important to consider what information stakeholders need and to present it in a way that highlights both achievements and areas for development.

Activity: Supporting effective assessment conversations

Think of a learner in your setting and map out all the assessment information you collect. Consider:

- Who needs to receive this information (learners, families, staff, governors).
- What is essential for each group of stakeholders to know, highlighting both achievements and areas for development.
- How the information should be communicated (meetings, reports, visual summaries, verbal feedback). Are different methods required?
- How you can present the information so that it supports dialogue and strategic planning.

Thinking points

- What does your baseline assessment process look like? How do you determine what learners already know and what gaps they have?
- What assessment information is requested for new learners joining your provision?
- For learners sitting traditional exams, which staff have responsibility for assessing and implementing access arrangements? What may be needed to accommodate these needs?

When used thoughtfully and holistically, summative assessment enables teachers to celebrate progress, identify emerging needs, and ensure that every learner's journey is recognised, celebrated, and shared.

Case study: How assessment can support parental engagement by Kimberley Legg, Assistant Headteacher at Addington School

In this case study, Kimberley illustrates how assessment is a tool not just for tracking progress but also for engaging families as active partners in their child's education.

☆

I had led on assessment in my previous school and when I moved to Addington I thought I could replicate my previous assessment model. However, this wasn't easy to do as schools are all at different stages and have different needs.

I picked Earwig as our assessment platform because of its ability to share progress with parents. This means it does two things; it tracks progress and supports parental engagement. A key consideration for leaders was how we would quality assure and monitor the information being shared with parents as this was a potential risk. Providing staff training and supporting staff with this element is important.

I started our journey towards implementing Earwig by asking 'what do our families need?'. As with our children, our families all need different things and what they need fluctuates throughout their time with us. I realised that there was a spectrum of needs and that all our families had different engagement levels. Some families were at a point where they were almost co-producing One Page Profiles and support strategies. Other families were beginning active engagement, whereas some just wanted to know what was happening in school but didn't want to get involved. We used these insights to create tiers of engagement and provided support for staff on how to support families at each tier. I came up with the concept of levels of engagement from my background working with children with Profound and Multiple Learning Difficulties. I was used to looking at the engagement of students through the Department for Education's Engagement Model (2020) and realised that I could transfer the concept across to parents.

When establishing Earwig, we wanted to avoid overwhelming families. At first, some thought they were being asked to replace school activities. However, by discussing how important it is for children to generalise and transfer skills, we helped parents understand that their support was about applying learning outside of school.

We're constantly tweaking and refining what we do with Earwig - we've even had a parent create a video for other parents on using the platform! Communicating with families via Earwig is now a core part of our induction package for new staff, including crib sheets on how to communicate effectively.

☆

This case study highlights one of the benefits of new online assessment systems - the ability to collaborate with families. Many can create a two-way dialogue, enabling families to share pictures and videos of their child learning at home or in the community. This approach is particularly valuable for non-speaking children who might not be able to share their experiences at home with school and vice versa.

Thinking points

- How does your current assessment system support meaningful, two-way engagement with families?
- Do you consider the needs of families when sharing pupil progress and do you tailor communication accordingly?
- Kimberley discusses a tiered approach to parental engagement. What might this look like in your setting?
- How do you quality-assure the accuracy and clarity of assessment information shared with families?

Although effective assessment can strengthen parental engagement, this also has implications for teacher workload and wellbeing. Leaders need to consider how assessment systems are designed and implemented so that staff can use them meaningfully without feeling overwhelmed. This consideration forms the focus of the section below.

Balancing assessment demands with staff wellbeing

One of the benefits of specialist provisions is that smaller class sizes make marking more manageable. However, reliance on cloud-based systems, often requiring photographs and the uploading of evidence, can be time consuming for teachers. Tomkins (2024) suggests a range of strategies to help manage these demands and support staff wellbeing:

- Provide clear expectations and guidance for staff through assessment policies, helping staff understand why, when, and how to assess.
- Create a shared understanding of what makes a good piece of photographic or video evidence. This is particularly useful for support staff who can then help teachers upload evidence.

- Identify a multi-tasking app or system which enables you to create reports and communicate with parents.
- Use a shorthand system or acronyms to tag evidence and reduce lengthy written comments.

Tomkins (2024) also suggests that a natural approach to assessment can help reduce teacher workload by making it part of everyday classroom practice, rather than an additional task. In this approach, Tomkins (2024) suggests that all staff capture learners' progress throughout the day with ongoing pupil observation incorporated into planning. This type of assessment helps with tracking incremental progress, capturing learning moments, and the sharing of highlights with parents.

It is important to help Early Career Teachers and staff new to specialist provisions to be aware of and celebrate small-step progress. Educators who are used to age-appropriate progress and expectations can feel sometimes disheartened and feel that their learners are not making any progress. Learning to focus on small improvements is important as Lucy Kreczak, Deputy Headteacher at River Tees Hospital School, explains:

> *Small steps, but every small achievement is a big success for the student.*

Helping staff understand what success looks like supports their self-esteem and tells them that their efforts are having an impact.

Beyond annual reviews: Making pupil voice part of the everyday

In specialist settings, understanding the lived experience of the children we serve is central to everything we do. We are here for the children and to be truly child-centred, we must use their voices to shape our provision. However, eliciting authentic pupil voice can be a complex task, particularly for non-speaking learners who may not have found their preferred method of communication yet. Many neurodivergent learners find redrafting work or reflecting on feedback difficult, often due to compartmentalised thinking patterns. A child may see a task as 'finished' and therefore see little value in returning to it. Rather than viewing this as defiance or disinterest, we must approach it with empathy, recognising that, for some pupils, 'finished' provides a satisfying sense of closure and therefore revisiting a task can feel confusing or overwhelming. Moreover, some learners experience feedback as a form of rejection - sometimes referred to as Rejection Sensitive Dysphoria - leading to intense emotional responses that can make redrafting feel threatening, uncomfortable, or painful.

Our approach to pupil voice must be responsive and creative. Research by Maloy et al. (2025) highlights the importance of listening directly to young people, rather than relying only on adults' interpretations of what young people have experienced. Lydia Colios, Assistant Headteacher at Addington School, explains their approach to pupil voice:

Pupil voice isn't just what we do at annual reviews. It's all the things we do every day to capture the voice of the child. We must advocate for our young people. Sometimes it can be hard to gain their voice, so a Total Communication approach is vital. It's important to get pupil voice on everything, from curriculum to safeguarding. In particular, we survey new pupils in September and July. Good pupil voice depends on relationships. I always include the literacy team to adapt resources for our complex learners to ensure they can partake. We need to ensure, through the curriculum, that we're enabling them to give their voice.

However, if pupils give us their voice, how do we feed back to them about how we're listening? We often use the school council for this, but as senior leaders sometimes we need to set the scene – it isn't possible to always agree to pupils' requests e.g. it might be financially unviable.

We want to equip learners with skills for life. We want them to have an approach for advocating for themselves that they can take with them when they leave us. We want to build on their own communication styles so that they can take that approach with them and use it post-16.

Lydia stresses that pupil voice is not something to be captured only at annual reviews – it should be embedded in the daily life of a provision. Crucially, it's not just about gathering opinions, but feeding back to learners so they understand how their input is being used. Lydia's approach reminds us that capturing pupil voice effectively requires intention, planning, and a collaborative team approach.

Many specialist provisions, particularly residential settings, will also have an independent listener and policy surrounding this. Independent listeners are external to the organisation and support the safeguarding and welfare of learners by being a trusted and impartial adult. This offers learners another way to be heard and supported. When pupil voice is genuinely embedded and responded to, it strengthens inclusion, safeguarding, and reinforces child-centred approaches.

Thinking points

- How do you embed pupil voice in your daily provision?
- How do you use a range of communication methods to ensure all learners can share their views?
- How do you ensure learners understand how their input is being acted upon or why some requests may not be possible?
- How do you equip learners with self-advocacy skills that can be used beyond your setting?

Author anecdote: the HEARD principle

> *Empathy, patience and listening are crucial. Sometimes schools listen but they don't hear. It's really important to actually hear what the children are telling you.*
>
> Emma Twell, Safeguarding and SEND Specialist and autistic adult

Most of us have probably experienced situations where the person we're talking to says, "You're not hearing what I'm saying". They don't mean that your ears aren't physically receiving their voice; they mean you're not understanding the message they're trying to communicate. This is what Emma is referencing above. There is no educational setting that would say they don't listen to children, but have they *really* understood what the child is saying, particularly if that child is non-speaking or has complex communication needs?

After a review of pupil voice in our setting, we introduced a feedback strategy called HEARD. This is a school-wide approach that reminds staff of the importance of listening for understanding - not what we *think* our learners have said, but what they actually want to say. When our learners' voices are heard then their views are acknowledged and respected.

HEARD stands for:

- Hear - actively listen without assumptions
- Empower - enable learners to advocate for themselves
- Accept - validate their feelings
- Reflect - consider what they've shared
- Decisions - give feedback on the decisions taken

Figure 4.1 The HEARD Approach used at The Springfields Academy

To support this, HEARD boxes are available across the school, including in classrooms and social spaces. Learners can share their thoughts in writing, through pictures, by circling visual images, or via a bespoke email address.

Figure 4.2 What HEARD stands for

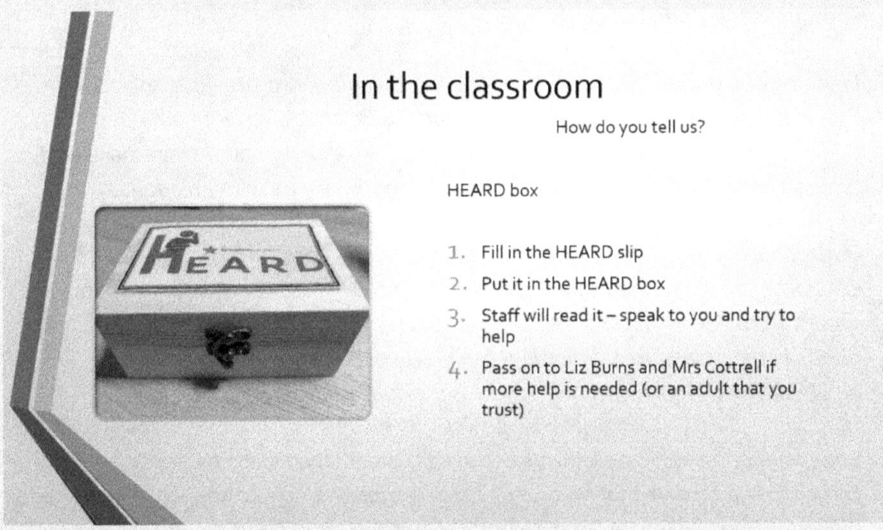

Figure 4.3 The HEARD Box and how to use it

By extending the same approach to parents and staff through boxes in Reception and the option to email HEARD directly, we've been able to engage our entire school community in the HEARD principle. This shared language is important as it creates a consistent system that stakeholders trust in, use, and signpost to others.

Case study: Listening, responding, empowering: Southfield's pupil voice strategy

Angela O'Rourke, Headteacher of Southfield SEN School, explains how they have embedded pupil voice into daily life, ensuring that children's views actively shape the school and learning environment. Southfield is a primary school for 103 pupils with Learning Difficulties, including Autism, Speech Language and Communication Needs, and Global Developmental Delay.

☆

Pupil Voice is imperative at Southfield. Children need to have their voice heard and be made to feel that they matter. We believe:

'A Southfield pupil will be confident, have self-esteem and self-belief which can be transferred into appropriate and accelerated learning inside the classroom and beyond. Our pupils will have emotional literacy, follow the school rules and know how and when to ask for help'.

Many of our pupils join us demonstrating trauma from previous experiences. This is supported in a variety of ways from daily 'check ins' with a named member of staff to weekly art or play therapy. Some of our pupils need a weekly timetabled slot where they can talk about their interests with an adult.

Our school council champion the ideas from their classes on to how to make 'their school better'. Meetings take place fortnightly where school council members (pupils from each class elected by their peers) will champion the thoughts from others in their class. Behaviour Leads are also established in each class and these pupils support others with our School Behaviour Charter.

Complaint and suggestion forms are accessible in each class by pupils and they can choose a format that works for them or get an adult to support. Pupils can make a complaint about something that has happened and say what they feel needs to happen. They can also suggest how we can make the school better.

These suggestions are read out in assembly on a Friday and each individual complaint or suggestion is responded to by a letter written by the Headteacher. Pupils' views are taken seriously and for most pupils being seen, being heard and action being taken in relation to this is a huge step in their development and progress at Southfield.

☆

In her case study, Angela explains how pupil voice can be embedded in daily practice. From School Council representatives and Behaviour Leads to accessible complaint and suggestion systems, Southfield's approach ensures that pupils are seen, heard, and empowered.

Thinking points

- Could any of the strategies outlined by Angela be useful in your setting?
- Southfield's approach ensures that all pupils, regardless of communication style or cognitive level, can share their views. How do you achieve this in your provision?
- Southfield uses a range of methods to help their learners contribute to school life e.g. Behaviour Leads, school councils. How might your learners take greater ownership of their school community?
- Southfield demonstrates a feedback loop where learners' suggestions are acknowledged publicly and responded to personally. How could you achieve this in your setting?

Activity: Reviewing your feedback loop

Map out the current pupil voice journey in your provision, from when a pupil shares an idea to when they receive a response. Think about:

- How learners share their voice
- How staff review input
- How and when actions are taken
- How and when learners are informed of outcomes

Can you identify any areas where this process breaks down? How could you strengthen this system?

Learning from lived experience: Assessment

It is rare to find people who enjoy assessments, however the pressures of assessment on those already experiencing anxiety can be significant. The Department for Education's *Curriculum and Assessment Review: Interim Report* (2025) describes the pressures of the examination system in England, driven by the large number of exams children sit. This echoes the concerns raised by our lived experience contributors below that formal assessments, such as exams, are not always effective assessment mechanisms.

At school I didn't know I had autism – nobody knew. Like most girls undiagnosed with autism, I suffered. I was a huge people pleaser, but I was also a selective mute. The pressure of assessments and the build-up to assessments was enormous, they were enormous events.

Personally, I need to see an example, a model. I need a model of what you're asking me for. If I have no idea what it looks like, how can I complete the task? I still need this now, as an adult. I ask, 'Can you show me what that looks like?'.

Different models of assessment are needed. If the assessment was different then children may perform differently. Alternative methods must be explored. We don't use technology enough – we need to harness technology and not impede our young people. Why don't we teach our children to touch type? They're so used to doing it! Needs like hypermobility and dyspraxia make writing incredibly difficult and we need to give alternatives.

Emma Twell, Safeguarding and SEND Specialist and autistic adult

Generally, my mainstream school assessments consisted of written exams as well as some group work and presentations. For me, there were numerous barriers to undertaking exams. These included struggling to hand write rapidly and finding it difficult to memorise information, particularly when in pressurised situations. In exams, there was often limited time to process information and present a comprehensive response. This resulted in heightened anxiety, which affected my ability to absorb information. The sensory environment was often overwhelming; just the thought of walking into a room full of people and the anxiety of how to correctly stack my chair at the end of the exam was enough to send my mind into shutdown mode.

Moreover, when I was expected to participate in group work and present in front of the class, I was distracted by the fear of being judged. I spoke quietly

so that nobody would notice the quivers in my voice. These barriers meant that unfortunately, my potential was not realised, and I didn't always achieve the results I was capable of. However, when I attended an alternative provision, I was allowed exam access arrangements, consisting of rest breaks, extra time, a separate room if needed and the provision of a laptop.

I urge leaders of specialist provisions to get creative when planning how to measure progress since written and oral exams may not yield the best results and may put young people under excess pressure. Reasonable adjustments may be required to meet learner's specific needs.

Lauren Smith, autistic adult and postgraduate researcher

I get anxious when we do quizzes – I don't want to come first and be the centre of attention, but I don't want to come last because others will think I'm stupid.

I find exams hard as it is a lot about memory and I find this difficult. I have to remember lots of theorists for English and Sociology as well as equations for Business as well and we can't take anything into the exam with us. I have my exams in a quiet room which is good, but I found it hard to know the rules for asking for rest breaks. I prefer coursework.

Zoe, autistic teenager

Collectively, these reflections show how traditional, exam-heavy assessment systems create barriers for learners with additional needs. Emma, Lauren, and Zoe all describe the pressure that surround assessments, whether it's the overwhelming build-up to exams, the physical demands of handwriting or the fear of being judged in group work. What is striking is how these experiences show that exams often fail to reflect the true ability of learners with additional needs, highlighting the limitations of a system that was designed with neurotypical learners in mind.

Yet, within their stories lies multiple thinking points for leaders. Emma explains the need for modelling and visual approaches, whereas Zoe reminds us of the importance of access arrangements. From Lauren, there is a clear call for creativity, flexibility, and a broader understanding of what assessment should be. They challenge us as leaders to rethink how we define success and how we measure progress.

Thinking points

- Written exams often reward memory under pressure rather than depth of understanding or creativity. How do you ensure that your assessments reflect the full abilities of your learners?
- Emma Twell mentions her need for models and clarity. Do we assume that all learners know what 'good' looks like? How do you ensure expectations are explicit and accessible for all?
- Lauren Smith reflects on the implications of sensory overwhelm. What can you do to create calmer and safer assessment experiences?
- Zoe didn't feel confident asking for a rest break, despite being entitled to one. How do you ensure learners understand and feel safe to use their access arrangements?

Activity 1: Rethinking assessment

Think of one assessment currently used in your setting.

Using the reflections from Emma, Lauren, and Zoe, redesign this assessment using at least two of the following strategies:

- Providing a model or example
- Offering multiple means of expression (e.g. video, audio, drawing)
- Reducing sensory load
- Including processing time
- Using assistive technology
- Allowing coursework or portfolio options

How does you redesigned assessment:

- Reduce barriers?
- Provide clarity?
- Increase fairness?

What would be your first step to trialling this assessment?

Activity 2: Understanding lived experience

Share with your leadership team the insights from Emma, Lauren, and Zoe. Ask them to reflect silently on the ideas they express, particularly the emotional and sensory experience of assessments.

Ask your leadership team to individually complete this short task: What is the purpose of assessment in our setting? Impose two or three of the constraints below.

- Time pressure - provide no more than 2–3 minutes to write a 100-word response in full sentences
- Cognitive load - don't allow time to think or discuss, they must start handwriting immediately
- Sensory disruption - create background noise or change the lighting
- Limit methods of completion - insist on handwriting

Discuss with your team:

- How did it feel to complete the task under those conditions?
- Did your output reflect your actual knowledge or ability?
- What helped or hindered your ability to concentrate or express yourself?
- What are the implications for how we assess our learners?
- What is one change we could make to our assessment processes to make them more inclusive?

Chapter summary

This chapter explores what formative and summative assessment looks like in the specialist sector. It thinks holistically about different progress measures, including social and emotional progress.

- Assessment helps leaders determine the effectiveness of their curriculum and how well learners are progressing socially, emotionally, and academically.
- It can be difficult to compare performance within and between specialist provisions meaningfully as designations and individual needs vary. This means success can look different across settings.
- Most specialist provisions will design their own assessment frameworks to ensure that small-step progress points match their context effectively, enabling every learner to show what they know in a way that works for them.
- Baseline assessments are particularly important in specialist settings, where it can be challenging to establish learners' starting points with confidence.
- Formative assessment provides powerful, real-time feedback to learners and staff.
- Standardised summative assessments tend to capture only a small part of a learner's progress and can sometimes mask a learner's potential.
- Many specialist provisions assess progress laterally, recognising that a child's development may not follow a linear or age-expected trajectory.

- Proactively gathering and responding to pupil voice helps children feel valued and understood. Crucially, it helps them develop the skills to advocate for themselves beyond our settings.
- Learning from lived experience encourages us to be innovative, harnessing technology and designing alternative methods to ensure that every child has the chance to show what they know and can do.

Further reading

- *Inside the Black Box: Raising Standards Through Classroom Assessment* by Paul Black and Dylan Wiliam (1998) continues to be a seminal text on formative and summative assessment.
- The Challenge Partners' *Assessment in Special Schools and AP Settings: A Challenge Partners Best Practice Guide* (n.d.) provides a good overview of policies, target setting, and how data should inform practice.

References

Black, P., and Wiliam, D. (1998). *Inside the Black Box: Raising Standards Through Classroom Assessment*. London: Granada Learning.

Challenge Partners (n.d.). *Assessment in Special Schools and AP Settings: A Challenge Partners Best Practice Guide*. Available online at: https://challengepartners.org/sites/default/files/files/Assessment%20in%20Special%20Schools%20and%20AP%20settings.pdf [accessed 23 March 2025]

Department for Education and Department of Health (2014, June). *Special Educational Needs and Disability Code of practice: 0 to 25 years*. Available online at: https://www.gov.uk/government/publications/send-code-of-practice-0-to-25 [accessed 15 June 2025].

Department for Education (2020, January). *The Engagement Model*. Available online at: https://www.gov.uk/government/publications/the-engagement-model [accessed 29 July 2025].

Department for Education (2025, March). *Curriculum and Assessment Review: Interim Report*. Available online at: https://assets.publishing.service.gov.uk/media/6821d69eced319d02c9060e3/Curriculum_and_Assessment_Review_interim_report.pdf [accessed 21 August 2025].

Encyclopaedia Britannica (2025). 'Uncertainty principle'. Available online at: https://www.britannica.com/science/uncertainty-principle [accessed 11 August 2025].

Happé, F. (1994). 'An advanced test of theory of mind: Understanding of story characters' thoughts and feelings by able autistic, mentally handicapped, and normal children'. *Journal of Autism and Developmental Disorders*, *24*(2), 129–154.

Maloy, L., Tolley, J., King, S., Barwell, N., Cross, E., and Brown, A. (2025). *Young Researchers Young Voices: Co-research SEND project. Final Report*. Available online at: https://www.researchgate.net/profile/Liam-Maloy/publication/394447746_Young_Researchers_Young_Voices_Co-research_SEND_project_Final_Report [accessed 13 August 2025].

Tomkins, A. (2024, 13 May). 'Assessing progress in special schools: Reviews and recommendations'. *Impact*. Part of My College, Chartered College of Teaching. Available online at: https://my.chartered.college/impact_article/assessing-progress-in-special-schools-reviews-and-recommendations/ [accessed 23 March 2025].

Yan, Z., Xiao, Y., Sin, K. F., Yang, L., and Guo, W. Y. (2021). 'Formative assessment practices in special school classrooms with the support of e-books: A case study'. *Frontiers in Education*, vol.6.

5

Building safe, independent lives: Personal Development and Preparation for Adulthood

Education is not about today, next week, next year, but about who our children will be at 16, 19 and 25. Will they be confident? As independent as possible? Know what they are good at? And have the most fulfilling future possible?

Angela O'Rourke, Headteacher of Southfield SEN School

You're only in secondary school for 5 years - what happens next?

Robert Bell, Headteacher of Consilium Evolve

Chapter overview

Arguably, the ultimate measure of an educational provision is how effectively it prepares its learners for adulthood and the world beyond its gates. We begin this chapter by exploring the unemployment statistics for adults with SEND and the moral imperative of supporting our young people into employment, education, training, or activities with meaningful purpose. We then explore what effective Personal Development and preparation for adulthood looks like and how these can be embedded across a provision. We end by considering how we can support our young people to understand and embrace their diagnosis, enabling them to be lifelong self-advocates.

A moral responsibility

Employment statistics for individuals with SEND make grim reading. Around a quarter of working-age individuals are recognised as living with a disability, but just over half of these are employed. In Quarter 2 of 2024, there was a stark difference between the employment rate for disabled people, 53.1%, compared with 81.6% for non-disabled individuals (Department for Work and Pensions, 2024b). Notably, the employment rate falls to just 31% for those with a neurodivergent condition (Department for Work and Pensions, 2025). Despite this, a co-research project by Maloy et al. (2025) exploring the views of learners with additional needs found that:

- 53% would like to be in paid employment as an adult
- 37% want to live independently

DOI: 10.4324/9781003601388-6

- 26% would like to live in their own property
- 32% would like to have children of their own

This shows that young people with additional needs and disabilities want many of the same things as their neurotypical and non-disabled peers, including careers, homes, and families. The fact that so few individuals with SEND currently achieve this goal is not a reflection of their want or potential, but of the systemic barriers that we need to remove. Knowledge of these employment statistics should motivate us as leaders to prioritise Personal Development curricula that address the real-world needs of our learners.

Hughes, Curley, and Kotera (2024) suggest that some parents of autistic children experience a sense of loss, akin to grief, when reflecting on the future they had envisioned for their child. This perspective is easy to empathise with, especially when confronted with the statistics above. Hughes, Curley, and Kotera (2024) also found that parents conveyed a deep hope that their child would be treated with respect and included and valued within society. This is sobering, given that these are basic expectations outlined in the European Convention on Human Rights, particularly Article 14, which protects against discrimination (Council of Europe, 1950). In the Introduction we referenced the social model of disability, conceptualised by Professor Mike Oliver in 1983. This model reframes disability as the result of barriers in society. As specialist provisions, we must lead the systemic change needed to dismantle these barriers and this process starts with effective Personal Development. By this, we mean supporting our young people holistically, building their confidence, skills, and sense of identity so they can live the lives they want to lead. Our Personal Development curricula must be rooted in the aspirations of our young people and enable them to participate and thrive in the world.

Specialist provisions promote the holistic development of the whole child with the aim of helping them become confident, independent, and fulfilled members of society. Tomkins (2025) suggests that when designing our Personal Development curriculum, it's important to consider the skills learners need to support their long-term goals and aspirations. This perspective is especially important given that our learners will spend significantly more of their lives as adults with additional needs and/or disabilities than as children, as Melissa Taylor, Lead Teacher at Ellesmere College, emphasises:

> *They're going to be adults longer than they're children. We want our learners to leave EYFS being able to use the toilet, feed themselves and regulate. These lay the foundation for independent life skills.*

The current life expectancy for men in England is 79.1 years and for women it is 83.1 years (Office for Health Improvement and Disparities, 2025). Hence, on average, our learners will spend around four times as long out of education as they do in it, underscoring Melissa's point about the need to get preparation for adulthood right. In fact, recent research from King's College London (Stewart, 2025) highlights just how important it is to view our young people's diagnosis in the context of a full lifespan. It found that older autistic adults face much higher risks of physical and mental health conditions compared with their non-autistic peers. Therefore, the work we do as educational settings lays the groundwork for a healthier, more engaged adulthood. By focusing on volunteering, hobbies, community involvement, and independent living, we're helping our learners be ready for their life beyond the classroom.

Although these findings may feel hard-hitting, it is important for us, as educational settings, to be aware of them. The prompts below encourage you to think critically about your curriculum and how it can be developed to meet learners' lifelong needs.

Thinking points

- How can your Personal Development curriculum directly address the barriers to employment that many adults with disabilities or additional needs experience?
- How do you integrate foundational life skills into your curriculum?
- Melissa Taylor says, "They're going to be adults longer than they're children." How does your Personal Development curriculum account for this?
- What opportunities are there for learners to practise decision-making, communication, and self-advocacy in your current Personal Development curriculum?

The importance of Personal Development

> *It's not just about getting them through their GCSEs. It's a nurturing approach. 50% of what we do is academic and 50% is Personal Development. How are we positively moving them away from exploitation, for example?*
>
> Juliette Baldwin, Headteacher at EOTAS

At the time of writing, Personal Development and Wellbeing is one of the judgement areas made by Ofsted during an inspection (Ofsted, 2025). This area examines how well a school supports its learners beyond academic learning. For example:

- Is there an enriching curriculum, including wider opportunities and experiences, to help learners develop their interests and talents?
- Does the curriculum support character development by building confidence, resilience, and independence?
- Does the curriculum promote physical and mental wellbeing?
- Are learners prepared effectively for future success in the next stages of their education, employment, or training?
- Are learners well-equipped for life in twenty-first century Britain through responsible citizenship, respect for others, an understanding of British Values, and an appreciation of equality and diversity?

Together, these elements reflect Juliette's point that Personal Development is not an add-on, but a vital part of the curriculum. It sits at the heart of how schools prepare their young people for a lifetime of success and the prompts below encourage you to consider this.

Thinking points

- Which of the above elements are already strengths within your provision? Where are there gaps? Where do learners need more support?
- How are you capturing the impact of Personal Development? What evidence shows that learners are becoming more resilient, more confident, or more independent?
- Are there any groups of learners who may be experiencing Personal Development differently? For example, students who are nonspeaking or who are experiencing disadvantage.
- How well does your setting connect Personal Development with safeguarding practice?

What is Preparation for Adulthood?

Preparation for Adulthood, often abbreviated to PfA, aims to give learners with disabilities or additional needs the best possible start as they move towards adult life. Developed by the National Development Team for Inclusion (NDTi, 2020), the PfA framework centres around four key areas for a meaningful adult life:

- Employment - supporting young people into work, vocational training, or other meaningful activities such as volunteering.
- Independent Living - helping young adults to have choice and control over where and how they live.
- Good Health - enabling individuals to access the right health support to stay well, both physically and mentally.
- Friends, Relationships, and Community - supporting young people to build relationships, feel connected to and play an active role in their community.

These four key areas form the foundation of our work in specialist settings, where preparing learners for adulthood goes beyond the academic. Transitions can be challenging (and scary) for learners who find forward thinking tricky, so there must be a strong emphasis on supporting learners and families through these changes.

A vital aspect of preparing for adulthood is financial literacy. For many learners with additional needs, managing money independently can be challenging. Impulsivity, difficulty with abstract thinking, or sensory overload may lead to financial vulnerability. Purchasing goods in 2025 is simpler than ever – from instant spending via one-click purchases to accumulating debt through 'buy now, pay later' schemes – and it's all too easy to spend money. The autistic and ADHD author Sarah Boon (2025) warns of the 'neurodivergent tax' – a term used increasingly within the neurodivergent community to describe the additional financial burdens that arise from managing everyday life. This includes the cost of replacing lost or damaged items, paying for taxis to avoid the overwhelming sensory environment on public transport, or supporting a special interest that, whilst providing comfort and joy, can be financially demanding. This insight into the everyday reality of living with SEND demonstrates why PfA is so important. If your mission statement in Chapter 1 was about enabling learners to thrive, not just in school but throughout life, then PfA is the bridge between that vision and reality. Our provisions offer a place where learners are safe, valued, and understood – the real work, however, lies in preparing them for a world that isn't yet fully inclusive.

Consequently, when preparing our young people for life beyond school, it's vital that learning environments and experiences reflect the world they will enter. Headteacher Alex Tomkins explains how his provision, Greenside School, has replicated this through working with The Hyde Shopping Centre in Stevenage.

> *Always think about the destinations of the students – when they are in the 'real world'. Classrooms are not real life. Classrooms only exist in educational settings, which for nearly all our learners is not their future destination. Most adults don't step back into a classroom when they get a job (except for teachers!). With this in mind, and community learning a destination for many of our cohort, we wanted to try and get our post-16 provision to replicate this. To begin with we just 'went out more' into the community, but this became logistically challenging.*
>
> *We first thought of The Hyde about 15 years ago, when a shop was up for lease. This was taken on by the school and opened as a sweet shop – to be run by our learners. We still run the shop but also have two other units in The Hyde area. These were old shops but converted into 'classrooms' that don't look like traditional classrooms. All have a kitchen, round tables and soft chairs so it's different to the main school.*
>
> *Being based in a shopping precinct, The Hyde has led to closer working in the community. Students go to the shops regularly and they take part in work experience in local charity shops. Being based in the community makes it feel natural. When schools think of external provision for post-16, I would always encourage them to think about using community spaces like we did with The Hyde.*

This approach highlights the power of educational settings moving learning into the wider community. It's a reminder to consider what 'real life' looks like for our learners and how we can replicate this within the curriculum.

Thinking points

- How can you move beyond your school site to create learning spaces that reflect the world your learners will enter?
- What local community settings could become 'extended classrooms' for your students?
- What might be your first step to exploring such opportunities and partnerships?

Activity: Enabling independence

Alex Tomkins stresses the importance of planning for learners' adult lives rather than just their next educational step. As a leadership team, choose one learner who may face financial, social, or practical challenges as they approach the age of 25.

Map out one week of independent adult life for that learner.

Consider:

- How they will manage money (budgeting, paying for accommodation, bills, transport, or food).
- How they will navigate daily tasks (shopping, travel, healthcare).
- How they will manage sensory or emotional regulation.
- How they will engage socially or pursue interests in the community.
- What work, volunteering, or meaningful purpose might look like for them.

Reflect as a leadership team on:

- What daily challenges might this young person face?
- How well does your current curriculum equip them to manage this week?
- What are you doing explicitly to teach or model the skills they need?
- Identify one gap in your current PfA provision and outline one action you could take this term to address this gap.

Careers and employability skills

> *The low levels of autism employment are terrible. We need to help our young people understand the world of work and upskill them to get into employment. Children need*

> *the skills to be in the workplace. We need to teach the things they need to be successful in their next steps.*
>
> Emma Twell, Safeguarding and SEND Specialist and autistic adult

Careers and employability are an integral part of the Personal Development curriculum in specialist settings. As Emma Twell highlights and as we explored above, the low levels of employment for individuals with SEND are a national concern and it's our role as educators to equip learners with the skills and experiences they need to succeed in the workplace. Maloy et al. (2025) found that learners with additional needs have high aspirations for themselves but are often asked to express these under pressure e.g. in annual reviews or at careers guidance meetings with unfamiliar adults. It's no wonder that young people sometimes struggle to voice their ambitions in these situations and this should prompt us to consider how we structure such meetings in our settings. The work of Maloy et al. (2025) suggests the need for ongoing, relationship-based careers conversations built into everyday interactions rather than confined to formal appointments with external advisers. To achieve this, we must ensure careers education is woven across the curriculum through functional learning, enterprise projects, and community engagement. Learning to travel independently, manage time, collaborate, and problem-solve are all essential employability skills. When pupils practise them in real contexts through workplace encounters or work experience, these skills become meaningful and relevant.

Leaders of specialist provisions should be given the time and recognition to prioritise employability skills alongside academic learning. As Charlotte Barton, Managing Director of Progress Schools, notes below, success in APs is often evidenced differently to success in mainstream settings, but that doesn't make it less valuable:

> *Policymakers need to enable Alternative Provisions to prioritise life skills as highly as academies and to acknowledge that 'success' is evidenced differently in AP. With the right framework and understanding, AP can foster aspirations and business acumen in non-academic students helping to integrate them into the world of work.*

Thinking points

- How are employability skills and vocational learning integrated into every stage of your provision?
- How do you ensure learners have the language, confidence, and relationships to articulate their goals and aspirations?
- Are you providing ways for young people to express their ambitions beyond formal meetings or reviews?

Leadership scenario

You are the Headteacher of an alternative provision for 11–16-year-olds. One of your learners is interested in coding and gaming and makes games online at the weekend. During their independent careers meeting, they're asked about their interests. After several verbal prompts to answer, the student says that they would like to do equine and farm-based studies at college, despite having shown no interest in this before.
What action do you take, if any? Consider:

- How you will follow-up with this learner.
- What training or guidance the careers adviser may need.
- How your setting enables learners to express their interests and aspirations safely and confidently.
- What curriculum adjustments or enrichment opportunities could turn this learner's passion for coding into practical workplace skills.
- How you might explore this new interest in equine and farm-based studies.
- How you could involve local businesses or mentoring schemes to create a pathway into employment for this learner.

Developing cultural capital

Cultural capital is the knowledge, skills, and cultural experiences our learners need to succeed in life and school. The term, originally introduced by sociologist Pierre Bourdieu (1986), highlights that having access to certain cultural norms and experiences can provide individuals with an advantage in education and society. This is important when we consider the socio-economic barriers that many of our families face: children with SEND are more than twice as likely to be eligible for free school meals compared with their non-SEND peers (Education Endowment Foundation, 2020). Research by the Sutton Trust (O'Regan and Latham, 2025) suggests that learners with SEND from lower-income backgrounds face compounded barriers that limit access to cultural capital and enrichment opportunities. As specialist provisions, developing cultural capital therefore becomes an important part of preparing learners with disabilities or additional needs for life beyond school.

Overall, children's participation in enrichment opportunities has deteriorated over the last 10 years (Centre for Young Lives, Leeds Beckett University and YMCA George Williams College, 2025). Nevertheless, the same report highlights that enrichment opportunities remain particularly vital for children identified as having SEND. The report also highlights a possible link between enrichment opportunities and attendance, suggesting that some learners attend school specifically to take part in enrichment activities. Findings by Hallgarten et al. (2025) suggest that enrichment activities support children's mental health and wellbeing, raise aspirations, and develop employability skills such as teamwork and resilience. Moreover, the Centre for Young Lives, Leeds Beckett University and YMCA

George Williams College (2025) suggest that building relationships is one of the most powerful benefits of enrichment activities. These findings align strongly with the direction of the government's new curriculum reforms which offer an enrichment entitlement of 80 hours a year across civic engagement, arts, nature, sport, and life skills (Department for Education, 2025).

Unfortunately, in specialist provisions, home to school transport can often limit before and after-school opportunities, meaning enrichment must be embedded creatively into the school day. Break and lunch clubs, off-site trips, community partnerships, and late stays onsite can all help build confidence, independence, and a sense of belonging. Maloy et al. (2025) suggest that independence matters to children with SEND. Many want to do things for themselves and only look for support when they genuinely need it because their goal is to be as independent as possible.

One development which could support specialist settings to enhance their enrichment offer is the increase in Artificial Intelligence (AI). Lomas and Baker (2025) suggest that AI has the potential to support learners' social development by creating interactive, real-world scenarios that adapt and grow to a learner's capabilities. Since visiting new places can be challenging for learners with SEND, AI and virtual reality have the potential to provide immersive learning environments from the safe space of a learner's own provision (Lomas and Baker, 2025). In particular, virtual experiences could provide targeted interventions to prepare learners for future real-world opportunities (Lomas and Baker, 2025).

The development of cultural capital, the provision of enriching experiences, and the promotion of independence are all interconnected. Yet, when access to opportunities can be affected by socio-economic factors, it becomes even more important that we provide access to these within our settings. Alongside teaching the knowledge and skills required for adulthood, we must also (literally) open the doors to it through community links, work experience, and enrichment opportunities. Reflect on your setting's approach to this using the questions below.

Thinking points

- What does the development of cultural capital look like in your setting?
- How accessible is your current enrichment offer? Are there any barriers that reduce uptake? How do you track engagement in your offer and its impact?
- Is there a link between attendance and enrichment in your setting? How do you know?
- What implications does the enrichment entitlement have for your provision?
- Lomas and Baker (2025) suggest that AI can be an important tool in enabling learners to access enrichment opportunities. How could you use this in your setting?

Case study: Jonny's journey

This case study, written by Andrew Poole, Director of School Improvement at The People's Learning Trust, highlights the vital role that personalised support and enriching experiences play in developing a young person's cultural capital and self-belief.

☆

Jonny joined Everton Free School at the beginning of Year.9 in September 2021. He had previously attended a mainstream school in Liverpool and was excluded following a number of incidents.

Our Key Stage 3 provision at Everton Free School was developed to rekindle students' 'love of school' with a holistic focus on developing social skills, self-esteem and confidence. As part of this provision, young people are provided with a class teacher who serves as their key adult during their school day.

The timetable for our Year.9 learners involved two days of excursions that aimed to increase cultural capital and allow young people to engage with their local area. Students visited the rich cultural heritage of Liverpool visiting local art galleries, museums and employers.

Towards the conclusion of Jonny's time in this provision, students were given the opportunity to visit The Rugby School on an exchange visit, allowing young people to experience the private education sector first hand. Students stayed in local accommodation, attended lessons and integrated with pupils from the school. Jonny was enthused by the visit to The Rugby School and stated his interest in applying for a scholarship for his further education pathway.

Jonny expressed his belief that he had gained the skills and confidence to return to mainstream education at the end of Year.9 and a managed return to mainstream education was facilitated. Unfortunately for Jonny, his return to a mainstream setting resulted in another exclusion and a transition back to Everton Free School.

Jonny returned at the beginning of his final year of studies. At first staff at Everton Free School had to work on remotivating Jonny as another exclusion had left him despondent. He was provided with the opportunity to extend his studies beyond the curriculum offer at Everton Free School and was provided with support to apply for his desired scholarship at The Rugby School.

Jonny was helped by support staff and teaching staff to understand his needs; this had been a source of angst for Jonny previously. Working on establishing healthy routines and understanding the viewpoints of others was explicitly taught, allowing Jonny to integrate more successfully with his peers.

Jonny was given the opportunity to travel to Barcelona on an exchange with nine of his classmates. Students were given the opportunity to explore all the cultural experiences of the city and experience living away from their parents for five days.

Jonny attended The Rugby School for an interview in December 2023 and was offered a conditional place with a full scholarship. Fantastically, Jonny achieved the required results to gain his place at The Rugby School. He has remained in contact with staff at Everton Free School since and staff have visited Jonny in his new home to assist with the transition to his new living and learning environment.

☆

Jonny's journey shows how intentional work around building cultural capital can re-engage young people, widen their aspirations, and create pathways they may not have considered before. The questions below encourage you to reflect on how you achieve this in your setting.

Thinking points

- How does your provision create meaningful, real-world experiences that broaden learners' cultural capital and aspirations?
- In what ways can partnerships with other educational provisions or organisations enhance the enrichment opportunities you offer?
- How do you track and celebrate the impact of enrichment activities on a learner's development?
- How do you gather pupil perspective to ensure enrichment activities are relevant, meaningful, and accessible?
- What adjustments, scaffolds, or environmental changes are needed so every learner, including those with high sensory needs, can participate without stress or overwhelm?

Leadership scenario

You are a senior leader with responsibility for Personal Development across your provision, an all-through special school for 150 learners with moderate and severe learning difficulties.

You have been offered 10 places on a 5-day cultural exchange programme to France, where you will visit famous landmarks and attractions. Although the programme offers huge benefits to your learners, it is costly, at over £1,000 per place. Many families in your provision face financial hardship, which could limit children's ability to take part.

Do you accept the places on the programme? Consider:

- How you would allocate places
- How you would fund the places
- What partnerships or fundraising streams could be explored to reduce financial barriers
- How you would ensure that the learners who stay behind don't miss out on developing their cultural capital
- How you would evaluate the impact of the programme

This scenario places you in a dilemma - the opportunity could significantly enrich some learners' experiences, yet it also risks leaving others behind due to cost and circumstance.

As leaders, we face such choices each day, balancing aspiration with fairness, wanting to open the world up for our children whilst being aware of the barriers that many families face. The answer to the above dilemma lies in knowing your learners and their contexts. This leads us into the next section and the importance of helping young people know themselves, their rights, and what makes them happy.

Positive wellbeing and self-advocacy

Helping young people understand who they are and to feel proud and comfortable in that identity, paves the way for happiness in life. Yet, how many of your learners know what an EHCP is and how it benefits them? Maloy et al. (2025) found that many young people with an EHCP had little awareness of what it is or how it affects them. Consequently, few young people value their EHCP as a working document. Maloy et al. (2025) suggest that some learners with additional needs or disabilities lack the expressive language and/or self-esteem to articulate their needs or request changes to their plan. This highlights the necessity for specialist provisions to support their learners to develop strong self-advocacy skills. Alarmingly, only 20 percent of learners with additional needs were reported to have communicated during their EHCP annual review (Maloy et al., 2025). This highlights how easily young people's voices can be overlooked in processes designed to support them. Consequently, helping our learners to understand and express their needs is fundamental to them being able to access the right support when they're older and this must be integrated into the curriculum. The case study below by Bridget Young, Headteacher of The Holmewood School, shows an innovative example of how schools can support young people to understand their diagnosis.

Case study: Project 101 at The Holmewood School

Bridget Young has recently been diagnosed with ADHD. Her passion for advocacy for neurodivergence led to the school creating a series of podcasts.

☆

We came up with the concept of 'Autism 101' and 'ADHD 101', which was coined by my colleague Jack, who is also neurodivergent. We were talking about our practice and he kept saying, 'People should know that – that's Autism 101!'.

I said, 'What's that? They obviously don't know it'.

Consequently, we began to unpick what 'Autism 101' and 'ADHD 101' look like at Holmewood and then we explicitly communicated it to everyone to create a shared language and understanding.

I have access to a recording studio and I love podcasts so we've created a podcast, 'The ND Pedagogy Podcast', which is led by myself and Jack, two neurodivergent colleagues. We reflect on lots of our neurodivergent pedagogy as well as our own experiences. Our students have been listening to it and the kids are the audience for it now. We've got two more episodes planned and I want to make sure it's really positive for them. Parents have also listened to it and given us positive feedback.

☆

'Project 101' shows what can happen when learners are given the language, tools and confidence to understand themselves and shape their own narrative. The questions below encourage you to reflect on how you achieve this in your setting.

Thinking points

- How do you support your learners to understand their needs so they can be their authentic self?
- How many of your learners attend their annual review? How many communicate in it?
- How well does your provision support learners to understand their unique strengths?
- What would your 'Project 101' be and what would it look like?
- What podcast could you create and what would it be about?

Learning from lived experience

Learning from lived experience ensures that our approaches are grounded in reality rather than assumption. Individuals with disabilities or additional needs are the experts in their own lives. When we take time to hear their voices, we gain genuine insight into what educational settings can do to prepare their learners for adulthood effectively.

Some of the things that would've really helped me to prepare for adulthood would've been more time focused on understanding my sense of self and identity, and how to support my wellbeing. Learning about my natural communication style, rather than being taught only the norms of "effective" communication, would've made a big difference, for example, knowing that it's okay not to make eye contact, and to take time to process information.

It also would've helped to have opportunities to explore what supports me to learn and thrive, and then translate this into a potential workplace setting, for example, exploring what adjustments might support me in the future as I move beyond education. Alongside this, being taught and having the opportunity to practise self-advocacy skills would have given me the tools to ask for what I needed.

Remie Colledge, Neurodivergent Speaker, Trainer, and Writer

Success is when my daughter does something she is proud of, whether it is in her driving lessons, feeling confident to look at university places and think about moving into her own university accommodation. I'm thrilled whenever she tells me something she has done with pride. For a long time, she appeared to find it difficult to see her strengths and all her skills. Recently she completed her Extended Project Qualification assessment, she did this by herself, researching in depth and then shared it with us. We were staggered at what she had achieved.

Miranda, autistic adult and parent to an autistic child

At school, I wanted to understand the world around me. I wanted to know that I'm not odd or shy and it's not my fault. I was told again and again, "you're not an extrovert like your sister" who did Brownies and Guides. I did Brownies and Guides and disliked every moment! I couldn't cope with the social aspect, the noise, the sensory overload. I still feel this now every day and have only realised this since my diagnoses!

We need a society that recognises, supports and learns that neurodivergent young people can be part of a world that needs them. As an adult who has been recently diagnosed, I feel I've been in a world that I do not understand and now, more than ever, have realised that I have masked all my life to fit in.

Jo Dennis-Minns, late-diagnosed neurodivergent with lived experience of autism, OCD, and situational mutism

These accounts can be difficult to read, but listening to lived experience helps us reflect on our own provision and the changes we can make to prepare our young people for adulthood effectively. The questions below help you to do this.

Thinking points

- How do you demonstrate the long-term impact of your provision and that learners are successful once they leave you?
- To what extent do you prioritise exam results at the expense of the broader Personal Development that individuals with SEND value most?
- How do you engage with families and adults with additional needs to understand better what 'success' looks like from their perspectives? How could this shape your curriculum and support?
- How do you create space for learners to make choices, co-design activities, or showcase their strengths, building confidence and self-advocacy?

Chapter summary

This chapter looks at the importance of Personal Development and the growth of the whole child.

- Education is the starting point of a child's Preparation for Adulthood journey. Our learners will be adults longer than they are children – preparing them for adulthood and their life beyond education is crucial.

- Educational leaders must ensure their settings are equipping learners not just academically but with the knowledge, confidence, and skills needed to succeed in society as adults.
- There are significant disparities in employment rates between neurodivergent, disabled, and non-disabled individuals in the UK. These figures pose a moral obligation to specialist provisions to prepare learners more effectively for the workplace.
- Research suggests that many learners with disabilities or additional needs have the same dreams and aspirations as their peers - our Personal Development curricula must help them achieve these.
- The rise of Artificial Intelligence has the potential to support learners' social development by creating interactive, real-world scenarios that adapt and grow with their needs.
- Research suggests that, by supporting mental health, raising aspirations, and developing employability skills, enrichment opportunities are particularly valuable for SEND learners.
- Children with SEND are often socially disadvantaged. Specialist provisions must support them to build cultural capital through accessible and plentiful enrichment experiences.

Further reading

- You can find out more about the Preparation for Adulthood framework and access resources on the National Development Team for Inclusion website: https://www.ndti.org.uk/
- To learn more about the origins of cultural capital you could read 'The forms of capital' by Pierre Bourdieu (1986).
- The *Buckland Review of Autism Employment: Report and Recommendations* (DWP, 2024a) provides a detailed overview of the employment of autistic adults and the significant pay gap they face.
- For a written interpretation of her A-Fest Webinar, see Sarah Boon's book *Young, Autistic and ADHD: Moving into Adulthood When You're Multiply-Neurodivergent* (2024).

References

Boon, S. (2024). *Young, Autistic and ADHD: Moving into Adulthood When You're Multiply-Neurodivergent*. London: Jessica Kingsley.

Boon, S. (2025). *Moving into Adulthood When You're Multiply-Neurodivergent - Autism and ADHD*. A-Fest Online 2025 Webinar, 6 March 2025.

Bourdieu, P. (1986). 'The forms of capital'. In: Richardson, J. (ed.), *Handbook of Theory and Research for the Sociology of Education*. New York: Greenwood Press, pp. 241–258.

Centre for Young Lives, Leeds Beckett University and YMCA George Williams College, (2025, February). *Beyond the Classroom: The Role of Enrichment in Tackling the School Absence Crisis*. A report for the National Citizen Service Trust and The Duke of Edinburgh's Award. Available online at: https://www.dofe.org/wp-content/uploads/2025/02/Beyond-the-classroom-enrichment-report-1.pdf [accessed 11 August 2025].

Council of Europe (1950). *European Convention on Human Rights*. Rome: Council of Europe. Available online at: https://www.echr.coe.int/documents/convention_eng.pdf [accessed 3 August 2025].

Department for Education (2025, 4 November). 'New curriculum to give young people the skills for life and work'. Press release. Available online at: https://www.gov.uk/government/news/new-curriculum-to-give-young-people-the-skills-for-life-and-work [accessed 16 November 2025].

Department for Work and Pensions (2024a, 28 February). *The Buckland Review of Autism Employment: Report and Recommendations*. Available online at: https://www.gov.uk/government/publications/the-buckland-review-of-autism-employment-report-and-recommendations/the-buckland-review-of-autism-employment-report-and-recommendations [accessed 25 July 2025].

Department for Work and Pensions (2024b). *The Employment of Disabled People 2024*. Available online at: https://www.gov.uk/government/statistics/the-employment-of-disabled-people-2024/the-employment-of-disabled-people-2024 [accessed 25 July 2025].

Department for Work and Pensions (2025, 30 January). 'Employment prospects for neurodiverse people set to be boosted with launch of new expert panel'. Press release. Available online at: https://www.gov.uk/government/news/employment-prospects-for-neurodiverse-people-set-to-be-boosted-with-launch-of-new-expert-panel [accessed 25 July 2025].

Education Endowment Foundation (2020, March). *Special Educational Needs in Mainstream Schools: Guidance Report*. Available online at: https://educationendowmentfoundation.org.uk/education-evidence/guidance-reports/send [accessed 25th July 2025].

Hallgarten, J., Stoddart, H., Wilby, F., and Ellis, S. (2025). *Enrichment for All: Benchmarks to Build Belonging, Skills and Opportunity*. The Duke of Edinburgh's Award. Available online at: https://www.dofe.org/wp-content/uploads/2025/06/DofE_external-benchmarks_v8_green-and-light-blue.pdf [accessed 11 August 2025].

Hughes, R., Curley, K., and Kotera, Y. (2024). 'Parents' experiences after their child's autism diagnosis: A reflexive thematic analysis'. *Psychiatry International*, 5(3), 370–394.

Lomas, C., and Baker, G. (2025, 9 June). 'Utilising AI and emerging technologies to support learners with autism'. *Impact*. Part of My College, Chartered College of Teaching. Available online at: https://my.chartered.college/impact_article/utilising-ai-and-emerging-technologies-to-support-learners-with-autism/ [accessed 12 August 2025].

Maloy, L., Tolley, J., King, S., Barwell, N., Cross, E., and Brown, A. (2025). *Young Researchers Young Voices: Co-research SEND project. Final Report*. Available online at: https://www.researchgate.net/profile/Liam-Maloy/publication/394447746_Young_Researchers_Young_Voices_Co-research_SEND_project_Final_Report [accessed 13 August 2025].

National Development Team for Inclusion (2020). *Preparing for Adulthood: Employment Resources* Available online at: https://www.ndti.org.uk/resources/preparing-for-adulthood-all-tools-resources [accessed 25 July 2025].

O'Regan, C., and Latham, K. (2025, October). *Double Disadvantage? Uncovering Inequalities in Access to Support within the SEND System*. The Sutton Trust. Available online at: https://www.suttontrust.com/wp-content/uploads/2025/10/Sutton-Trust-Double-Disadvantage.pdf [accessed 23 October 2025].

Office for Health Improvement and Disparities (2025). *Public Health Outcomes Framework: Commentary, May 2025*. Available online at: https://www.gov.uk/government/statistics/public-health-outcomes-framework-may-2025-data-update/public-health-outcomes-framework-commentary-may-2025-2 [accessed 5 July 2025].

Office for Standards in Education, Children's Services and Skills (Ofsted) (2025). *Education Inspection Framework: For Use from November 2025*. London: GOV.UK. Available online at: https://www.gov.uk/government/publications/education-inspection-framework/education-inspection-framework-for-use-from-november-2025 [accessed 23 October 2025].

Oliver, M. (1983). *Social Work with Disabled People*. Basingstoke, UK: Macmillan.
Stewart, G. (2025, 3 September). 'What we do (and don't know) about autism and ageing - new research'. *King's College London News*. Available online at: https://www.kcl.ac.uk/news/what-we-do-and-dont-know-about-autism-and-ageing-new-research [accessed 23 October 2025].
Tomkins, A. (2025, 19 May). 'Using research to refine an inclusive curriculum for children with severe learning difficulties'. *Impact*. Part of My College, Chartered College of Teaching. Available online at: https://my.chartered.college/impact_article/using-research-to-refine-an-inclusive-curriculum-for-children-with-severe-learning-difficulties/ [accessed 12 August 2025].

6

Therapy first: Developing a therapeutic culture

We do not believe in pushing for compliance and control. Our job is to walk with our learners, to build empathy, to be on their side and be their advocate.

Sarah Cullip, Behaviour Lead, Greenside School

Chapter overview

This chapter explores the central role therapeutic approaches play in specialist and alternative settings, particularly how emotional safety, regulation, and wellbeing form the foundation for learning. We start by outlining what a therapy first culture is and why it matters. We look at the importance of wellbeing, the link between wellbeing and attendance, and how therapeutic approaches support these. Through the perspectives of practitioners and advocates, lived experience illustrates how relationships, trust, and co-regulation support children to engage meaningfully in the classroom. For many learners with SEND, progress in literacy, numeracy, and other areas can only take place if they feel safe, calm, and in control of their emotions. Finally, we discuss the principles of Universal Design and the importance of creating environments that are calm, predictable, and responsive to individual needs.

Why is a therapy-first culture important?

Dr Luke Beardon (2020) contends that it's the environment that should be adapted to meet the needs of autistic children, rather than expecting the child to change their behaviour to align with neurotypical norms. The autistic advocate and author, Pete Wharmby (2025), suggests that schools can sometimes be hostile places for the neurodivergent because they are designed to meet the needs of the neurotypical majority. This is supported by the Children's Commissioner (2023), who found that children identified as having SEND experience greater challenges in feeling safe. Among the areas explored in 'The Big Ask', this was the most pronounced difference between children with and without SEND. Feeling safe is a fundamental prerequisite for learning – it's difficult to receive and process new

DOI: 10.4324/9781003601388-7

information when you're worried or anxious (Bindreiff, 2023). This is why a therapy-first culture is important. Sarah Cullip, Behaviour Lead at Greenside School, explains:

> *Our approach at Greenside is a therapeutic approach. My mission is to understand how the learners I support experience the world. I need to consider the factors and barriers that exist for them in being able to successfully navigate the world. The starting point is not to look solely at any behaviour that could be considered difficult, dangerous, anti-social or in any way detrimental to themselves or society. It is to invert your viewpoint away from the behaviour and to analyse why it occurs. What's the learner experiencing? What do those experiences make the learner feel? Analysis is key to determining how we can have a positive impact. Fundamental to this is the forging of a positive and trusting relationship – we are on their side and here to help.*

Sarah's approach demonstrates how therapeutic principles can be embedded into daily practice rather than delivered as discrete interventions. It illustrates what we explored in Chapter 1 – a culture is the pervading feeling or atmosphere that characterises an organisation. In a therapy first culture, therapeutic principles are woven into the daily actions and interactions of everyone in the organisation, recognising that emotional safety, regulation, and wellbeing are essential for meaningful learning and growth. Factors of key importance to a therapy first culture are:

- Enabling environments – understanding that environment is the first intervention.
- Multi-disciplinary collaboration – placing equal value on therapy and education and seeing therapy as the gateway to attendance and education for some learners.
- A wellbeing curriculum that supports academic learning and explicitly teaches self-regulation and self-care.
- Leaders who model taking a therapeutic lens and help every adult to see through it.
- The understanding that a therapy-first approach is enacted by everyone in your organisation, not just therapists.

Ultimately, a therapy-first culture positions therapy not as something that happens to a child in a room with a therapist, but as a collective, whole-school framework that supports everyone to learn and thrive. Remie Colledge, Neurodivergent Speaker, Trainer, and Writer explains this further:

> *Small differences could have made a massive impact. For example, recognition and validation of both my strengths and challenges, the opportunity to stim freely without fear of judgement, having a buddy or role model to go to for support, curiosity around my individual differences, having designated quiet spaces when I was overwhelmed, support to learn about, make sense of and communicate my emotions, and guidance to develop self-regulation strategies. What I wish most, is that school had given me permission to be myself, without needing to mask or hide who I am. This would have meant I could have left education with greater self-awareness and self-esteem.*
>
> *An ideal school environment for me would have been defined less by the building itself and more by how it felt as I walked through the gates. Instead of fear, I would have felt a sense of safety, supportiveness and acceptance. This comes from whole-school*

education and culture, where differences are not only understood, but valued and celebrated, and where children are encouraged to be themselves. For me, the ideal school environment would have been one where belonging was the foundation, and from this, my learning and aspirations could grow.

Remie effectively describes the environment we want for our learners - to be safe, to be understood, and to be supported to be themselves. A therapy first culture provides this feeling of belonging and enables learning and engagement to occur. The case study below demonstrates this further.

Case study: Supporting therapeutic thinking

Sarah Cullip, Behaviour Lead at Greenside School, describes how she supports staff to develop a therapeutic thinking approach.

☆

Being a Behaviour Lead allows me to work as a conduit for positive change and to support learners and the staff team at Greenside. Greenside has a therapeutic approach to behaviour underpinned by our Hertfordshire County Council backed training programme known as Therapeutic Thinking. I consider the essence of the therapeutic approach to be the focus on building a positive, symbiotic relationship. Once we have created a therapeutic relationship that has generated trust and understanding, we can plan to facilitate change by developing intrinsic motivation. Allied to this is a deep commitment to differentiation and adaptation. Each learner is a unique individual who must be considered in the round, including a holistic understanding of their needs and what will create success for them. I spend time creating Therapeutic Thinking plans in conjunction with the class team.

It's important to accept that staff may not arrive at Greenside with a comprehensive knowledge of a therapeutic approach; it takes time to develop a full understanding. It is incumbent upon us that we offer an immediate induction on the key fundamentals of our expectations of how staff should be offering support and what practice falls outside a therapeutic remit. The ethos is not to catch staff getting it wrong, but to offer support to build their skills and understanding. Working in specialist settings is incredibly rewarding but it can also present emotional and physical challenges which will be experienced differently by each member of staff. It's important that staff wellbeing is prioritised in the same way as learners' needs. New staff need to know that we're working to help them and be comfortable approaching us for support.

☆

Sarah describes how developing positive relationships, knowing learners holistically, and attending to wellbeing are central not only for learners but also for staff. She reminds us that developing a therapeutic approach requires supporting staff to develop their skills and confidence – something we will explore in Chapters 7 and 8.

Thinking points

- How do leaders in your provision model therapeutic thinking in their own practice and interactions with staff and students?
- How do you support new staff to understand what a therapeutic approach looks like in your setting?
- What ongoing professional development opportunities exist to deepen staff's understanding of therapeutic approaches?
- How do you balance the emotional demands of working in specialist settings with staff resilience and wellbeing initiatives?

Supporting attendance

In the academic year 2024/25, children with SEND in England experienced much higher rates of absence compared with their peers without additional needs or disabilities (Department for Education, 2026).

Learners with additional needs or disabilities also tend to be unhappier than their peers without SEND in several areas. Barnes and Harrison (2017) used a 7-point scale to identify happiness and unhappiness. They found that children with additional needs or disabilities rated themselves:

- 0.6 points less happy with their schoolwork
- 0.4 points less happy with their school
- 0.3 points less happy with their friendships

These findings suggest that learners with additional needs or disabilities generally report lower levels of wellbeing compared with their peers without SEND, particularly in relation to school, schoolwork, and friends. A therapy first culture has the potential to overcome this by supporting wellbeing and emotional regulation. If children with SEND feel less happy with their school, schoolwork, and friendships, it's not surprising that their absence rates are higher. By embedding therapeutic principles across a setting, learners are more likely to experience school as a safe and supportive place, potentially lowering the anxiety or distress that can lead to persistent absence. A wellbeing curriculum that provides strategies for self-regulation can help children feel more positive and increase their ability to learn. When children experience education as a place where they are understood and their needs are met, they are more likely to attend regularly.

Thinking points

- How embedded is a therapy-first culture within your provision? What could be your next step towards strengthening this?
- How can leaders ensure that all staff feel confident applying therapeutic approaches?
- How can settings measure the impact of a therapy-first culture beyond attendance data?

Perspectives on practice

The following perspectives from practitioners and advocates illustrate how a therapy first culture takes shape in specialist and alternative provisions. Collectively, they highlight that self-regulation, trust, and relationships underpin learning. From recognising that a child's academic ability is meaningless without the capacity to regulate, to questioning the deficit-driven labels we use, these perspectives remind us that therapy first cultures start with how we see and understand each child.

> *How will they achieve the best for their life? They might be really good at Maths but if they can't regulate, then they can't use the subject purposefully.*
>
> Gemma James and Melissa Taylor, Lead Teachers

> *I'd like to get rid of the word 'defiant' from the English language. I want us to change our language around children. We need to look at it from a point of understanding, we need to keep asking 'why?'. It's not because they're defiant, it's because they're anxious and a whole host of other things. We are the child's safe space. They want us to keep them safe. We strip everything back and we meet their basic needs. In Alternative Provision you see children being children – they can thrive in this space.*
>
> Juliette Baldwin, Headteacher at EOTAS

> *It is imperative to be calm, kind and consistent. And that applies to everyone the learner interacts with. Consideration is always centred on what's in the learner's best interests.*
>
> Sarah Cullip, Behaviour Lead, Greenside School

Across these perspectives, some key themes emerge:

- self-regulation is a prerequisite for learning
- trust and relationships are central
- the language we use shapes how we understand and respond to learners

The questions below encourage you to reflect on these points further.

Thinking points

- How do you establish regulation, trust, and safety as prerequisites for learning?
- How do you build trust and relationships with learners, families, and staff?
- What role does language play in shaping how learners in your setting are understood and responded to?

Managing emotion or managing behaviour?

A recurring theme throughout this book has been that language matters – a point that Juliette Baldwin echoes above. The words we choose to describe our setting, policies, and procedures shape the way learners, families, and staff understand the ethos of our provision. Headteacher at Consilium Evolve, Robert Bell, provides a good example of the importance of language:

> *We don't have a behaviour policy – behaviour policies are for adults. We have a communication policy instead. One of our guiding mantras draws on the work of Catherine Hope and Seth Godin who suggest that curiosity and anger can't coexist as it's hard to stay angry when you're genuinely curious. We stress the importance of being curious and asking questions, particularly 'what works?'.*

Robert's distinction between 'behaviour' and 'communication' is more than semantics. This reframing shifts the focus from managing behaviour, which often implies a compliance model, towards managing emotions, which sees behaviour as communication. If we view behaviour as a form of expression, especially if the learner is non-speaking, the emphasis is placed on understanding and interpreting the behaviour, rather than simply reacting and correcting. In specialist and alternative provisions, this is especially important, as behaviours in young non-speaking children often reflect unmet needs, struggles with regulation, or difficulties expressing themselves effectively. By continuing to use deficit-based language, we risk reinforcing a cycle of misunderstanding, where young people are defined by their challenges rather than by their strengths.

Thinking points: What's in a name?

- What name is given to your policy relating to managing behaviour and/or emotion?
- What does the name suggest about the ethos of your provision? You might like to ask other stakeholders for their ideas.
- Consider some alternatives e.g. communication policy, connection policy, regulation policy, or relationships policy. Do any of these better reflect the culture you wish to create?

Managing emotion: Co-regulation and self-regulation

The American educator John Taylor Gatto (1992) suggests that emotional regulation is a prerequisite for successful learning. Autistic advocate and speaker Dean Beadle (2025a) notes that we often ask young people what makes them upset, but we rarely ask what makes them calm. Arguably, knowing what makes an individual calm and then effectively implementing these strategies, reduces the likelihood of upset occurring. Beadle (2025a) argues that calm should be a constant, not a destination, and therefore we should schedule calming activities throughout the school day.

Co-regulation refers to the supportive process through which a caring, attuned adult helps a young person navigate their emotions, particularly during moments of dysregulation. Co-regulation helps young people develop the capacity for self-regulation and independent emotional organisation. It creates the emotional safety for learning to occur as Headteacher Robert Bell explains:

> *Learning is an emotional risk and what happens to your body when there's risk? We need to make children feel safe enough to take that risk to learn. We understand that some of our learners wear ear defenders. They also might choose to wear a hood because it suppresses the auditory system and helps them feel safe. We also move staff around the school site rather than the learners, so there's less transitions.*
>
> *Our provision at Evolve draws on self-determination theory, a psychological framework that explores motivation. Developed by the psychologists Edward Deci and Richard Ryan in the 1980s, Self-Determination Theory suggests that individuals are most motivated when their basic psychological needs are met. Consequently, we give learners something motivating to look forward to, for example, I come in and first thing I've got music – I meet my favourite teacher and we bang some drums. Our learners need a successful start to come into. Our young people are more likely to engage if they're doing something they enjoy.*
>
> *We ensure that there's a team of staff there to meet them, so we can unpick and support if they've not had a well-regulated evening. If they're not ready to learn then students don't go to period 1.*
>
> *You have a golden hour in the morning to make education attractive to children. We make it therapeutic, and that's how we make it attractive. Our pupils come to school because they're excited about what they're learning. In traditional settings you often start the day with a compliance check e.g. pens, rulers, equipment. Who's that compliance check for? Is it for the children?*
>
> *We plan by emotion, not by content. There's a physiological reaction when you're panicked and stressed. When you relax and feel successful then you're more open to challenge. We praise and acknowledge in public. We tell our learners how proud we are of them and we constantly reinforce this.*
>
> *We also use Rest, Restore and Acknowledge for staff. We never want a staff member to leave today anxious about tomorrow. We want them to be able to go and enjoy their life outside of work, being a mum or a dad, a brother or a sister. It's an opportunity to talk to someone and get rid of any anxiety.*

Robert reminds us that learning is an emotional experience and that pupils need to feel safe before they can engage. At Consilium Evolve, co-regulation, supportive environments, and activities that excite learners help them to engage in learning and to succeed.

Building on Robert's emphasis on emotional safety, Sarah Cullip discusses how she develops learners' self-regulation:

> *To develop self-regulation, we need to start with co-regulation. To develop the skills of co-regulation we need to build a positive trusting relationship. Intensive Interaction is an amazing way to build relationships and communicate in a nurturing and positive way. We need to understand why the learner is dysregulated - what is driving them into crisis? What can we change about their world at school? Is their behaviour controlling them or do they have an element of conscious control? Can they understand that changing their behaviour will impact on their regulation and reduce their anxiety?*
>
> *An essential element to self-regulation is developing emotional literacy. Emotional literacy teaching needs to be woven into learning throughout the day in a way that's accessible to each learner. Allied to emotional literacy, communication differences must be assessed. Without a method to communicate how they feel and think we cannot be effective in our support or growth towards self-regulation. Collaboration with a Speech and Language Therapist is key.*

Sarah emphasises the importance of understanding the reasons behind dysregulation and of working collaboratively as a staff team to identify these. The questions below encourage you to reflect on the insights that Sarah and Robert provide into the importance of co and self-regulation.

Thinking points

- How can we design environments and routines that embed calm as a constant?
- Safety and familiarity are vital to our learners. What benefits are there to having the same teacher for 2 years? Is this something that might work in your setting?
- Robert refers to the 'Golden Hour' principle. What might this look like in your provision?
- How can Self-Determination Theory guide the way you plan learning experiences, ensuring pupils have agency, choice, and motivating activities to start the day positively?
- Robert refers to the Rest, Restore, and Acknowledge approach for staff. What could this look like in your setting?

Activity: Creating calm- environmental learning walk

This activity invites you to explore your setting from a learner's perspective, recognising that, as Dean Beadle (2025a) reminds us, calm is not a destination but a constant that we work to maintain.

Spend 20–30 minutes on this activity and ask a therapist or member of your leadership team to join you. Do not speak for the first 5 minutes.

Imagine that you are a young person who is dysregulated, anxious, or overwhelmed.

As you walk, reflect on:

- Which aspects of this space support regulation?
- What might increase anxiety or sensory overload?
- Where could a learner go if they needed calm, reassurance, or space?

After 5 minutes, discuss:

- What did you see, hear, smell, taste, and touch?
- Which aspects of the environment are intentionally therapeutic?
- How does the environment help or hinder calmness?
- Which supports rely on staff and which can be accessed independently by learners?
- Identify one practical change you could make to enhance the environment for learners.

Enabling environments

Dr Luke Beardon (2020) stresses the importance of environment, suggesting that the wrong setting can cause anxiety for autistic learners. Equally important is a positive workplace environment for staff. Camilleri, Rockey, and Dunbar (2024) emphasise that, as leaders, it's our responsibility to shape environments where everyone can succeed. Reflecting on the environmental strategy of fast-food giant McDonald's, Camilleri, Rockey, and Dunbar (2024) suggest that McDonald's approach of a consistent look to each store builds customer confidence. If each branch looks and works the same, then that provides customers with a sense of predictability and safety. We can apply the same principle to our settings – familiar environments reduce anxiety and build confidence for learners, families, and stakeholders. Investing time and resources in buildings and estate management is therefore essential for creating spaces that support positive outcomes for everyone. After all, as Alexander den Heijer (2018) suggests, when a flower struggles to bloom, it's the environment that needs to be altered, not the plant itself.

Since a child's reaction to sensory input can be fluid, you will often need to teach hyposensitive and hypersensitive learners in the same space, making flexibility of the environment crucial. Some environmental aspects to consider include:

- Using unscented cleaning products. Some provisions also have restrictions on strong smells (e.g. perfumes) as part of their staff dress code.
- Personal protective equipment for learners to accommodate sensory differences e.g. gloves for messy play.
- School uniform adjustments. For every learner that finds a hood comforting and sensory reducing, there will be another one who finds it lumpy and bulky. Providing options is important - some learners will want to wear shorts all year and some will want to wear a coat.
- Personal Emergency Evacuation Plans (PEEPs) for fire alarms and other emergencies e.g. lockdowns.
- Quiet eating areas and/or solitary eating areas for those conscious of eating in front of others.
- The ability to adjust lighting e.g. dimmer switches or blinds.
- The ability to adjust acoustics e.g. sound proofing, ear defenders.
- Clear, functional signage with visuals.

Although these might seem like small changes, creating the right environment can reduce anxiety and, rightly, Beardon (2020) stresses the importance of meeting individual needs through modifying the environment. Importantly, these practices benefit everyone, not just neurodivergent individuals (Beardon, 2020) and this reflects the principles of Universal Design. Created by architect and designer Ronald Mace in 1998, Universal Design is the practice of creating buildings and environments that are inherently accessible and usable by everyone, without the need for adaptations. Universal Design aims to be proactive, removing literal and metaphorical barriers before they become obstacles. If you are designing your provision from scratch, or can have input into the design, then you can incorporate Universal Design principles from the start.

Schools are busy places - minimising intense stimuli creates a calming environment which supports focus and wellbeing. Our occupational therapist conducts regular monitoring of our school environment, looking at classroom layout, equipment, and even how messy the teacher's workstation is. This is particularly important for our autistic learners who often take in more information at once than non-autistic learners, reflecting a naturally higher perceptual capacity (Brinkert and Remington, 2020). Ensuring that environments are clutter-free can help learners focus on the materials relevant to learning rather than the chip in the teacher's cup or the stack of marking on their desk.

Leadership scenario

As the Head of a Pupil Referral Unit, you've noticed that some of your classrooms feel rundown. You understand that environment plays a part in how safe and regulated learners feel and you believe that a fresh coat of paint, some calm displays, and soft furnishings could make a real difference to learning and emotional wellbeing. You raise the proposal with your Business Manager, only to be told that the budget cannot accommodate it this year.

What action do you take? You could consider:

- How you advocate for the needs of your learners whilst operating within the financial constraints of the provision.
- Any alternative approaches you could explore e.g. low cost or no cost ways to improve the environment.
- Any alternative funding streams you could utilise.
- How pupil and stakeholder voice could help support your argument.

This scenario reflects a familiar reality for educational leaders - we understand exactly what our learners need, yet the budget isn't always available. Sourcing donations, bidding for grant funding, and gathering stakeholder voice to strengthen your argument can all provide small but purposeful steps toward creating an environment that helps learners feel safe, calm, and ready to learn.

Sharing therapeutic expertise

One of the benefits of being in a Multi-academy Trust (MAT) are economies of scale and the ability to share resources. One exciting development for therapeutic practitioners is the growing creation of centralised therapeutic provision within MATs. Some MATs now provide a central therapies hub as part of their core offer, enabling universal and targeted therapeutic support across schools. Kimberley Legg explains how Ascendency Partnership MAT, comprised of three special schools, including Addington School where Kimberley is Assistant Headteacher, is developing such a model:

> *One of the things Ascendency Partnership MAT is doing is looking to create a therapies hub. Someone will be appointed to lead therapeutic provision across the MAT and*

oversee that in the different schools. We've been working with Wokingham Council on a programme called Therapeutic Thinking and this has helped develop our own curriculum called 'Feel Better to Learn Better'. It can sometimes be daunting for teachers because there is so much therapy on offer. What do they use? When do they use it? This helps clarify that and brings different therapeutic offers together.

There are many benefits to implementing the approach described above where therapists are directly employed by a MAT to work across its settings. These include:

- The ability to recruit staff that fit an organisation's ethos and vision.
- Therapists become part of the school community, developing strong relationships with learners, families, and staff.
- Learners benefit from familiar, trusted adults, which supports emotional security and therapeutic engagement.
- Therapists can work alongside teaching and support staff, embedding strategies into daily routines and enabling multi-disciplinary planning.
- The ability to respond quickly to the needs of each provision.
- Therapists can deliver training, coaching, and modelling for staff, increasing staff confidence and skill in using therapeutic approaches.

Case study: The Support Square

Ashley McCormick is SENCO and Senior Leader at Archers Brook School, a school for learners with Social, Emotional and Mental Health needs. Ashley has recently led the implementation of the Support Square, a holistic tool that enables staff to co-regulate emotionally with children, providing the foundations for academic learning and progress.

☆

Ashley is an advocate for behaviour as communication. He emphasises the importance of children being emotionally regulated for learning to occur. He argues that if a child is not emotionally regulated, they are unable to engage in learning, meaning subject content is unlikely to be retained or prioritised. When Ashley started as SENCO he encountered situations where one teacher would say a child was fine in their lesson and well-regulated, with another teacher describing the opposite. Ashley wondered why this mismatch occurred.

Ashley's efforts to unpick what was happening led to the creation of the Support Square. This has five components and starts by building on Maslow's Hierarchy of Needs (1943), specifically safety, before progressing onto the metacognitive strategies a child needs for success e.g. task cards. Archers Brook has 103 young people, and this approach has helped the school develop a detailed picture of each individual. Ashley describes it as a toolbox that supports emotional regulation for every child – it's the key document that runs throughout the school. Archers Brook have created bespoke datasets which link with the Support Square, meaning it's fully integrated into school life. New staff come to realise quickly that the Support Square is the one document they need to understand and know each child.

The Support Square is co-constructed and Ashley stresses the importance of getting input from the whole team, telling staff 'I'm not the expert – you are!'. Staff ask questions like, 'What's the win for this student?' and collaboratively problem solve to create positive, enabling environments. The Support Squares are reviewed termly and incorporate each child's EHCP outcomes. The feedback from staff has been overwhelmingly positive and staff confidence has grown as they understand the strategies which work for each child. Ashley's next step is to make a child friendly version of the Support Square and to develop a website for families and other professionals to use the tool.

A challenge that Ashley encountered along the way was in trying to change people's language: for example, changing informal and emotive phrases such as 'kick off' to 'dysregulated'. The Support Square encourages staff to apply an inquisitive and analytical approach to situations. Many of the children at Archers Brook have an emotional range below that of their chronological age, meaning that they need a trusted adult to analyse and respond to complex behaviour situations with them.

Ashley talks with pride about how Archers Brook has moved from a behaviourist to a humanist approach, underpinned by trauma-informed practice. Providing staff with autonomy and ownership has been important. Ashley is proud that staff now update the Support Square independently and have collaborative, child-centred conversations with the Support Square in the middle. It's created a standardised approach that has enabled Ashley to focus on other SENCO tasks and strategic leadership priorities, supporting his workload.

Another important factor in the evolution of the Support Square was the focus on Rational Emotive Behaviour Therapy (REBT). REBT draws upon stoicism, a school of philosophy derived from Ancient Greece, and the stoic principle that you cannot change events, but you can change your perspective of events. Archers Brook School worked with Manchester Metropolitan University to develop this approach and incorporate it into the Support Square. They worked closely with Dr Martin Turner who visited the school to provide training. Ashley explains that he asked Martin, 'How do we adapt REBT for our kids?'. The mutually beneficial nature of the partnership with the university has supported the development of the Support Square. Ashley describes how 'Martin challenges us and we challenge him'. He describes asking Martin, 'Where's your neurodivergent approach to using REBT?' This close working relationship, coupled with visits to the school, have enabled Martin to understand Archers Brook fully.

The impact of the Support Square has been substantial and helped the school gain National Autistic Society Advanced Accreditation. There has also been positive feedback from Ofsted and Social Services. Ashley says that it's been easy to see the proof because the kids are going to college and the colleges have assumed that it was a product the school purchased. The response has been so positive that Archers Brook's outreach service has started to share the Support Square across their borough. Ashley is extremely proud of this and the validation it brings that the Support Square works across settings. Sharing the Support Square has provided Archers Brook with feedback from multiple users, enabling them to refine the tool further. Additionally, the use of the Support Square from outreach colleagues has enabled more mainstream placements to be maintained.

☆

The introduction of the Support Square highlights how intentional, co-constructed systems can transform both staff confidence and learner outcomes. The questions below encourage you to reflect on how you could implement such an approach in your setting.

Thinking points

- How might a document like the Support Square work in your provision?
- How do you create the conditions for staff to innovate and trial new approaches?
- Ashley describes how staff have moved to a model of co-construction and ownership of key documents. To what extent does this occur in your organisation?
- Ashley describes a successful partnership with Manchester Metropolitan University. What partnerships could bring fresh perspectives and innovation to your setting?

Learning from lived experience

To truly understand the impact of a therapeutic approach, we must listen to those with lived experience. Lauren Smith, autistic adult and postgraduate researcher, reflects on her time in mainstream secondary school and the challenges she faced when her needs were not recognised or met.

I found mainstream secondary school overwhelming and frightening; I was socially isolated and was ostracised by three girls who I considered to be my friends. I was unable to use the toilet or eat lunch for six weeks due to severe anxiety. Due to funding constraints, there was no learning support assistant or quiet space available for me. I had to struggle for two years and almost reach crisis point before my family and I were listened to and any support was implemented. The school advised against applying for a statement of SEN, which would now be called an Education, Health and Care Plan which would entitle me to additional support.

Eventually, at the beginning of year 10, the autism outreach team was called in to provide one to one support. The support worker helped me to deliver a presentation to my peers, detailing my specific needs and how my peers could help me. This was well received however it came a little too late.

The outreach team supported me in and outside of school, with confidence building and anxiety management. I recommended having in-depth autism training for all staff, having a designated quiet area for students to retreat to, being flexible with expectations and having an individual learning plan shared with all staff from the outset. I wish I had been listened to and wish there had been greater support for when I was being bullied. I also wish the friendships I forged were accepted and nourished by staff.

Lauren Smith, autistic adult and postgraduate researcher

Lauren's experience can be difficult to read but it is a powerful reminder of the responsibility leaders have to create an environment and culture where young people feel safe, understood, and included.

Thinking points

- What implications does Lauren's account have for your setting?
- Does your provision offer quiet, low-stimulation areas for learners who need them?
- How do you enable learners to understand and support each other?

Lauren's story brings us back to the core message of this chapter - a therapy-first approach is a culture we need to build through our daily practice and interactions. Lauren's experience highlights the importance of listening to learners, shaping environments around their needs, and supporting staff to respond with curiosity and compassion.

Chapter summary

This chapter explores the important role therapeutic approaches play in specialist settings.

- A therapy-first approach recognises that before learners can engage with learning, their sensory and emotional needs must be met. It reframes therapy not as an intervention, but as the foundation for learning.
- Prioritising therapeutic approaches, such as co-regulation, communication, or sensory support, creates the safety, trust, and stability learners need to engage in academic work.
- When adults see behaviour as communication and respond with therapeutic strategies first, learners are less likely to reach crisis point.
- Findings from the Children's Commissioner (2023) suggest that children with SEND experience greater challenges in feeling safe. A therapy-first culture can support children to feel calm and ready to learn.
- Everyone has a sensory profile and experiences the world in different ways.
- Specialist and alternative provisions need to create environments that reduce sensory overload, provide flexibility, and promote autonomy.
- Universal Design principles can be a proactive approach to inclusive environments, ensuring that our provision is usable and welcoming for everyone.

Further reading

- The Children's Commissioner's Big Ask set out to 'hear the voices of as many children in England as possible, to amplify them, and to deliver improved life chances for this generation and beyond'. A report on the findings of the Big Ask can be found in *The Big Ask - The Big Answer*: https://assets.childrenscommissioner.gov.uk/wpuploads/2021/10/the_big_ask_the_big_answer_2021.pdf
- Archers Brook's Support Square incorporates aspects of Rational Emotive Behaviour Therapy. You can read more about Dr Martin Turner and his work on the Rational Practitioner website: https://thesmarterthinkingproject.com/

- Dr Luke Beardon's (2020) book *Avoiding Anxiety in Autistic Children* is an accessible and informative guide for those looking to learn more about the link between environment and anxiety.
- Robert Bell references the work of Catherine Hope and Seth Godin. You can read more about this at Seth's blog: https://seths.blog/2018/02/you-cant-be-curious-and-angry-at-the-same-time/
- If you're interested in reading more about moving from a traditional behaviour policy to a relational policy, then you may like to read *Guidance for Developing Relational Practice and Policy* (2020) by Babcock Learning and Development Partnership and Devon County Council.
- To think further about what makes young people calm, this blog by Dean Beadle (2025b) explores sensory regulation and emotional safety from a lived-experience perspective: https://ndwisehub.substack.com/p/the-unasked-collection-4
- For more information on Intensive Interaction, as discussed by Sarah Cullip, see: https://www.intensiveinteraction.org/

References

Babcock Learning and Development Partnership and Devon County Council (2020). *Guidance for Developing Relational Practice and Policy*. Available online at: https://cumbria.gov.uk/elibrary/Content/Internet/537/6381/6388/44573151759.pdf [accessed 24 August 2025].

Barnes, M., and Harrison, E. (2017). *The Wellbeing of Secondary School Pupils With Special Educational Needs*. Research Report, Department for Education. Available online at: https://assets.publishing.service.gov.uk/media/5a82201fe5274a2e8ab57a08/Wellbeing_and_SEN.pdf [accessed 28 May 2025].

Beadle, D. (2025a). *A-Fest keynote speech* [in-person talk]. A-Fest, 24 February 2025.

Beadle, D. (2025b). 'The Unasked Collection #4: "What makes you calm?"' NDwise Hub (Substack). Available online at: https://ndwisehub.substack.com/p/the-unasked-collection-4

Beardon, L. (2020). *Avoiding Anxiety in Autistic Children: A Guide for Autistic Wellbeing*. London: Sheldon Press.

Bindreiff, D. (2023, 21 May). 'How a sense of safety shapes student learning and behavior'. *Education Week*. Available online at: https://www.edweek.org/leadership/opinion-how-a-sense-of-safety-shapes-student-learning-and-behavior/2023/05 [accessed 22 August 2025].

Brinkert, J., and Remington, A. (2020). 'Making sense of the perceptual capacities in autistic and non-autistic adults'. *Autism*, *24*(7), 1795–1804.

Camilleri, T., Rockey, S., and Dunbar, R. (2024). *The Social Brain: The Psychology of Successful Groups*. London: Penguin.

Children's Commissioner for England (2023, October). *We All Have a Voice: Disabled Children's Vision for Change*. Available online at: https://assets.childrenscommissioner.gov.uk/wpuploads/2023/10/We-all-have-a-voice-Disabled-childrens-vision-for-change_final.pdf [accessed 29 May 2025].

Deci, E. L., and Ryan, R. M. (1985). *Intrinsic Motivation and Self-determination in Human Behavior*. New York: Plenum.

den Heijer, A. (2018). *Nothing You Don't Already Know: Remarkable Reminders About Meaning, Purpose, and Self-Realization*. CreateSpace Independent Publishing Platform.

Department for Education (2026, 26 March). *Pupil Absence in Schools in England. Academic Year 2024/25*. Available online at: https://explore-education-statistics.service.gov.uk/find-statistics/pupil-absence-in-schools-in-england/2024-25 [accessed 1 April 2026].

Gatto, J. T. (1992). *Dumbing Us Down: The Hidden Curriculum of Compulsory Schooling*. Gabriola Island, BC: New Society Publishers.
Godin, S. (2018, 26 February). 'You can't be curious and angry at the same time' [blog]. Seth's Blog. Available online at: https://seths.blog/2018/02/you-cant-be-curious-and-angry-at-the-same-time/ [accessed 28 July 2025].
Mace, R. L. (1998). 'Universal Design in housing'. *Assistive Technology, 10*(1), 21–28.
Maslow, Abraham H. (1943). 'A theory of human motivation'. *Psychological Review, 50*(4), 370–396. Available online at: https://www.academia.edu/9415670/A_Theory_of_Human_Motivation_Abraham_H_Maslow_Psychological_Review_Vol_50_No_4_July_1943 [accessed 1 February 2025].
Turner, M. (2025). *The Smarter Thinking Project*. Available online at: https://thesmarterthinkingproject.com/ [accessed 24 August 2025].
Wharmby, P. (2025). *A-Fest keynote speech* [in-person talk]. A-Fest, 25 February 2025.

7

Attracting, keeping, and caring for great people

Employ diverse staff - do not employ anyone like you. Have a strong team around you who will challenge you and tell you as it is. Build a team who understand that the role is for the greater good and that the reputation of the school is everything.

Angela O'Rourke, Headteacher, Southfield SEN School

Chapter overview

Recruitment and retention in specialist education is more than filling vacancies - it's about finding, keeping, and developing individuals who share your values and vision. Knowledge alone is not enough - people stay and give their best when they feel understood, supported and working towards a purpose bigger than themselves.

This chapter explores how to attract, keep, and care for your greatest asset - your staff team. We'll look at the current recruitment and retention landscape through a SEND lens, recognising the unique challenges and opportunities facing specialist and alternative settings. We'll explore the strategies used by specialist leaders to attract staff and how to set them up for an effective start. We'll discuss succession planning and leadership development, making sure that the care, expertise, and shared purpose that leaders build continues to grow after they've moved on. Finally, we'll discuss staff wellbeing and its importance in specialist settings.

Recruitment and SEND - the national picture

As practitioners in schools, we understand the challenges educational settings face around recruitment and retention. Over the education system, although trainee teacher numbers have slightly increased, most secondary subjects are still underrecruited (McLean, Worth, and Smith, 2024). Retention rates are particularly concerning, with more than 25% of new teachers leaving within their first three years and a third leaving by the end of their fifth

DOI: 10.4324/9781003601388-8

year. Just over 50% of teachers are teaching a decade after qualifying (Department for Education, 2025a).

Although specialist provisions tend to have fewer pupils than mainstream primary schools, the complexity of need means they require substantially more staff. On average, special schools have around 75 full-time-equivalent staff members, whereas mainstream primary schools average 30 (Scott, 2025). This means that special schools generally employ one staff member per two pupils (Scott, 2025). Specialist provisions are therefore likely to face greater recruitment challenges, especially among teaching assistants (TAs), who constitute most of the staff body in specialist settings. On average, special schools employ around 41 TAs, significantly more than the 11 typically found in primary schools and 14 in secondary schools (Scott, 2025).

However, there are disparities in staffing between different types of specialist provisions. On average, alternative provisions and pupil referral units (PRUs) employ 33 staff whereas social, emotional, and mental health (SEMH) provisions have a staff body of around 43. Provisions specialising in cognition and learning average a staff group of 87, with over 50% being TAs (Scott, 2025). In a 2023 NFER (National Foundation for Educational Research) survey, 63% of special school leaders said that it was very difficult to recruit TAs, a higher percentage than mainstream leaders. Special school leaders also reported significantly lower success rates in filling TA vacancies within a 2-month window, citing challenges in recruiting adults with the skills required to support children with SEND (NFER, 2023). This has real implications for the classroom, as Gemma James and Melissa Taylor, Lead Teachers at Ellesmere College, explain:

> *It's difficult to get TAs, which is tough as they're at the heart of the classroom. The wages are so low it makes them difficult to retain. TAs don't always realise the physicality of the setting, particularly working with little ones. The salary and the intensity combined is difficult. TAs often have to adapt their language and expectations, particularly if they've come from mainstream and that can be a learning curve.*

The picture varies slightly when looking at teacher vacancies within the specialist sector, with special schools having fewer teacher vacancies than pupil referral units (PRUs) and alternative provisions (APs) (Scott, 2025). APs also see a greater number of teacher vacancies being temporarily filled compared with mainstream and special schools (Scott, 2025). Special schools with a SEMH designation also tend to have higher teacher vacancy rates than specialist provisions with other designations (Scott, 2025), possibly due to the emotional intensity of working in these settings. Taken together, these figures highlight that there are ongoing recruitment and retention challenges across the specialist sector. For leaders, this underlines the importance of proactive workforce planning and supporting staff wellbeing so that all children receive the high-quality support they need. The questions below invite you to reflect on these statistics and the implications for your setting.

Thinking points

- Do any of these statistics surprise you? Do they reflect your own experience?
- How can specialist and alternative provisions make TA roles more attractive and sustainable?
- What mentoring, induction, or support structures can help staff adapt to specialist settings?
- How do you support staff wellbeing?

Building a specialist workforce

Strength in difference

Specialist and alternative provisions require a highly skilled, values-driven workforce capable of meeting the complex and varied needs of its learners. From therapists and TAs, to pastoral managers and auxiliary staff, the range of roles required is significant. In specialist settings, effective leadership is not about knowing everything yourself but about building a team with the right mix of skills and experiences to find the answers together. It's essential for specialist leaders to be comfortable with not being the expert in every area but with being able to find and deploy the required expertise effectively. Headteacher at Southfield SEN School, Angela O'Rourke, suggests actively recruiting staff dissimilar to yourself:

> *Employ diverse staff - do not employ anyone like you. Have a strong team around you who will challenge you and tell you as it is. Build a team who understand that the role is for the greater good and that the reputation of the school is everything.*

What Angela O'Rourke alludes to is being wary of homophily. Homophily, descending from the Greek for 'love of the same', is the tendency of individuals to associate and bond with those who similar to themselves. This can refer to characteristics such as gender or ethnicity, as well as values, attitudes, and beliefs. Homophily can lead to hiring biases, so slowing down decision making and using techniques such as blind shortlisting can help. This reduction in hiring biases aligns with a growing body of research on the positive impact diverse teams have on organisational performance (McKinsey & Company, 2020). By actively challenging homophily and embracing diversity, your organisation will benefit from a fairer, more inclusive culture. You will also position yourselves to perform better by making innovative and well-rounded decisions. A benefit of mixed economy multi-academy trusts (MATs) is the ability to draw on multiple perspectives during the recruitment process, including staff from both mainstream and specialist provisions, each offering valuable insight into which setting would best suit an applicant (Flemons and Walker, 2024).

Grow your own team

As a leader, one of your most important responsibilities is to ensure your team has the right expertise. When you can't recruit the specialists you need, then you need to look at growing them from within, as these leaders explain:

> *In terms of recruiting teachers, we adopt a grow your own model. We've been helping support staff study for degrees so they can go down a teaching route. We've been working with a local university on a teaching apprenticeship and currently have two apprentices.*
>
> Karen Parker, Head Teacher, Sir Charles Parsons School

> *We try to grow our own teachers. We have a clear process of development for our Learning Support Assistants (LSAs) and we support them to get any qualifications that they missed out on at school. We'll support them to get a degree and go through Initial Teacher Training (ITT). Our trust are looking to develop our own ITT model so that we have a clear method of progression and staff can grow. This supports staff retention. We've also supported one of our LSAs to become a play therapist.*
>
> Kimberley Legg, Assistant Headteacher, Addington School

Grow your own staffing models were a frequent strategy cited by our case study contributors. This situation reflects findings from the National Foundation for Educational Research (NFER, 2023) which shows that fewer than 20% of those beginning teaching roles in special schools in 2022–23 had entered directly from ITT routes, significantly lower than the 30% average for mainstream primary and secondary schools.

Supporting staff to gain Qualified Teacher Status (QTS) is likely to be a common occurrence, given that around 10% of teachers in special schools and 11% in AP settings lack QTS, much higher than the 3% in mainstream schools (Scott, 2025). Teaching apprenticeships are a cost-effective way to support staff who already have a degree, and some Teaching Schools Hubs are now providing part time educational degrees to support TAs to gain one.

Moreover, there's an increasing number of apprenticeships that will develop different staff groups, including specialist apprenticeships, such as the Thrive Advanced Practitioner Apprenticeship, the Pastoral Support Practitioner Apprenticeship, and the AI Practitioner for Schools Apprenticeship, all delivered by Best Practice Network. There are also university level apprenticeships, particularly in therapies, for example the Speech and Language Therapy apprenticeship with Birmingham City University or Occupational Therapy with the University of the West of England. There are also a range of apprenticeship for colleagues across site, Human Resources and Information Technology roles. Your organisation will begin paying into the government's Apprenticeship Levy once you exceed an annual wage bill of £3 million, so it is worth being aware of this (and your spending strategy) as your provision grows (HM Revenue & Customs, 2026).

Values-based interviewing

As discussed in Chapter 1, recruiting staff who align with your values is crucial, and values-based interviewing can help you achieve this. Values-based interviewing focuses on recruiting individuals whose personal values align with the ethos and culture of your provision. By exploring candidates' motivations and behaviours through scenario-based questions, leaders can identify those who are not only capable, but who are also aligned with your purpose, helping to build a resilient, values-driven team. The following insights from leaders illustrate the importance of recruiting staff who not only have the right skills but who also share the ethos and culture of a provision:

> *Do staff go the extra mile? Do they get the vision and values of the school? Are they prepared to challenge the status quo?*
>
> Angela O'Rourke, Headteacher, Southfield SEN School

> *We have to use supply, but we won't keep them if they don't fit with our values. If they do fit then after 12 weeks we encourage them to apply for a job. It's imperative that they match our values – if you're not aligned with them then it's not going to be the job for you. We're really open about the skills needed. We have lots of open days with local universities and colleges. We have lots of apprentices. We're very open-door. We invite people to come and spend a day shadowing us, meeting us, talking about our jobs. We encourage staff to share their experiences and put these videos on our website. Our young people support our People and Culture Team at careers fairs.*
>
> Julliet Doherty, Head of Adult Services, Ascent Autism Specialist College

These types of 'try before you buy' approaches are popular within the specialist sector. Having staff on temporary contracts through agencies provides both the organisation and the individual the opportunity to see whether they share a similar ethos. The questions below invite you to reflect on the recruitment process in your setting.

Thinking points

- How could you apply values-based interview approaches in your setting?
- What strategies could help temporary staff understand and align with the vision and ethos of your organisation?
- How do you provide opportunities for potential applicants to experience working in your setting?

Hiring for heart and skill

Appointing staff in specialist settings is about more than someone's qualifications. You're looking for individuals who understand the pace and complexity of the work and who will keep children and your school's values at the heart of what they do. Regardless of the role, appointing the right staff is a crucial task for school leaders. Headteacher at EOTAS, Juliette Baldwin, discusses part of her interview process:

> *In interview I make it clear that this is a hard place to work. I explain to candidates what we will do to support them, but we're open and honest that AP isn't for everyone. I explain that it's not a reflection on them if they decide that it's not the right setting during the interview day.*
>
> *When appointing a leader, I do a scenario-based fishbowl activity. I give them three scenarios and they have a discussion. I try to see what their resilience is like. I'm also looking for curiosity – why is this happening? I don't want somebody who's going to say as an action 'these children need suspending' – that's not our ethos.*

It's important to remember that an application form only tells us so much about an individual, particularly given that half of job applications are now thought to be written by artificial intelligence (Milmo and Almeida, 2025). Many of the leaders we spoke with recommended interviewing multiple individuals and not discounting candidates too quickly. Several emphasised the value of seeing applicants supporting children across a provision to identify those who can truly connect with learners with additional needs and disabilities. Several leaders stated that some individuals may not stand out on paper but shine when interacting with pupils and that this should form a large part of the interview plan. Headteacher at Greenside School, Alex Tomkins, emphasises this in his approach:

> *The big thing about recruitment is seeing a person around the learners. An interview is different to the actual job, some TA applicants can struggle with the interview but be great in the classroom. You can make an interview more class based. I always expect at least 2 hours in a classroom prior to a simple interview. The emphasis is always on how well they do in the classroom around the children.*

Some leaders we interviewed recommend that candidates experience different age groups and curriculum pathways during interviews. This helps leaders make informed decisions about where candidates would have the greatest impact and connection with children.

Recruitment dilemmas – quantity or quality?

As discussed above, recruitment nationally in education is challenging and leaders might have to choose between appointing a candidate who may not be ideal or leaving a role vacant – a decision that can leave gaps in support for learners. Julliet Doherty, Head of Adult Services at Ascent Autism Specialist College, advocates only appointing staff who will have an impact, rather than simply filling vacancies quickly:

> *It's not just about getting staff. I'm a real stickler for quality over quantity. This might be the best that our young people get in life and I want it to be the best. Since COVID it's been really hard getting staff to commit. It's a very difficult job, it's draining and it can be demoralising at times. We could grow even further but I don't want to grow and not give the children the best. Every person we employ is about the students. It's not about glory, it's not about Ofsted, we want them to make a difference to our young people.*

Some schools have introduced golden handshakes or cash incentives for staff who successfully refer new recruits. Although these schemes can be beneficial for individuals and can help fill vacancies quickly, they also contribute to a more competitive marketplace. Moreover, this approach carries the risk of attracting candidates driven by financial reward rather than alignment with values and culture.

Thinking point: The Eton Example

In his book *Centennials*, Alex Hill explores how House Masters at Eton typically remain in their roles for 13 years. A statistic which stands out when compared with the wider teaching profession in England, where only around 60% of teachers remain in the profession after the same period (Department for Education, 2025a). Eton's success encourages us to look at retention differently. Rather than asking whether we want to retain an individual for 13 years, we should consider the support and opportunities that would encourage someone to stay for that length of time. In other words, instead of focusing on what an individual can offer our provision, we should consider what our provision can offer them. By investing in staff development and providing a sense of belonging, you encourage loyalty and create a thriving, stable team. Being open and honest about your purpose and culture also helps attract the right applicants for your organisation as teachers applying to Eton understand its ethos and traditions. The questions below invite you to reflect on Eton's approach and how it relates to your setting.

- When recruiting and onboarding, how do you help applicants understand your ethos and values?
- How can you make an individual's work purposeful and interesting so that they will stay for a decade or longer?
- How do you ensure that long-serving staff professionally develop rather than stagnate?
- Speak with some of your long-serving members of staff. What connects them to your organisation and how do you reward this loyalty?

Onboarding and Induction

Transitioning from a mainstream to a specialist provision can be challenging, requiring a period of professional and personal adjustment for staff, as Headteacher at Consilium Evolve, Robert Bell, explains:

> *When we recruit someone into AP from mainstream, I often love the pace of their teaching and the quality, but it takes time for them to adjust. Most teachers did well at school so they don't know what it's like to be asked to read aloud in front of your peers when you can't.*

A structured induction programme helps new colleagues feel settled and supported, enabling them to reach their full potential quickly. To support what can be an emotionally demanding time, you could consider offering reflective supervision to staff. This provides staff with a dedicated space to process their professional experiences and maintain their wellbeing in what can be an emotionally intensive working environment.

Your induction programme will become even more important as your provision grows - not only will you employ more staff, but your staff turnover is likely to increase. You will need to consider:

- How your induction process adapts and supports colleagues in different job roles
- How new staff will get to know the wider staff team
- The mandatory training new staff need and when this will be completed
- The operational knowledge staff need to manage day-to-day and how you will provide this
- How you track and get feedback on induction
- Who is responsible for delivering induction
- Whether a buddy or mentor system will support new staff to settle in

Many of the staff you appoint will be new to specialist settings so providing the right support and training is essential for an effective transition. For teachers, you could look at additional PPA (Planning, Preparation, and Assessment) or a period of team teaching - even experienced mainstream staff may feel like an Early Career Teacher again! The following insights from leaders illustrate different approaches to induction and training, highlighting the importance of aligning learning with both staff needs and the ethos of the provision.

> *Staff can join us at any time. We have a rigorous induction package. Quite a lot of people who join us have no understanding of education - for us it's more about do they align with our values? There's lots of work around safeguarding. Our therapy team will do work on sensory integration. There's also things on health and safety as well as autism specific training. Our Lead for Admissions is involved and explains the process of admission and transition. It means that anybody starting with us knows where our young people start from and where they're going to get to. We also prioritise and fund individual CPD.*
>
> Julliet Doherty, Head of Adult Services, Ascent Autism Specialist College

We have a thorough induction programme. Learning Support Assistants often come in with no SEND background or very little. The role is very complex – it's hard to find someone who can come in ready to go with all the skills and knowledge that you need.

One thing we'd like to develop is a training week. This means having new staff off-timetable and on training for their first week. A bespoke training week would help new staff develop those solid foundations before they go off into class and meet the students. At the moment our induction programme is a rolling programme that takes place on a Wednesday after school. As it's a rolling programme, it means that sometimes people start and you're on Week 16 of induction and you're not focusing on what they need right now. So, we're looking at how we can change that. With the training week you'd start at the beginning of term, have a full week of training and be prepared to go into class.

We also offer lots of video and online training. We record team meetings and give people the opportunity to join remotely. Lots of staff are keen to engage and if they're given the option to come and it's possible then they will.

Kimberley Legg, Assistant Headteacher, Addington School

Kimberley raises a valid point about the relevance and timing of induction. The questions below encourage you to reflect on the approach to induction in your setting.

Thinking points

- Is there any merit to trialling a training week in your organisation? Would it provide a stronger foundation for new starters? What are the opportunities and barriers to this?
- If you currently utilise a rolling induction model, does it meet the needs of your new starters effectively or does it risk not providing what they need, when they need it?
- Do you offer flexible, blended learning opportunities (e.g. video content, remote access) for staff who want to revisit training or catch up on missed sessions?
- How accessible and inclusive is your induction programme for part-time or agency staff?

Activity: Reflecting on the impact of induction

Work with a group of recent starters and map their induction experience from recruitment to classroom/role readiness.

- What supported them?
- Where were there gaps?
- How can this insight refine your induction programme?

Succession planning: Supporting and growing leaders

As highlighted in the Introduction, the expansion of specialist settings has brought with it a growing need for committed and capable leaders. Consequently, supporting and developing new leaders must be a priority for existing ones, not only to retain and maximise talent but to ensure that the next generation of leaders is ready (Leithwood, Harris, and Hopkins, 2008). By providing opportunities, mentoring, and pathways for progression, we can grow aspiring leaders, ensuring our organisation continues to thrive after we've moved on.

In January 2024, the football manager Jurgen Klopp announced his intention to retire from managing Liverpool FC at the end of the 2023/24 season. Many football followers were devastated by the news, Liverpool were performing well and Klopp was a solid fan favourite. Klopp's arrival at Liverpool, just before the 'special one' Jose Mourinho was about to be sacked from Chelsea for the second time, was notable for its humility. In fact, you used to be able to buy a mug from the Liverpool FC shop with a picture of Klopp and 'The Normal One' on it. Klopp's achievements at Liverpool were immense, including Premier League, Champions League, and FA Cup success. Charismatic, passionate about developing youth players, and committed to knowing the names of his 1,000 strong staff team (Pearce, 2024), Klopp was going to be a leader who was hard to replace.

Although fans were said to have favoured the appointment of previous club legend Xabi Alonso, the recruitment board at Liverpool took a data-driven rather than a sentimental approach to replacing Klopp (Arnold, 2024). They were also determined not to be rushed, taking around 4 months to confirm a successor (most football managers are replaced within days). On 20 May 2024, Dutch football manager Arne Slot was appointed, leaving many fans disappointed (McNulty, 2024), even though comparisons showed clear similarities with Klopp, such as his attacking style and ability to nurture young players. At his last game in charge of Liverpool, Klopp chanted Slot's name in a bid to excite and reassure fans about the change to come.

Despite never having managed in England, Slot led Liverpool to Premier League victory in his first season, being crowned champions with a phenomenal four games to spare. Over 300 managers have managed in the Premier League (Wikipedia, n.d.), yet Slot is only the fifth to win the title during their first season in charge. (Souter, 2025). To the surprise of fans, one of the first things Slot did upon becoming crowned champions was to reciprocate Klopp's gesture, chanting his name back to the stands. It was beyond the wildest dreams of Liverpool fans and a fitting culmination to one of the finest leadership handovers in Premier League history.

Even if you're not a football fan, there's a lot to admire in how Liverpool FC approached leadership succession. In particular, they spent time and effort appointing someone who matched the club's ethos and style, demonstrating that thoughtful succession planning ensures success isn't person dependent.

Former U.S. presidential candidate, Ralph Nader (2001), suggests that it's the responsibility of leaders to create more leaders by developing and championing the individuals that will lead after them, a bit like Klopp did when he chanted Slot's name to the fans. As educational leaders, it's our job to make sure that individuals within our teams feel encouraged, trusted and ready to step into leadership themselves. This becomes even more important as an organisation grows and succession planning at all levels becomes integral to success.

Hill (2024) warns that most organisations struggle to identify their next generation of leaders early enough. Without time to grow into their roles, or receive coaching and mentoring from existing leaders, handovers can become disjointed rather than smooth. Of course, succession planning is not the responsibility of one individual - it requires each leader in an organisation to commit to the success of the person who comes after them. To develop this, as part of your annual appraisal cycle, leaders should consider:

- Who is your successor?
- How can you support them to be ready to do your role?
- What opportunities are there for them to shadow or work with you?
- Are there opportunities for secondments or role rotations that might help your successor gain key skills or experiences?

Of course, your successor can only step into your shoes if you are ready to step into someone else's. Therefore, it is also important for you to consider the role you are looking to step into and how you can work with the current postholder to ensure that you're ready.

Lydia Colios, Assistant Headteacher at Addington School, explains how her provision invests in aspiring middle leaders:

> *Talent spotting is a key part of the senior leader role. It's about giving somebody opportunities and broadening their experiences. We identify aspiring middle leaders. You need to ensure that there are lots of opportunities for leaders to step up and shine. There are always opportunities in special schools since teachers often do what is expected of a SENCO in a mainstream school. We invest in our middle leaders and give them time out of class. There are clear channels down from senior leaders to middle leaders with everybody having a senior leader link.*

As well as considering your own successor, you'll also need to think about who will succeed the other leaders in your organisation, particularly as your provision grows and your leadership team expands. Hill (2024) suggests proactively identifying a successor 4 years ahead of the current leader's departure. Given that many headteachers leave within 5 years, and only a minority remain beyond a decade, the typical tenure of a headteacher is often estimated to be around 5 to 7 years (NFER, 2017; Department for Education, 2025b). In this context, succession planning should be, ironically, one of the first considerations for any new head.

Consequently, long-term thinking is key for leaders. Having studied the success and lifespan of a number of US businesses, Hill (2024) suggests a strategy of developing internal talent to fill 80% of leadership roles, while bringing in external candidates for the remaining 20%

to incorporate new perspectives. This means that most of your future leaders are already in your organisation. However, with only 42% of deputy and assistant heads saying they aspire to headship (Teacher Tapp & SchoolDash, 2025), providing the time, exposure, and opportunities to work alongside current headteachers who can role model and champion the role becomes even more important. The questions below invite you to reflect on succession planning in your setting.

Thinking points

- Who in your organisation will be ready for leadership or additional leadership responsibility over the next 5 years?
- How could you incorporate shadowing or secondments into your leadership development programme?
- What systems do you have in place that allow leadership expertise to be transferred across tiers of leadership?
- What does a leadership handover look like in your setting?
- How will you know when it is time to move on?

As educators, we give feedback to children as a matter of course – we wouldn't dream of letting them learn without it. In fact, we'd be concerned if we didn't see any form of feedback during our learning walks. So why are we often less willing to seek or offer feedback as adults? One possibility is because it makes us feel vulnerable to open ourselves up to criticism (even if it supportive, constructive, and given with the intention of making us get better). For effective feedback to occur within a leadership team, trust must come first. In Chapter 1 we explored psychological safety – an important foundation if we want our colleagues to give meaningful feedback about our leadership. Individuals will only provide honest feedback if they feel safe, yet this sort of feedback is crucial to help you develop as a leader. The questions below allow you to reflect on how you elicit feedback in your setting.

Thinking points

- How do you create opportunities for you and your leadership team to receive meaningful feedback?
- How do you use the feedback you receive?
- How will you help create a culture that views feedback as an opportunity, not a threat?
- Too often feedback gets mistaken for judgement or performance appraisal. How will you develop clear and separate systems for both so that leaders receive developmental feedback focused on growth?

Staff wellbeing - putting people first

One of the positives of the Covid-19 pandemic has been an increase in the openness of discussions around wellbeing. Education is never easy work and your team will experience moments of significant pressure. It's therefore becoming more common for educational settings to have a wellbeing policy or charter to demonstrate their commitment to supporting staff. Small but important steps, such as an open-door policy, valuing staff loyalty, and employee assistance programmes, can all help.

Although there is no legal obligation for schools to provide a staffroom, there are benefits to providing a place for staff to eat and socialise. Neuman (2024) suggests that eating together supports social bonding, trust, and cooperation between group members. This is further supported by Helliwell et al. (2025), who found that sharing meals greatly impacts our sense of wellbeing - people who regularly eat with others report feeling more satisfied with life and experience more positive emotions. Given that over 20% of teachers eat lunch in their classroom (McInerney, 2017), providing a staffroom and encouraging staff to use it could be a quick win in establishing and maintaining relationships.

Providing opportunities for your team to eat and meet together can also help cultivate psychological safety. Google's 'Project Aristotle' (Pretty, 2024), which set out to explore team performance, suggests that psychological safety is the most important aspect of effective teamwork. Psychological safety creates the foundation for discretionary effort, meaning that staff are more likely to go above and beyond because they feel respected and supported. At Springfields, we build in time for all staff to eat together at the end of every long term by providing a lunchtime buffet. It's not just about eating lunch - it's about the social opportunities to get to know each other and the connections it creates. Our staff wellbeing group also offers a range of activities for staff through our termly Wellbeing Wednesdays e.g. playing computer games or a walk to a local café. They also arrange staff awards at Christmas and in the summer, and keep our Staff Shout-out Board updated.

As your provision grows and your team gets bigger, you'll probably see more varied working patterns, with different start and finish times and staggered breaks. Be mindful that this can limit opportunities for staff wellbeing and collaboration, meaning you may need to make a conscious effort to build these opportunities in elsewhere (Camilleri, Rockey, and Dunbar, 2024). Additionally, if you're a residential provision, it's important to consider staff on unsociable working hours, who may have fewer opportunities to collaborate and fewer colleagues to connect with. Some strategies that may support collaboration and connection include:

- Ensuring wellbeing activities are offered at different times - e.g. before school as well as after school - to incorporate different shift patterns.
- Record training sessions or briefings so staff can access them asynchronously.
- Ensuring that your open-door policy spans across different shifts so that all staff have access to the leadership team.

- Include and celebrate colleagues on different shift patterns in whole-school communications so their work is clearly connected to the life of the school.
- Ensure staff on unsociable hours are included in celebrations by publicly acknowledging their contribution and providing alternative ways for them to join in.

Although buffets and wellbeing days are appreciated, real staff wellbeing comes from thoughtful calendar design – making sure there's a balance between busy, accountable periods and weeks where little else but teaching and learning is happening. By thinking ahead and designing the school year with this equilibrium in mind, leaders can create a calendar that supports wellbeing and a sustainable work/life balance. Helen Parry, Mental Health and Wellbeing Lead at Three Towers Alternative Provision Academy, explains how they've established a whole-school approach to wellbeing:

> *Whole school staff mental health and well-being questionnaires are sent annually to all colleagues. They are anonymous and questions are consistent to monitor feedback and any changes. Results are fed back to staff and actions are taken, such as improvements within the layout of the staffroom. Alongside the questionnaire, a workload review took place. Consequently, changes were made to reduce workload and policies were updated. A mental health policy was created and 'well-being Wednesday' implemented into the timetable which allows staff to engage in activities with students which they may not usually access such as fishing, hair and beauty or trampolining.*
>
> *Staff PPA is timetabled for Friday afternoon which allows the flexibility for staff to take at home if they choose to do so. Feedback is consistently positive, some examples from the questionnaire being 'Three Towers makes me feel valued', 'there is support as soon as you walk in the building', 'I think we care for each other well'. A bank of wellbeing resources for staff has been created and are updated regularly.*
>
> *I have learnt that listening to staff and communicating with them about future plans is key. Explaining why some suggestions cannot be carried out is the foundation to establishing a wellbeing focus with mutual trust. My main advice for others looking to develop a mental health and wellbeing strategy would be that the key issues need to be addressed before what might be considered 'superficial activities' are encouraged.*
>
> *Once we established our formal priorities, additional well-being initiatives were developed such as afternoon tea boxes for all staff, staff quizzes and social activities. In 2024 the school was re-accredited to Gold status for the Carnegie Mental Health Award. In 2025 Three Towers were recognised at Bronze level for the Pearson Education Awards and went on to win 'Specialist Provision of the Year' at the TES awards.*

Helen effectively describes how a supportive approach to wellbeing can be woven into an organisation's culture. Our own leadership ethos and values, as outlined in the

Introduction and Chapter 1, align with what Cameron and Quinn (1999) call 'Clan Culture', a workplace environment that fosters a close-knit, collaborative, and values-driven community. Many organisations say they are like a family and Clan Culture resembles this, focusing on strong relationships and valuing people. Cameron and Quinn (1999) suggest that education is well-suited to developing Clan Cultures as it is a sector that requires innovation, flexibility, and collaboration. Janna, Olynick, and Li (2020) suggest that organisational culture can significantly impact employee wellbeing and performance. Their research into Canadian organisations found that individuals working within a Clan Culture experienced less stress and more enjoyment at work. They suggest that creating a Clan Culture supports staff retention as these workplaces experience lower staff turnover - most likely because when people feel valued and part of something meaningful, they are more likely to stay.

Clan Cultures can also encourage the conditions for psychological safety by helping staff feel that their voice matters and enabling them to speak up. Crucially, this helps staff share any concerns early, not just around safeguarding, but any changes in their wellbeing or mental health. Moreover, there are likely to be greater numbers of neurodivergent adults entering the workplace, either through becoming of working age or through gaining a diagnosis later in life. In a psychologically safe workplace, people know they can be their authentic selves without fear of being judged or excluded by others (Edmondson, 1999). Given that, in March 2025, more than 232,000 adults were waiting for an ADHD diagnosis (House of Commons Library, 2025), the number of neurodivergent staff in the workplace is only likely to increase. By intentionally building inclusive, clan-style cultures, leaders can make sure all staff feel valued, heard, and supported. The questions below invite you to reflect on how your organisation supports staff wellbeing.

Thinking points

- Do leaders in your setting ever eat lunch together? Does the evidence suggest that they should?
- How can leaders be visible in the staffroom without compromising staff members' need for a safe space to offload?
- Does your current staff wellbeing offer support and include those on non-typical working hours?
- How do you celebrate and recognise staff contributions in ways that reinforce a sense of belonging?
- How prepared is your organisation to support an increasing number of neurodivergent or disabled staff?

Leadership scenario

You've noticed a recent increase in staff absence and low morale in your setting. While exit interviews have been positive, there's a sense among staff that there have been fewer opportunities for collaboration this year and people are feeling disconnected. A new staff member, who recently received a diagnosis of ADHD, says they feel unsure whether they can be their authentic self at work. You reflect on your leadership values and recognise that although your setting talks about being 'like a family', that feeling of collaboration and care is missing.

Using the prompts below to help you, what action would you take and why?

- What feedback mechanisms could you use to understand how staff are currently feeling?
- What actions could you take to rebuild a sense of community and belonging within your team?
- How might you develop an inclusion strategy to support neurodivergent staff?
- How will you know that your wellbeing strategy is making a difference?
- What would you expect to see, hear, or feel in 6 months' time to demonstrate that your culture is changing for the better?

Positive leaving

As your organisation and workforce grows, staff leaving will become a more frequent occurrence. It is natural, particularly if you're spending time developing others, that some staff members will move on to take up leadership positions of their own. There will also be some staff who drift apart from the ethos and culture of your provision, choosing to leave in search of a renewed sense of belonging and purpose. Spend time with your leadership and HR team thinking about how you want people to leave you. Consider:

- What does positive leaving look like in your organisation?
- How do you use exit interviews to reflect and refine the employee experience?
- How do you retain links and build partnerships with those employees moving on to promotions or new opportunities?
- How can you leave the door open for people to seek reemployment with you?

Thinking about how people leave your organisation brings us full circle - we started by thinking about recruitment and have finished by considering positive leaving. Supporting staff to arrive, grow, and positively move on is vital and demonstrates that every stage of your employee experience matters. How people leave your organisation says as much about your ethos and values as how they join.

Chapter summary

This chapter explores how to attract, keep, and care for a school's greatest asset - its staff team.

- Specialist and alternative provisions require more staff than mainstream settings, particularly TAs.
- Nationally, the education sector faces a range of recruitment and retention challenges and therefore having a strategy which encompasses growing your own staff is key.
- A growing research body highlights the importance of building a diverse team.
- It's important to look beyond an application form and get a sense of how each applicant interacts with young people.
- Values-based interviewing may help organisations identify staff who are a good cultural fit.
- It's vital to identify and develop the next generation of leaders effectively.
- Although there's no legal obligation to have a staffroom, research suggests that there are benefits from staff eating together.
- Adopting a Clan Culture can help support staff wellbeing and retention by creating a close-knit community with psychological safety at its core.
- As your provision grows, staff turnover will increase. Positive leaving is about creating a culture where staff departures are handled with dignity, reflection, and appreciation for the contribution someone has made.

Further reading

- If you'd like to learn about how other public sector settings use values-based interviewing, you could read the National Health Service's National VBR Programme and Framework, which is available on the NHS England website (Health Education England, 2016).
- If you'd like to know more about Google's 'Project Aristotle' and what makes an effective team. You can read some insights uncovered by Project Aristotle at https://www.aristotleperformance.com/post/project-aristotle-google-s-data-driven-insights-on-high-performing-teams (Pretty, 2024).

References

Arnold, L. (2024, 28 January). 'What approach Liverpool will take when choosing who will replace Jürgen Klopp this summer'. *TBR Football*. Available online at: https://tbrfootball.com/what-approach-liverpool-will-take-when-choosing-who-will-replace-jurgen-klopp-this-summer/ [accessed 30 July 2025].

Cameron, K. S., and Quinn, R. E. (1999). *Diagnosing and Changing Organizational Culture: Based on the Competing Values Framework*. Reading, MA: Addison-Wesley.

Camilleri, T., Rockey, S., and Dunbar, R. (2024). *The Social Brain: The Psychology of Successful Groups*. Penguin, London.

Department for Education (2019). *Teacher Recruitment and Retention Strategy*. London: Department for Education. Available online at: https://www.gov.uk/government/publications/teacher-recruitment-and-retention-strategy/teacher-recruitment-and-retention-strategy [accessed 22 June 2025].

Department for Education (2025a, 5 June). *School Workforce in England: November 2024. Accredited Official Statistics*. Available online at: https://www.gov.uk/government/statistics/school-workforce-in-england-november-2024 [accessed 26 April 2026].

Department for Education (2025b). *School Workforce in England, Reporting Year 2024*. Available online at: https://explore-education-statistics.service.gov.uk/find-statistics/school-workforce-in-england/2024 [accessed 25 April 2026].

Edmondson, A. C. (1999). 'Psychological safety and learning behavior in work teams'. *Administrative Science Quarterly, 44*(2), 350–383.

Flemons, L., and Walker, M. (2024). *The MAT Factor: Exploring How Multi-academy Trusts are Supporting Pupils with SEND*. Slough: NFER.

Health Education England (2016). *Values Based Recruitment*. National Health Service England. Available online at: https://www.hee.nhs.uk/our-work/values-based-recruitment [accessed 22 June 2025].

Helliwell, J.F., Layard, R., Sachs, J.D., De Neve, J.-E., Aknin, L.B., and Wang, S. (eds.). (2025). *World Happiness Report 2025*. Oxford: Wellbeing Research Centre, University of Oxford. Available online at: https://files.worldhappiness.report/WHR25.pdf?_gl=1*1u571sg*_gcl_au*MzgxNTEyMjQyLjE3NTUxNjg1Mzg [accessed 14 August 2025].

Hill, A. (2024). *Centennials: The 12 Habits of Great Enduring Organisations*. London: Penguin Books, Random House Business.

HM Revenue & Customs (2026). *Pay Apprenticeship Levy. Guidance* [update 6 April 2026]. Available online at: https://www.gov.uk/guidance/pay-apprenticeship-levy [accessed 26 April 2026].

House of Commons Library (2025, 4 March). *FAQ: ADHD Statistics (England)*. Available online at: https://commonslibrary.parliament.uk/faq-adhd-statistics-england/ [accessed 6 August 2025].

Janna, O., Olynick, J., and Li, H. (2020). 'Organizational culture and its relationship with employee stress, enjoyment of work and productivity'. *International Journal of Psychological Studies, 12*(2), 14–30.

Leithwood, K., Harris, A., and Hopkins, D. (2008). 'Seven strong claims about successful school leadership'. *School Leadership and Management, 28*(1), 27–42.

Lynch, S., Mills, B., Theobald, K., and Worth, J. (2017). *Keeping Your Head: NFER Analysis of Headteacher Retention*. Slough: NFER. Available online at: https://www.nfer.ac.uk/media/0tqlfvg0/keeping_your_head_nfer_analysis_of_headteacher_retention.pdf [accessed 26 April 2026].

McInerney, L. (2017, 24 September). 'Lunch: How do teachers eat theirs?' *Teacher Tapp* Available online at: https://teachertapp.com/uk/articles/lunch-teachers-eat/ [accessed 8 August 2025].

McKinsey & Company (2020, 19 May). *Diversity Wins: How Inclusion Matters*. Report. Available online at: https://www.mckinsey.com/featured-insights/diversity-and-inclusion/diversity-wins-how-inclusion-matters [accessed 19 July 2025].

McLean, D., Worth, J., and Smith, A. (2024). *Teacher Labour Market in England Annual Report 2024*. Slough: National Foundation for Educational Research.

McNulty, P. (2024, 14 May). 'Is Slot an underwhelming appointment?' *BBC Sport*. Available online at: https://www.bbc.co.uk/sport/football/articles/c3g55xpwde8o [accessed 30 July 2025].

Milmo, D., and Almeida, L. (2025, 13 July). 'Teach First job applicants will get in-person interviews after more apply using AI'. *The Guardian*. Available online at: https://www.theguardian.com/technology/2025/jul/13/graduates-teach-first-in-person-interviews-ai [accessed 23 October 2025].

Nader, R. (2001). *Crashing the Party: How to Tell the Truth and Still Run for President*. New York: St. Martin's Press.

National College for School Leadership (NCSL) (2008). *School Leadership Labour Market*. Available online at: https://www.ncsl.org.uk/files/school-leadership-labour-market.pdf [accessed 25 October 2025].

National Foundation for Educational Research (2023). *Cost-of-living Crisis: Impact on Schools*. Slough: National Foundation for Educational Research. Available online at: https://www.nfer.ac.uk/publications/cost-of-living-crisis-impact-on-schools/ [accessed 22 June 2025].

Neuman, N. (2024). 'Commensal attraction: Eating together as a social tool'. *Journal for the Theory of Social Behaviour, 54*(4), 556–570.

Pearce, J. (2024, 17 May). 'The real Jürgen Klopp, part five: The manager who made Liverpool believe again'. *The New York Times (The Athletic)*. Available online at: https://www.nytimes.com/athletic/5496187/2024/05/17/jurgen-klopp-manager-liverpool-secrets/ [accessed 30 July 2025].

Pretty, N. (2024, 1 December). 'Project Aristotle: Google's data-driven insights on high-performing teams'. Aristotle Performance. Available online at: https://www.aristotleperformance.com/post/project-aristotle-google-s-data-driven-insights-on-high-performing-teams [accessed 26 April 2026].

Scott, M. (2025, 25 February). 'Exploring the special schools workforce: What's the current picture?' Blog post. Slough: National Foundation for Educational Research. Available online at: https://www.nfer.ac.uk/blogs/exploring-the-special-schools-workforce-what-s-the-current-picture/ [accessed 22 June 2025].

Souter, J. (2025, 27 April). 'Arne Slot, Liverpool next: No manager lasts long after winning Prremier League in first season'. Football 365. Available online at: https://www.football365.com/news/arne-slot-liverpool-next-manager-win-premier-league-first-season [accessed 26 April 2026].

Teacher Tapp & SchoolDash (2025). *Teacher Recruitment and Retention in 2025*. Available online at: https://teachertapp.com/app/uploads/2025/04/RELEASED_Teacher-Recruitment-and-Retention-in-2025.pdf [accessed 25 October 2025].

Wikipedia (n.d.). 'List of Premier League managers'. *Wikipedia*. Available online at: https://en.wikipedia.org/wiki/List_of_Premier_League_managers [accessed 26 April 2026].

8

Everyone a SEND practitioner: Staff development

My progression, from Teaching Assistant to teacher, from youth worker to project leader, has been shaped by strong mentorship, trust and a shared commitment to the young people we serve. More than anything, it has reaffirmed that with the right people, vision and support, we can transform lives.

Danielle, Everton Free School

Chapter overview

Having considered how we can recruit and retain staff, this chapter explores how to turn them into a strong, well-developed team. It also explores what high-quality Continuing Professional Development (CPD) looks like in specialist and alternative provisions, and how leaders can balance individual interests with organisational priorities as their provision grows.

The importance of teams

Educational leadership expert Michael Fullan reminds us:

> An organization cannot flourish - at least, not for long - on the actions of the top leader alone.
>
> (2002, p. 20)

This view echoes Aristotle's famous observation that, 'the whole is greater than the sum of its parts'. Effective leadership is not just about managing people but about creating a team whose collective strengths exceed any individual achievement. This principle is vital in specialist contexts, where the needs of young people are becoming ever more complex, meaning that adults require increasingly specialised knowledge and skills.

The power of working collectively means that developing others should be a constant in your organisation, not an add on. As Sir Richard Branson (2014) suggests, leaders should

DOI: 10.4324/9781003601388-9

equip staff with the skills to grow and move on but create the working conditions that encourage them to stay. In education, a powerful driver of staff retention is the provision of meaningful learning that supports professional growth. Poekert (2012) emphasises that educational leaders can achieve this through fostering a culture that values collaboration and continuous development There is also a growing body of research which suggests that investing in staff not only builds their skills and capacity but is associated with improved retention and workforce stability (Skills for Care, 2025).

Developing staff in specialist settings

Supporting the professional development of others is a vital part of leadership (Leithwood, Harris, and Hopkins, 2019). Within your budget, staffing costs are likely to be your biggest expenditure. However, it's not just about good financial return for your investment in staffing, but the moral imperative - if staff are at their best, equipped, and confident to do their roles, then children receive the best. When you invest in your staff, the impact spreads throughout your organisation. From increased discretionary effort to higher staff attendance and retention, these effects all transfer into benefits for your learners and school community. The questions below invite you to reflect on your organisation's approach to CPD.

Thinking points

- How much time do you spend thinking about others' professional development?
- Who leads the professional development strategy in your organisation and how much of your budget is devoted to it?
- How can you, as leader, creature a culture in your setting in which professional development is valued and prioritised?
- How can leaders model the importance of continuous professional growth?

What do we mean by CPD?

Our definition of CPD draws on that of Coldwell (2017), who views CPD as encompassing a wide variety of formal and informal activities, underpinned by the aim of developing teachers as professionals and increasing their knowledge and skills. Of course, CPD isn't just for teachers, but for all staff (and, arguably, governors and families). Including all staff groups in your programme is essential, as specialist provisions are complex organisations with a range of roles - such as therapists - not typically found in mainstream provisions.

The breadth of activities that Coldwell (2017) considers to be CPD echoes our own understanding and professional learning programme. We believe that grassroots, informal, and collaborative CPD all count - from social media discussion, to reading blogs and attending educational conferences. For us, CPD is anything that helps staff learn, reflect, and change their practice to benefit young people or their wider school community. As well as benefitting individuals, CPD should also strengthen overall organisational capacity and growth. Encouraging staff to take up membership of professional bodies, e.g. the Chartered College of Teaching, is an effective way to give them access to up-to-date research, accreditation pathways, and a sense of professional community beyond your organisation.

Designing CPD for specialist contexts

Giving time to CPD is important - leaders need to model the prioritisation of CPD and the value of being a learning organisation. We believe that the traditional five INSET (In-Service Education and Training) day model is outdated. INSET days, often called 'Baker Days' after Kenneth Baker, the Education Secretary who introduced them, first appeared in 1989. Let's think about the world then. For us, we were still in primary school. Indiana Jones was gearing up for his last crusade, whilst Robin Williams was inspiring future English teachers (like Nicola B!) in the film the *Dead Poets Society.* 'Eternal Flame' and 'Like a Prayer' boomed out from cassette players to a backdrop of world events that included the fall of the Berlin Wall and the Hillsborough Disaster. It was also the year that Tim Berners-Lee submitted his proposal for something called the World Wide Web . . . meaning there was absolutely no need for GDPR (General Data Protection Regulation), cybersecurity, or online safety training! Likewise, *Keeping Children Safe in Education* (Department for Education, 2015), which overhauled safeguarding training, wasn't published until March 2015. In 2026, the amount of mandatory training required takes around two full INSET days to complete. We have campaigned hard and written a business case for specialist settings within our trust to have ten INSET days per academic year. This may sound a lot, but the specialist knowledge and training that staff in specialist settings require to be effective is significant. Which would you choose: 190 pupil days with staff who are adequately trained, or 185 days with staff who are highly trained, confident, and able to make a difference to their learners?

Prioritising and finding time for CPD is important because, as Coldwell (2017) implies, once staff engage in CPD, they're more likely to continue to do so, and crucially, perceive positive benefits from their learning. Coldwell (2017) also found a link between the frequency of engagement with CPD and positive evaluation of its impact. Practitioners who engaged in CPD frequently were more likely to report positive impacts across a range of outcomes. This suggests that CPD creates a virtuous cycle - the more you engage in it the more you (and arguably your learners) feel the benefit.

Although some staff will be motivated learners who pursue their own professional development outside of working hours, we cannot assume or rely on this. Some staff will not have the financial means to do so; others may have second jobs or caring commitments that require their time. It's therefore vital that time is set aside during the working week for CPD. Your professional learning programme is important and deserves as much thought and input as we give to our pupils' schemes of learning. After all, it is a curriculum - just one designed for staff.

Case study: Planning a professional learning programme

Our approach to planning our annual CPD programme is described below:

- We start with our ten INSET days, as they form the foundation of our core CPD offer. We try to ensure that INSET days take place on different days of the week so that staff on part-time working patterns are not always missing out. We record as much of our CPD as we can to create an on-demand library to enable staff to join in asynchronously.
- We begin by mapping out all the mandatory training (e.g. safeguarding, health and safety, compliance) that must be covered during the year.
- We then map out the specialist training that staff require, such as Elklan, Makaton, and Team Teach.
- On top of this, we add the operational knowledge that staff require - for example, recaps on school structures and systems, or on our instructional approach.
- Next comes the curriculum and subject development that drives school improvement priorities for the year.
- Finally, we map in the annual events that form part of directed time - for example, parents' evenings and community events such as the summer fete.
- However, as we are part of a multi-academy trust (MAT), we must also ensure there is time to complete centrally directed training and to participate in whole-trust events.
- We then publish the whole calendar in September, along with a more detailed breakdown each half-term.

The questions below encourage you to think about your approach to planning your annual training programme.

- What similarities and differences are there in how you approach the planning of CPD in your setting?
- What professional learning would you want for staff if time and money were no object?

Our weekly professional learning programme is also mapped out in its entirety across the year. Alongside tailored programmes for groups of staff - Middle Leaders, Teachers, Teaching Assistants, pastoral staff, and therapy staff - there are also sessions that bring these groups together to develop shared understanding and foster a sense of belonging to the whole school team.

All these groups have directed time for CPD within their working week. Although building opportunities for weekly CPD carries a financial cost, and school budgets are under immense strain, it pays dividends. Staff are likely to increase their discretionary effort if they feel you're concerned about them and their development. For settings where staff work night shifts or unsociable hours (as discussed in Chapter 7), exploring models of asynchronous learning may be beneficial. For example, for those on term-time contracts, incorporate additional days into their contracts that can be disaggregated into weekly learning. Other flexible modes of delivery include watching recordings of sessions, followed by online discussions forums for reflection and the sharing of ideas.

We also have common elements between the different CPD for different teams that provide a structure for each term:

- Safeguarding briefing
- Headteacher's briefing
- Solution-focused surgeries
- Line management and/or appraisal
- Curriculum/subject development
- SEND development
- Events e.g. parents' evening
- Wellbeing Wednesday (where staff can select an activity that supports their wellbeing)
- Instructional coaching time

These elements provide a consistent structure and ensure a balanced approach to CPD across the areas of safeguarding, teaching and learning, wellbeing, and individual development.

Activity: Designing a professional learning programme

Imagine that you are designing next year's professional learning programme:

- How will you baseline staff needs?
- How will you provide time for all staff (including Governors) to engage in CPD?
- How will your CPD programme complement the Golden Thread of CPD available nationally?
- How will you balance specialist CPD with subject/role-specific CPD?
- How will you utilise external and internal expertise?
- What will your annual, termly, and weekly CPD programme look like?

Thinking point: Alternative models of CPD

Most CPD takes place at the end of the working day when colleagues are tired and likely to have reached cognitive overload. Is this really the best time for staff to learn new things? Swiss Cottage School, a special school in Camden, provides time for professional learning at the start of the day. Staff engage in training and collaborative planning between 8.30 am and 9.15 am (in addition to PPA). The school day for pupils then runs from 9.30 am to 3.30 pm.

- What are the benefits of this model?
- How could this model work in your setting?

The power of professional learning communities

There is widespread agreement that teachers benefit from collaborative learning (Avalos, 2011). Therefore, finding your own professional learning community is crucial, particularly in specialist and alternative contexts. For many provisions, being part of a MAT provides a peer network, but specialist settings can still be the only one of their kind within the group. Within the South West, we are lucky to have SWALSS - the South West Association for Leaders in Special Schools. SWALSS runs a range of professional development opportunities, including leadership conferences, training for Governors, and training for those new to specialist settings. These events also provide valuable networking opportunities, strengthening expertise and reducing feelings of professional isolation. Secondary special schools, PRUs, and APs frequently have departments of one. As Charlotte Barton, Managing Director of Progress Schools, notes, this makes it essential to create opportunities for peer collaboration between settings.

> *We know about the teacher retention crisis but workload in AP is often greater due to the small, multi-disciplinary teams that funding dictates.*

There is also growing recognition that Early Career Teachers in specialist settings benefit from opportunities to collaborate, with many delivery partners now providing SEND-specific groups.

Balancing individual and organisational needs

Alongside a structured learning programme, you will likely have mechanisms for individuals to request CPD relevant to their interests or role. However, as your organisation grows, so too does the challenge of balancing multiple individual aspirations with your organisational priorities. In Chapter 1, we looked at the time pressures created by weekly check-ins with staff, and, financially, the same principle applies when considering individual CPD requests. For example, in a provision of 100 staff, if each year everyone attended a £100 course of their choice, the CPD budget for this alone would exceed £10,000. Although scholarship funding for programmes such as the National Professional Qualifications (NPQs) can reduce costs, and some forms of CPD – such as peer observations or school visits – can be accessed at little or no expense, the reality remains that, as your staff body grows, it becomes increasingly difficult to fund individual CPD requests for every member of staff each year. Leaders therefore need to strike a balance between equity and organisational needs – your core CPD programme needs to provide a consistent core offer of professional learning for everyone, with the flexibility to offer targeted individual development opportunities that align with wider organisational goals. Other strategies that may help are listed below:

- Offer choice, which is a key element in increasing engagement in professional learning (Fraser et al., 2007). You could increase the relevance of CPD by incorporating sessions where staff choose what to attend. This underpins our approach to A-Fest, where staff select four workshops from a programme of more than 25, enabling them to create a bespoke day of CPD.
- Use expressions of interest to support equity of opportunity for any high cost or external CPD.
- Maximise scholarships/funded opportunities e.g. NPQs and apprenticeships.
- Consider how staff will disseminate their learning to others to ensure every individual CPD benefits the whole team.
- Explore 'train the trainer' opportunities for licensed training such as Elklan or Makaton. This will make it easier (and cheaper) to upskill staff across your organisation.
- Consider how you will track CPD to ensure that multiple individuals do not access the same learning and that the same individual does not access multiple opportunities.
- Implement a training agreement so that staff in receipt of substantial investment commit to a retention period subsequent to the CPD.
- Clarify the expected outcomes with staff before CPD begins. This will enable you to be clear about your impact measures and expected outcomes (Earley and Porritt, 2014).

These strategies will help you combine a core CPD programme with targeted individual opportunities, creating a professional learning culture that develops skills, knowledge, and confidence across the whole staff team. The questions below enable you to reflect on the CPD offer in your setting.

Thinking points

- How many of your staff participate in wider professional learning communities?
- How do you balance individual CPD aspirations with your organisation's strategic priorities, particularly when budgets are limited?
- How do you ensure that individual learning is shared to benefit the whole team?
- How do you measure the impact of CPD on staff practice and learner outcomes?

Leadership scenario

You're an Assistant Head with responsibility for CPD in a residential special school. You have a staff body of 120, including residential care staff and night staff. Several staff have approached you to request expensive external CPD that would take up most of your budget. You discuss these requests with other leaders. Your Deputy Headteacher argues that you should approve these requests since individual choice will boost engagement and retention. Your Headteacher stresses that you have a limited budget for CPD and should prioritise the core offer to ensure equity and meet organisational priorities. Do you approve the individual CPD requests? Consider:

- How do you make decisions about who accesses high-cost CPD without demotivating other staff?
- How could you incorporate more choice and autonomy into the core offer whilst ensuring CPD aligns with organisational needs?
- What strategies could you implement to ensure that any individual learning benefits the wider team?
- How would you communicate your decisions transparently to maintain trust and morale?
- Is it worth making the case for a larger CPD budget? What would the rationale for this be and how would you use the money?

The importance of line management

Good line management goes beyond accountability; it's about developing staff, helping them to feel confident, supported, and effective in their roles. The writer Marcus Buckingham highlights the pivotal role managers play in employee retention, observing that individuals don't leave an organisation – they leave a line manager (Buckingham and Coffman, 1999). This suggests that it's the daily support and guidance from managers that affect whether staff feel valued, confident, and committed. More recent research reinforces the vital role line management plays in staff engagement and retention. Zenger and Folkman (2022) found a strong correlation between effective line management and employee engagement, while Allas and Schaninger (2020) report that the relationship staff have with their line manager has a strong impact on how satisfied they feel in their role. Unfortunately, they also note that many people lack a positive experience of line management, with 75% of the individuals surveyed citing their line manager as a source of stress.

However, maintaining regular, high-quality line management becomes harder as your provision grows, simply because more staff equates to more line managers. Camilleri, Rockey, and Dunbar (2024) propose that weekly contact between managers and their teams strengthens relationships and fosters trust. For this to occur, leaders need to consider both the size of line management teams and the day-to-day accessibility of line managers to the staff they manage. Camilleri, Rockey, and Dunbar (2024) also suggest that the constant reshuffling of teams can unsettle individuals and diminish their energy and motivation. For this reason, at Springfields we have committed to ensuring that staff keep the same line manager for a full academic year - a situation that will change only if their line manager leaves the organisation.

Supporting line managers takes intentional effort and practice and may include:

- Providing induction programmes both for new line managers and for experienced line managers joining your organisation.
- Giving regular training in aspects of management e.g. coaching skills, giving feedback, and handling difficult conversations.
- Providing peer support networks, and allowing time to role-play and practise management techniques.
- Giving clear guidance on what is expected from them and providing adequate time for line management to happen.
- Helping line managers to understand the impact they can have on their teams.
- Ensuring that line managers understand the concept of psychological safety and the important role they play in creating the conditions for it to occur.

Because a key part of line management is to support staff with operational context and guidance, it's worth considering how soon new starters will gain the knowledge required to be an effective line manager. It's also important that line managers look after their own well being so that they can support the wellbeing of others. For this reason, it is also worth considering who provides the self-care for line managers. Although line managers should receive support through their own line management structure, it may also be beneficial to provide additional individual or group supervision specifically for this group.

Line managers can provide you with an effective snapshot of how your organisation is feeling. Simple questions can help you explore how connected staff feel to your vision and purpose while also enabling line managers to demonstrate empathy and curiosity. For example:

- Are you proud to work here?
- Would you recommend working here to your friends and family?
- Do you feel connected to your colleagues and the provision?
- Do you feel that your current role makes the most of your experience, knowledge, and skills?
- What would make your job more interesting?
- What can I do to make tomorrow easier?
- What role would you like to be doing in 3 years' time and how can I help prepare you for it?

Positive answers mean you have staff who are more likely to stay, whereas more reserved or negative answers may warrant further exploration. These questions not only generate useful insights but also model a culture of openness and trust, which can support psychological safety. They can also support effective succession planning, as discussed in Chapter 7.

Thinking point: The Dunbar Graph

Acharjee, Bora, and Dunbar's (2020) work on the Dunbar Graph suggests that humans can only sustain a limited number of high-quality relationships at any one time. Their findings indicate that the ideal number of people to line manage is around five. This has significant implications for staffing structures, particularly in large organisations. For example, a staff body of 100 would require 20 line managers. The prompts below invite you to reflect on the size of line management teams in your setting.

- What is the average size of line management teams in your organisation?
- Do you have many individuals line managing more than five people?
- If, as the Dunbar Graph suggests, the optimum number of people to line manage is five, what implications does this have for your current staffing structures?

Leadership scenario

Due to growth in pupil numbers, you have recently appointed three new middle leaders. Although they all have more than 3 years' teaching experience, they're all stepping into their first leadership role. Between September and Christmas, you notice differences in how they're supporting their teams in relation to feedback, check-ins, and navigating operational issues. You have limited time and budget for training, and your provision is expanding rapidly in terms of staff and students. As a senior leader, consider:

- How do you support each new line manager to develop the skills needed to support their team effectively?
- How do you ensure that staff wellbeing is not affected while the line managers are bedding in?
- How do you balance the operational demands of the provision with the need for line manager development?
- What actions do you take between Christmas and Easter?

Remember: the way you support these line managers will not only shape their confidence and effectiveness but will also influence the wider culture of staff development and wellbeing across your provision.

In the case study below we see how staff can flourish when provided with strong line management.

Case study: Danielle's story - from TA to teacher

This case study, by Danielle from Everton Free School in Liverpool, is a powerful example of how strong mentorship and talent spotting can develop staff members.

☆

My journey into education began at Liverpool Hope University, where I studied Education and Special Educational Needs and Disabilities, graduating with First Class Honours. I was passionate from the outset about working with vulnerable young people and creating opportunities where they might otherwise be lacking.

In 2017, I joined Everton Free School as an agency Teaching Assistant. I was employed by Andrew Poole, the school's SENCO at the time, who would go on to become a pivotal mentor in my professional journey. My first assignment was working 1:1 with a student with an Education, Health and Care Plan who was also in Local Authority Care. She presented with highly complex SEND and Social, Emotional, and Mental Health (SEMH) needs, having experienced significant trauma and instability. Everton Free School was her twelfth school placement since starting secondary education.

With Andrew's guidance, we created a bespoke therapeutic timetable built around her strengths and interests - integrating horse riding and hairdressing alongside core academic subjects. This approach provided structure, purpose and healing. The progress she made was truly life changing. When she arrived, she had been disengaged from formal education, refusing assessments and declining support. By the time she left, she had achieved eight qualifications, including six GCSEs at grade 4 and above. She was honoured with Knowsley Council's 'Educational Achievement of the Year' award, later securing an apprenticeship in hairdressing and moving into full-time employment. She now lives independently and has her own car. Supporting her transformation was one of my first profound reminders of why this work matters.

Andrew saw potential in me and consistently championed my development. In 2019, Everton Free School funded my PGCE in Secondary English, offering me a pathway into qualified teaching through in-school placements. This investment in my future built not only my confidence, but also my commitment to staying and growing within the world of AP.

In 2021, the Department for Education selected Everton Free School to pilot its new Taskforce programme, designed to reduce criminal exploitation, improve attendance and raise aspirations among vulnerable young people. Under Andrew's leadership as Project Coordinator, a multi-disciplinary team was assembled, including youth workers, mental health and speech and language practitioners, family support workers and a Youth Offending Team liaison.

I was offered the opportunity to work as a Youth Worker within the Taskforce, where I developed a more holistic and trauma-informed approach to student support – an approach I had always believed in but was now able to put into practice systematically. After a year, I was appointed Assistant Project Coordinator, with Andrew continuing to mentor me through leadership training and strategic development.

One of the students I supported during this period was "M", a young boy from a large family facing chronic socio-economic hardship, with a background marked by domestic violence, criminality and repeated school exclusions. M had become disengaged and distrustful of professionals due to prior trauma, including experiences with restraint at previous schools. When he joined us in Year 9, he was isolated, anxious and deeply vulnerable.

Working alongside our Taskforce team, we built a tailored support plan for M and his family. We provided daily transport, organised engagement through sport, supported the family with food, furniture and addiction services, and integrated practical life-skills into his weekly routine. He was introduced to Everton in the Community, where he joined a football programme that ultimately took him to the Street Kids World Cup in Qatar. For the first time in his life, he travelled abroad, met Prince William and, most importantly, began to believe in his own potential.

M eventually received a diagnosis of ADHD – something that had been missed due to his fragmented education. With appropriate support in place, he sat his GCSEs, leaving with six qualifications and a plan for the future. In interviews with the Department for Education, he spoke candidly about the difference our support made and how it diverted him from the pathways so many of his peers had taken carrying knives and selling drugs.

My work with M and others like him solidified my belief that sustainable change requires collaborative, family-focused and trauma-aware interventions. Over time, I worked closely with Andrew and other colleagues to build Everton Free School's pastoral and holistic offer into a fully embedded part of our school's ethos.

In 2023, I was honoured to be named Inspirational Leader in Alternative Provisions by The Worshipful Company of Educators, a nomination put forward by Andrew and the school Principal. A year later, I was awarded the British Empire Medal (BEM) in His Majesty The King's Birthday Honours List for services to vulnerable children and young people. I was later invited to Buckingham Palace for the Royal Garden Party, hosted by the Prince and Princess of Wales – an experience that brought reflection on just how far I'd come and how many lives had been touched through my work.

My progression, from Teaching Assistant to teacher, from youth worker to project leader, has been shaped by strong mentorship, trust and a shared commitment to the young people we serve. More than anything, it has reaffirmed that with the right people, vision and support we can transform lives.

☆

Danielle's journey shows what can happen when the potential of staff is identified and nurtured. Her story is a valuable reminder that investing in staff development is akin to investing in children – both benefit from the experience. The questions below encourage you to reflect on how you develop staff in your setting.

Thinking points

- How do you identify, nurture, and develop staff talent?
- How do you show staff that you value their potential long-term contribution, not just their current role?
- Danielle's story is powerful. How do you use case studies to inspire current and future staff about what's possible in your setting?

Danielle reflects on the importance of Andrew's mentorship to her development.

- Who are the best mentors in your organisation?
- How do you know?
- How do you give them the time to mentor and develop other staff?
- How do you identify and develop future mentors?

Against a backdrop of increasingly complex learner needs, sector growth, and recruitment challenges, staff development has become an essential part of leading a specialist provision. By creating a strong, structured CPD programme, establishing effective line management practices, and enabling access to wider professional networks, leaders can equip their team with the skills, knowledge, and resilience they need. Ultimately, this ensures that learners benefit from staff who are confident, well-supported, and continually developing their expertise.

Chapter summary

This chapter considers how to build a strong, skilled and well-developed staff team. It explores what continuing professional development looks like and how leaders can balance individual interests with organisational priorities as their provision grows.

- A key leadership responsibility is developing everyone in your team, since children benefit when adults are at their best.
- CPD encompasses a wide range of formal and informal activities, all aimed at increasing knowledge and skills for the benefit of an organisation and its young people.
- Building a culture of organisational learning creates a virtuous cycle in which staff who engage in CPD are motivated to keep learning and can see the impact it makes.
- Your CPD curriculum should be mapped with as much thought and intention as your curriculum for pupils.
- Engaging in specialist peer networks provides valuable collaborative opportunities that can reduce professional isolation and workload.
- As your provision grows, thought must be given to the balance between individual developmental priorities and organisational needs.
- Research suggests that line management is crucial, providing the small, everyday interactions that influence job satisfaction and wellbeing.

Further reading

- The specialist National Professional Qualification in Leading Teacher Development is designed for those interested in and leading CPD. Available online at: https://assets.publishing.service.gov.uk/media/66c4908b057d859c0e8fa7c4/NPQ_Leading_Teacher_Development_.pdf
- The Educational Endowment Foundation guidance report *Effective Professional Development* (2021) outlines 14 key mechanisms to consider when planning CPD.
- To find out more about reflective supervision you could read *Using Supervision in Schools: A Guide to Building Safe Cultures and Providing Emotional Support in a Range of Education Settings* (2023) by Penny Sturt and Jo Rowe or *Reflective Supervision in Education: Using Supervision to Support Pupil and Staff Wellbeing* (2023) by Hollie Edwards.

References

Acharjee, S., Bora, B., and Dunbar, R. I. M. (2020). 'On M-polynomials of Dunbar graphs in social networks'. *Symmetry, 12*(6), article 932.

Allas, T. C., and Schaninger, B. (2020, 22 September). 'The boss factor: Making the world a better place through workplace relationships'. *McKinsey Quarterly*. Available online at: https://www.mckinsey.com/capabilities/people-and-organizational-performance/our-insights/the-boss-factor-making-the-world-a-better-place-through-workplace-relationships [accessed 26 August 2025].

Aristotle (1924). *Metaphysics* (W. D. Ross, Trans.). In *The Works of Aristotle Translated into English* (Vol. 8, p. 1017). Oxford: Oxford University Press. (Original work published ca. 4th century BCE.) This is a paraphrase of 'The whole is something besides the parts'.

Avalos, B. (2011). 'Teacher professional development in "Teaching and Teacher Education" over ten years'. *Teaching and Teacher Education: An International Journal of Research and Studies, 27*(1), 10–20.

Branson, R. (2014). 'Train people well enough so they can leave, treat them well enough so they don't want to' [Tweet]. X (formerly Twitter). Available online at: https://x.com/richardbranson/status/449220072176107520 [accessed 25 August 2025].

Buckingham, M., and Coffman, C. (1999). *First, Break All the Rules: What the World's Greatest Managers Do Differently*. New York: Simon & Schuster.

Camilleri, T., Rockey, S., and Dunbar, R. (2024). *The Social Brain: The Psychology of Successful Groups*. London: Penguin.

Coldwell, M. (2017). 'Exploring the influence of professional development on teacher careers: A path model approach'. *Teaching and Teacher Education, 61*, 189–198.

Department for Education (2015, 26 March). *Keeping Children Safe in Education*. Statutory Guidance. Availableonlineat:https://www.gov.uk/government/publications/keeping-children-safe-in-education-2 [accessed 25 April 2026].

Earley, P., and Porritt, V. (2014). 'Evaluating the impact of professional development: the need for a student-focused approach'. *Personal Development in Education, 40*(1), 112–129.

Education Endowment Foundation (2021). *Effective Professional Development: Guidance Report*. Availableonline at: https://d2tic4wvo1iusb.cloudfront.net/production/eef-guidance-reports/effective-professional-development/EEF-Effective-Professional-Development-Guidance-Report.pdf [accessed 18 August 2025].

Edwards, H. (2023). *Reflective Supervision in Education: Using Supervision to Support Pupil and Staff Wellbeing*. London: Jessica Kingsley Publishers.

Fraser, C., Kennedy, A., Reid, L., and Mckinney, S. (2007). 'Teachers' continuing professional development: Contested concepts, understandings and models'. *Journal of In-Service Education, 33*(2), 153–169.

Fullan, M. (2002). 'The change leader'. *Educational Leadership, 59*(8), 16–20.

Leithwood, K., Harris, A., and Hopkins, D. (2019). 'Seven strong claims about successful school leadership revisited'. *School Leadership & Management, 40*(4), 1–18.

Leonard, P., and Madonna (1989). *Like a Prayer* [Song recorded by Madonna]. On *Like a Prayer*. Sire Records.

Poekert, P. E. (2012). 'Teacher leadership and professional development: Examining links between two concepts central to school improvement.' *Professional Development in Education, 38*(2), 169–188.

Skills for Care (2025). *The State of the Adult Social Care Sector and Workforce in England 2025*. Skills for Care. Available online at: https://www.skillsforcare.org.uk/Adult-Social-Care-Workforce-Data/workforceintelligence/resources/Reports/National/The-state-of-the-adult-social-care-sector-and-workforce-in-England-2025.pdf [accessed 25 April 2026].

Steinberg, B., Kelly, T., and Hoffs, S. (1988). *Eternal Flame* [Song recorded by The Bangles]. On *Everything*. Columbia Records.

Sturt, P., and Rowe, J. (2023). *Using Supervision in Schools: A Guide to Building Safe Cultures and Providing Emotional Support in a Range of Education Settings*. 2nd ed. Shoreham by Sea, UK: Pavilion Publishing and Media Ltd.

Weir, P. (Director). (1989). *Dead Poets Society* [Film]. Touchstone Pictures.

Zenger, J., and Folkman, J. (2022, 4 November). 'The single most important factor in improving employee engagement in today's workplace'. Zenger Folkman. Available online at: https://zengerfolkman.com/articles/the-single-most-important-factor-in-improving-employee-engagement-in-todays-workplace [accessed 10 August 2025].

9

Every family matters: Building parental and family engagement

Every child deserves a champion - we will be the champion for your child.

Angela O'Rourke, Headteacher of Southfield SEN School

Chapter overview

After considering how to get the best from the adults inside your organisation, we now turn our attention to the adults who matter outside of it. Parents, carers, and families are powerful advocates for their children and knowledgeable about their needs, interests, and strengths. They are experts and ambassadors, having often negotiated multiple and complex systems to secure a diagnosis and a place in a specialist provision. Research tells us that working closely with families is essential, with Leithwood et al. (2019) finding that parental involvement is key to raising achievement. In specialist and alternative settings, particularly where families have needed to fight for the right provision for their child, these partnerships must be intentionally built and carefully nurtured. This chapter considers the important role of Family Liaison Officers, how to support children and families with transitions, the importance of on-going communication, and the creation of wider community links.

Helping families feel connected

Absences for children identified as having SEND are frequently complex, with many being authorised to accommodate health or therapeutic requirements. That said, children with additional needs are more likely to miss school than their peers, with absence rates in special schools being noticeably higher than in mainstream settings (House of Commons Education Committee, 2023). When children are excluded or absent from school, families can begin to feel isolated from education. This makes it even more important for specialist provisions to respond with empathy and care, taking time to understand the reasons behind absence and build trust with families. Research by Hughes, Curley, and Kotera (2024) into the lived experiences of parents of autistic children suggests that stigma remains a persistent and

DOI: 10.4324/9781003601388-10

often painful reality for families following diagnosis. As the leaders below highlight, supporting families is crucial in helping them reframe their view of education so that they feel confident that their child is safe, understood, and nurtured.

> *It's really important to get parents on board. Quite often the parents haven't parted on good terms with the previous school and their own experiences sometimes haven't been great, so we have to rebuild parents' views of education.*
>
> Juliette Baldwin, Headteacher, EOTAS

> *Families and children often join us disillusioned. Parents can often be at their wits end.*
>
> Robert Bell, Headteacher, Consilium Evolve

> *We have lots of emotionally based school avoidance students and the parents need that support and reassurance. It is normal for them to feel anxiety, but we make the school safe – we will look after your child. That reassurance is important.*
>
> Lucy Kreczak, Deputy Headteacher, River Tees Hospital School

> *Working closely with families leads to better outcomes for our learners, helps parents/carers understand the school's approach and is more likely to lead to collaboration and therefore consistency for their child. Information sharing is a fundamental key to this process. It is easy to share news on how well a child is doing but it is just as important to be transparent when they are struggling. We aim to make the parent/carers understand that we want to help their child by working together to consider solutions.*
>
> *We offer meetings in school or by Teams and share Therapeutic Thinking plans so that they understand how we are interacting with their child and what strategies we are implementing. We also signpost to other professionals that might help, provide resources to use at home and direct to other information that can support.*
>
> Sarah Cullip, Behaviour Lead, Greenside School

These perspectives demonstrate that families are key partners in a child's learning and wellbeing. In specialist and alternative settings, families often arrive feeling anxious and disillusioned. By offering reassurance, sharing strategies, and involving families in problem-solving, we can create consistency and build relationships between home and school.

Leadership scenario

A new learner, Callum, is due to join your provision after being out of school for nearly a year. Callum was previously in a mainstream setting where he experienced multiple exclusions and was eventually placed on a part-time timetable. His family feel angry, judged, and exhausted. They have spoken openly about being let down by the education system and are wary of promises made by professionals. Callum presents with emotionally based school avoidance and high anxiety, particularly around transitions. He has moderate learning difficulties and sensory-processing differences. He finds busy environments particularly stressful.

You are preparing for Callum's transition into your provision. The family is reluctant to engage with your transition process, missing initial meetings and expressing doubt about whether your setting will be any different.

What action will you take? Think about:

- How you can rebuild trust with Callum's family
- How to balance your expectations for high attendance with empathy for the family
- How to prepare staff so that they understand Callum's context and can respond without judgement
- What Callum's transition plan might look like

First impressions matter

For all families, the first contact with an education provider is important. Whether it's a phone call, a visit to site, or an interaction on social media, first impressions matter. For families of children with additional needs, especially those who have navigated a long path to specialist provision, this moment can be a mix of hope and anxiety. It is therefore important to consider who families will interact with first in your provision, ensuring it is someone who not only understands and embodies your organisational values but is also skilled at building relationships and putting families at ease. Many specialist and alternative settings benefit from having a Family Liaison Officer (FLO), or similar role, built into their staffing structure. These roles send a clear message that families matter and that communication is a two-way process.

Word of mouth plays a powerful role in all school communities and through modern technology, families can quickly share their experiences across multiple platforms. Although we cannot stop these conversations occurring, we can control our online presence through our website and social media. This could be something your FLO leads on, ensuring that interactions are clear, consistent, and welcoming. They can also follow up on any concerns or comments that have the potential to escalate. Having someone as part of your social media team who knows families well helps reinforce that their voices are heard and valued.

Site tours are also important in establishing positive working. For families, a tour is more than a chance to view your site - it can often be the first time that they feel their child's needs are heard and understood. We find that individual tours work best - they may be time consuming, but those first interactions are crucial. Individual tours provide the quality time needed to build relationships, allow sensitive questions to be asked, and give families the space to share worries in confidence. Crucially, we can ensure that families understand our provision and whether it is a good fit for their child. Not everyone who comes to look around will go on to seek a place, or gain one, but that positive experience, or that comment that may appear on social media as word-of-mouth feedback, is invaluable. Remember, though, that honesty and empathy go hand in hand - be clear about your admissions process, timelines, and how likely it is for a place to be available.

Thinking points

- How does your staffing model reflect your commitment to working with families?
- How do you currently manage tours of your provision? Are they having the impact you desire? What are the benefits of group tours versus individual tours?
- How can your FLO help shape your online presence and interactions with families?
- What training, supervision, or support might your FLO need to handle sensitive situations confidently and effectively?

Supporting transitions

Transitioning to a new school can be an emotional and uncertain time for both children and their families. Many neurodivergent individuals find transitions overwhelming, and there is a growing body of research indicating that neurodivergent children experience the transition from primary to secondary school as particularly stressful (Sideropoulos et al., 2024). Although specific research on the transition into a specialist provision is scarce, it seems logical to suggest that it is the transition itself which creates the anxiety and therefore this is likely to be present alongside any change of placement. Some factors that Sideropoulos et al. (2024) suggest make transitions tricky include:

- A different environment can be emotionally and physically challenging, particularly if there are multiple new buildings.
- Learners often worry about getting lost.
- A change in teacher(s) and adjusting to new expectations and routines can be worrying.
- New peers and navigating peer relationships can often be accompanied by worries about bullying.

Consequently, it is important to think about more than just a child's first day. Instead, map out the transition to make it a gradual process that supports the child to build confidence and independence. Some approaches that support transition as a gradual approach include:

- Sharing One Page Profiles of key staff.
- Creating video tours of your provision that can be watched multiple times at home or in a learner's current setting.
- Visiting learners in their current setting or at home so they feel comfortable meeting new staff.
- Offering visits to your setting with current staff or family members who know the child well and can support them.
- Holding a transition evening that gives families the opportunity to ask questions, explore the environment, and meet staff informally.
- Inviting other professionals to attend transition events - for example, home to school transport - is useful in that it encourages families to connect with the broad range of individuals who will be supporting their child.
- Holding a transition day where only new pupils are on site, enabling a quieter environment and higher levels of staff support to help them settle in.
- Organising staggered starts for new pupils. This may involve gradually increasing the amount of time new learners spend on site, or spreading the start date of new children across the first few days of term, to ensure they all receive a high level of transition support.

A common barrier to family engagement in specialist provisions is that admissions are based on need rather than locality. Consequently, many learners travel considerable distances to attend education and this usually occurs via home to school transport arranged through the local authority. Living at a distance can affect a family's ability to visit your site, especially if they rely on public transport. Attending a 10-minute parents' evening appointment may not feel worthwhile for a family facing a 90-minute round trip. Consequently, it's important to consider how to make onsite visits meaningful by incorporating multiple opportunities into a single event, such as giving families the opportunity to network with other families, meet teachers, and receive training by professionals at the same time. The questions below encourage you to reflect on your setting's current approach to transitions.

Thinking points

- What implications do the findings of Sideropoulos et al. (2024) have for your transition processes?
- How do you provide a gradual approach to transition?
- How do you seek feedback from learners and families on the transition process?
- What systems are in place to sustain support after the initial transition period? Are there any follow-ups or check-ins with new families during the academic year, or bespoke events designed specifically for them?

On-going communication

Effective engagement with families is on-going and doesn't stop after the first week of term. Headteacher Juliette Baldwin explains the need for communication to be frequent, compassionate, and two-way:

> *We give the parents time and we listen. We overly communicate. We communicate everything. They might get several calls during the day. We involve them if a child is dysregulated, for instance we might say, 'let's get mum on the phone and have a chat'.*
>
> *We go out into the car park and we see parents at the start and end of the day. We have that high visibility. We invite them in for afternoon tea parties. We have restorative conversations with them. It's about meeting them halfway – if we can't get them in can we get them on the phone? Many of our children haven't had the opportunity to have an education and it's about working with parents as much as it's about working with the child. Our staff ratio is important and enables us to do that.*

Juliette reminds us that families benefit from consistency, visibility, and empathy, building trust through everyday interactions. The prompts below encourage you to reflect on communication with families within your setting.

Thinking points

- How do you know your communication strategies are effective?
- Who is responsible for reaching out to families, how often, and through which channels?
- How can leaders model high visibility and accessibility for families?
- How are difficult situations or dysregulation handled in partnership with families?

Choosing a communication system to support regular communication can be a compromise. You may be required to use a trust-wide platform or want something that integrates with your other information management systems. It's also important to consider what method works best for families – some will prefer a quick phone call; others might want an email. Taking the time to ask families what works for them shows that you're not just giving information, you're inviting a dialogue. In our setting, teachers ascertain a family's communication preferences at the start of the academic year so that we can contact them in their preferred manner.

We must also recognise that some parents and carers may have additional or undiagnosed needs. In some cases, a child's journey to diagnosis can help adults identify neurodivergent traits or characteristics in themselves (Hughes, Curley, and Kotera, 2024). This reminds us that clear, accessible communication matters for everyone – lengthy written letters may be best accompanied by a video or visual summary. In fact, findings commonly attributed to Forrester Research (as cited in Altura Learning, 2024), suggest that it may be better to forego written communication altogether, as people are up to 75% more likely to choose to engage with a video than with an online article. Consequently, your termly Headteacher's newsletter may be better received as a video.

Consequently, as leaders we must ensure that our communication is accessible, both in format and in tone. This means offering information in multiple formats (e.g. video summaries, easy-read guides, or translated materials) and using platforms that families access daily. Feedback opportunities should also be inclusive - families aren't only the recipients of information; we want their ideas and experiences too. Alongside surveys, other feedback mechanisms include:

- Google or Microsoft Forms with the option to leave a voice note.
- 'Tell us one thing . . .' sticky-note prompts at events such as parents' evenings. Alternatively, you could use sound buttons to enable families to leave you a message.
- A visitors' book or comment box in Reception.
- Interactive feedback boards at coffee mornings where families can write or draw responses to prompts such as: "What's working well?" or "What's one thing we could do better . . ."
- A bespoke email address for family feedback (we have a HEARD email for families, as discussed in Chapter 4).
- Use termly breakfast or afternoon tea with the Headteacher to carry out focus groups.
- For expressing a quick opinion, or selecting between options, try social media polls or comments.

These strategies help establish a two-way dialogue between home and school and provide feedback regarding what's working well and what isn't with regards to family engagement. The questions below invite you to reflect on your current communication strategy and how this may need to evolve in the future.

Thinking points

- UK adults spend more than 4 hours a day online (Ofcom, 2024). How might your digital communication strategy need to evolve over the next 3-5 years to reflect this? What training or staffing implications might this have?
- What systems are in place to quality assure the frequency and consistency of your communication with families?
- Is family voice genuinely influencing what you do, or are you only asking for feedback once decisions have been made?
- How do you ensure your communication and feedback methods are inclusive and accessible for all families?

Leadership scenario

You are a Deputy Head with responsibility for curriculum and timetabling in an alternative provision for 11-16-year-olds. One morning you receive a frustrated email from a parent which says:

> *Nobody told me that my child changed GCSE pathway last week. I only found out yesterday when she mentioned it during tea. I've asked before to be kept updated on her pathway as this will affect her application to sixth form. Why isn't anybody updating me?*

You check your internal communication log and see that the Head of Key Stage 4 agreed the change and had noted that the form tutor would tell the parent. The form tutor thought the Head of Key Stage 4 would communicate the change because they had authorised it. The form tutor also assumed that the parent would see the change through a notification on their timetable app; however, a look at the analytics shows that the family has only logged in twice this year.

What action will you take? Think about:

- How and where has communication broken down?
- How do you restore trust with the family?
- Is there a training need?
- Are any changes needed to structures and systems?
- How do you communicate the learning points with staff?

Beyond communication to community

Enabling families to feel a sense of belonging and contribute to the success of your organisation is vital. Being part of a specialist provision provides families with more than access to education – it gives them the opportunity to feel part of a community. It has been reported that a sense of belonging is linked to improved physical and mental health (Michalski et al., 2020), something that is likely to improve the lives of both learners and their families. Some simple ways to create a sense of school community include:

- Celebration events, such as leavers' events and proms, where families can celebrate and share their child's achievements.
- Festive events, such as carol concerts, nativities, and fairs.
- Summer events e.g. sports days and fetes.
- Setting up a 'Friends of . . . Group' or Parent Teacher Association, giving families a way to fundraise and support your provision.
- Stay and play events. These can be particularly helpful for new families, providing a low-stakes way to explore the school environment, building relationships and trust.

Headteacher Robert Bell suggests rethinking common approaches to celebration events and describes the powerful impact this can have on attendance and attitudes to education.

> *Most provisions put celebration events at the end of term. Why? It doesn't make sense! We celebrate all the good they've done and then send them home for the holidays. Instead, we celebrate that success at the start of the term. This sets a positive tone that helps learners and families feel motivated and prepared for the term ahead. Those relationships and connections you form during rewards and celebrations, put them at the start of term and you'll see the benefits throughout. Some of our learners come to us with an attendance of 18%, we get them to 80 or 90%. We celebrate a lot with our families, our parental engagement is amazing because we listen and work together.*

In specialist and alternative provisions, where families may have experienced challenges or disillusionment in the past, celebrating the positives is especially powerful. Robert's creative thinking has flipped the traditional approach to rewards, leading to a positive impact on attendance in his setting. The questions below invite you to reflect on how this approach could work in your provision.

Thinking points

- Could holding celebration events at the start of term set a more positive tone and encourage greater engagement from learners and families?
- How does your provision ensure families feel part of the school community?
- How can you ensure all families, including those who might struggle to access your site in person, feel included?
- How do you know that family engagement and community initiatives are having a meaningful impact on learners?

Learning with families

There is growing evidence that families can feel lost, overwhelmed, or drained after receiving a diagnosis or securing an Education, Health and Care Plan for their child.

Hughes, Curley, and Kotera (2024) found that receiving a diagnosis for a child can cause initial feelings of isolation, sadness, or inner turmoil in parents. They suggest that post-diagnosis, families often engage in an extended phase of exploration and discovery on how to support their child. However, it is often left to the family to do this independently. Headteacher Robert Bell explains an innovative approach to staff and families learning to support children together.

> *We have Community Days. This is where, once a term, we invite a professional to provide CPD. Staff sit alongside a learners' family and this can be everyone - grandmas,*

brothers, daughters. We all sit in a group - staff, families, professionals and we all learn together about the same topic e.g. sleep, mental wellbeing, diet. We want happy, healthy children and we sit shoulder to shoulder with families to create that. It creates a community and a powerful, joined up message between families and staff. 5 INSET days just isn't enough to do all the training we need, so this provides training, but it also provides a forum for families.

Author Anecdote: The Springboard Series

We firmly believe that if we support the family, we support the child. At Springfields, we have recently created a free series of webinars for carers and families called The Springboard Series. We respond to parent feedback regarding the topics and speakers that they wish to see and offer a free event per half-term. We have seen parents beyond our own setting sign up and it's great to know that we're having an impact beyond our school community. I love Robert's example of Community Days and, as a result, we've decided to offer a hybrid model at future Springboard Series so that we can benefit from the collaboration that comes from sitting shoulder to shoulder with families.

Thinking points

- How do you help families to understand their child's needs?
- Hughes, Curley, and Kotera (2024) suggests that parents feel the benefits of engaging with peer groups to share knowledge and grow support systems. How do you help facilitate peer-to-peer support for families?
- Gaining a diagnosis doesn't just affect parents, it can affect other children in the family too (Hughes, Curley, and Kotera, 2024). How can you support the siblings of your learners, even if they do not attend your provision?

Managing family engagement across split sites

For leaders working in multisite settings, family engagement brings an additional layer of complexity. It's no longer just about frequency and content of communication but about ensuring equity and consistency across different locations. Families need to feel that they belong to one school community, regardless of which site their child attends. Strategies that can support this include:

- Ensuring that any family forums or advisory groups include representation from all sites.
- Establishing working weeks where senior leaders rotate between sites, ensuring families can see them regularly at all locations.

- Ensuring that, across the academic year, events are held on different sites so that everyone feels included.
- Using short video updates to give families a sense of personal connection when leaders aren't physically present at their site.
- Ensuring that safeguarding and wellbeing support are equally accessible, so no family feels disadvantaged by geography.

The questions below help you reflect on the challenges of supporting family engagement across multiple sites.

Thinking points

- How do leaders remain visible across multiple sites when they can't be there in person every day?
- How do you ensure that families receive the same quality of communication, welcome, and support on all sites?
- Do families perceive one site as being "the main one"? If so, how can you prevent this from creating inequality or disengagement?
- Is there a clear point of contact (e.g. a Family Liaison Officer or Office Manager) for each site?

Case study: Using social media to engage with families

Lydia Colios, Assistant Headteacher at Addington School, has been reviewing and refining their use of social media as part of her Level 7 Apprenticeship in Leadership and Management. In this case study, she shares her advice for settings looking to develop their social media profile.

> *Social media is the outward facing part of the school. Before I started focusing on our use of social media platforms, our online profile was pretty much non-existent. I wanted to develop a social media strategy, that built our public face and celebrated success. Our strategy is about putting our staff and young people front and centre, bringing others onboard and building a brand.*
>
> *I started by looking at what other schools do. I asked, 'what do they do well?' and 'what could we replicate?'. The key thing to remember is that social*

media is a different style - it's not a formal email or letter to parents conveying information, it's meant to bring you closer and be more intimate. My top tips are:

- *Be conversational and informal.*
- *Post high quality photos, with a watermark to prevent copying, little and often.*
- *Be clear on your pupil photo permissions before sharing anything.*
- *Don't overcomplicate content but do vary it to include different types of post e.g. photo, video.*
- *Don't dilute your brand by reposting other things. Make clear what are your posts and if you repost, think carefully about what you are sharing. Be clear on your rationale for resharing and why?*
- *Schedule posts in advance so that you continue the little and often approach during busy times or holidays.*
- *Ensure staff tell you in advance of each half-term what scheduled posts they need.*
- *Prepare staff and provide clear protocols that allow them to engage in a safe way.*

We've focused on building engagement from local businesses. This has led to work experience, placements and trusted connections. We've seen really good engagement and positive feedback from parents - they enjoy seeing their children online and the children do too. Alumni parents say really nice things and the posts and photos give them an opportunity to reminisce. I know we've been successful because I now have local primary schools asking whether we can share our social media strategy with them!

☆

Utilising informal, frequent, and multimodal posts, Lydia has used social media to increase family engagement and strengthen community links, gaining interest from other schools in the process. The questions below support you in considering the effectiveness of your setting's social media strategy.

Thinking points

- If an outsider viewed your school's social media, what would they learn about your setting?
- How do you use social media play to build trust, celebrate learning, and foster a sense of community?

- Are your social media posts inclusive and accessible for all families, including those who may have limited digital access or communication needs?
- Which of Lydia's top tips could help you develop your social media presence?
- As online engagement continues to grow (Ofcom, 2024), how might you develop your social media strategy to enhance communication and reputation? What resources, knowledge, skills, or roles might be needed to do this effectively?

Activity: Social media audit

Use the questions below to review your current social media presence:

- Who leads on your social media strategy and when was it last reviewed?
- Which platforms do you use and which gain the most interactions?
- What's working well?
- What's missing from your online content?
- What types of posts receive most engagement?
- How do you gain feedback on the impact of your social media presence?
- What's one change that you can implement next term?

Chapter summary

This chapter has highlighted the importance of being family focused as well as child focused.

- Specialist and alternative provisions are more than learning environments - they can sometimes be the first place where families feel accepted and understood.
- Special schools and children with SEND have higher absence rates - helping families feel supported, heard and connected to education during these times is critical.
- Many learners live at a distance from specialist and alternative provisions. Consider combining events together to provide a meaningful experience that makes travelling to site worthwhile.
- The role of the Family Liaison Officer is key to making a good first impression with visitors and families.
- Partnerships with parents and carers require a genuine commitment to two-way dialogue. This means involving families in shaping provision, not just informing them of decisions that have already been made.

- Communication should be frequent, accessible, and inclusive - meeting families where they are and using platforms they know and understand.
- A sense of community and belonging can have a positive impact on physical and mental wellbeing and is just as important for families as it is for learners.
- With more adults spending time online, reviewing and developing your social media strategy will help you stay connected with parents and your wider school community.

Further reading

- For insight into the lived experiences of parents, you may find it interesting to read Jessie Hewitson's *How to Raise a Happy ADHD Child* (2025) or *How to Raise a Happy Autistic Child* (2024).

References

Altura Learning (2024, 8 August). '5 reasons to use video-based content in your training strategy'. Available online at: https://www.alturalearning.com/5-reasons-to-use-video-based-content-in-your-training-strategy [accessed 31 July 2025].

Hewitson, J. (2024). *How to Raise a Happy Autistic Child*. London: Orion Spring.

Hewitson, J. (2025). *How to Raise a Happy ADHD Child*. London: Orion Spring.

House of Commons Education Committee (2023, December). *Persistent Absence and Support for Disadvantaged Pupils. Government Response to the Committee's Seventh Report*. Available online at: https://dera.ioe.ac.uk/id/eprint/40928/[accessed 25 April 2026].

Hughes, R., Curley, K., and Kotera, Y. (2024). 'Parents' experiences after their child's autism diagnosis: A reflexive thematic analysis'. *Psychiatry International*, 5(3), 370–394.

Leithwood, K., Harris, A., and Hopkins, D. (2019). 'Seven strong claims about successful school leadership revisited'. *School Leadership & Management*, *40*(1), 5–22.

Michalski, C. A., Diemert, L. M., Helliwell, J. F., Goel, V., and Rosella, L. C. (2020). 'Relationship between sense of community belonging and self-rated health across life stages'. *SSM - Population Health*, *12*, 100676.

Ofcom (2024). *Online Nation 2024: Understanding Digital Habits in the UK*. London: Ofcom. Available online at: https://www.ofcom.org.uk/siteassets/resources/documents/research-and-data/online-research/online-nation/2024/online-nation-2024-report.pdf?v=386238&utm [accessed 31 July 2025].

Sideropoulos, V., Palikara, O., Burchell, E., Ashworth, M., and Van Herwegen, J. (2024). 'Anxiety during transition from primary to secondary schools in neurodivergent children'. *JCPP Advances*, 5(2), e12262.

10

Growing specialist provisions through people and place

Managing estates is not easy. Training is limited and NPQs are often quite generalised.

Alex Tomkins, Headteacher, Greenside School

Chapter overview

All organisations make regular changes to maintain alignment between their strategy, people and processes. In the spirit of Darwin's insights, all organisations must evolve, but it is their capacity to adapt that determines their future success.

This chapter focuses on transformational development – the kind of change that affects an entire organisation and accompanies growth. We'll consider how to balance the challenges and opportunities that come with expansion, while retaining the elements that make our provisions unique. We will explore two key considerations for leaders seeking to grow a provision while maintaining strong outcomes for learners.

- How to accommodate more learners and staff through the management and development of estates.
- How to ensure you have the right staff by developing effective organisational structures.

While I (Nicola B) was completing my PGCE in 2005, Netflix sent DVDs directly to people's homes. Fast forward to 2025 and it's a struggle to buy a DVD player – most of our learners have never seen one! The world changes daily and education is no different. Educational provisions evolve in response to shifts in national policy, funding, and accountability frameworks, as well as factors such as staff changes and site expansion. Consequently, managing change is something educational leaders do all the time. Winston Churchill (1925) reminds us that improvement comes through change, and the pursuit of excellence means embracing it regularly.

DOI: 10.4324/9781003601388-11

Responding to the need for more places

The number of children with EHCPs has risen sharply, more than doubling since 2016 (Roberts, 2025). This suggests expanding demand for places across the specialist sector. Some individual schools have grown substantially in size over the past decade and we have seen such growth in our own provision Over 50% of special schools are over capacity (Roberts, 2026).

Growth can be pro-active and planned (e.g. the Free Schools programme) or re-active in response to local need (e.g. the rise in internal alternative provision and resource bases). The pressure to expand and provide more places was a recurrent theme in our conversations with leaders. Julliet Doherty, Head of Adult Services at Ascent Autism Specialist College, states:

> *We've got a waiting list with children on it as young as three. We started with six Post-16 students we're now at forty-three students and growing.*

Although growth means having the capacity to provide more children with the specialist support that they need, it can also bring challenges. Camilleri, Rockey, and Dunbar (2024) suggest that as organisations grow, it can be harder to maintain relationships and effective communication. Over time, this can lead to fragmentation, as different parts of an organisation lose sight of one another's work, creating potential risks and inconsistencies. For successful and effective growth, forward-thinking and proactive management is therefore essential. By viewing change not as a threat but as an opportunity, leaders can focus on not only getting bigger, but also getting better, ensuring any expansion strengthens the provision and the core business of delivering high-quality education for learners. A good example of how this looks in practice comes from Julliet Doherty, who, in the case study below, shares how student voice shaped their new building.

Case study: Designing with us, not for us – embedding student voice in a new specialist environment

Ascent Autism Specialist College, where Julliet Doherty is Head of Adult Services, is currently experiencing an exciting period of growth as they transition into a new, purpose-built environment. She reflects on how they've incorporated student voice into the design of their new building.

☆

> *We showed pictures of the new school building to the student council and the students asked, 'Will there be this? Will there be that?'. The whole college went to visit the proposed site. It was really important we got student voice. In particular, we wanted them to experience the smell and the atmosphere of the building.*

We're now thinking about what we need. The pupils were really clear that they wanted laptops and not computer rooms. They also wanted mini-kitchens outside of the classrooms because they wanted to be able to make cups of tea and be independent. They also wanted a common room and a games room. We're close to a motorway so we need soundproofing. The children have also asked for Amazon Alexas in their rooms. That way they can control the music and the noise. We've had masses of input from the students.

We're having a lovely kitchen/dining area where the students will be able to make all their own meals as part of their learning. The students also run a horsebox café and they offer event catering as well.

We've gone for colours to define areas, for example green for social areas as it's relaxing, pink for break-out spaces and blue for classrooms. If the students get dysregulated they can follow the colours to calm – they don't need to ask someone. It gives them a sense of autonomy. If they're dysregulated and they need a calming space then they follow the green colour.

We really want the new building to be welcoming and inviting and it's vital that it's a flexible space. We need to manage all the needs of the individuals and that's why we've been led by the students. Our therapy team have been heavily involved and they've looked at things like blinds. We've also gone for slightly rounded walls because it's less intimidating as our learners can see everywhere closely and easily. I want people to come in and feel part of our family.

☆

Julliet highlights the importance of designing a space that meets the needs of the young people who use it. Establishing a newbuild provision enables leaders to embed the principles of Universal Design (Mace, 1998), such as blinds and rounded walls, from the start (as discussed in Chapter 6). The prompts below guide you to reflect on how student voice affects the design of your provision.

Thinking points

- How do you incorporate pupil perspectives into decisions that affect their learning environment?
- What mechanisms can be used to capture input from learners with different needs and communication styles?

- How can student preferences be balanced with practical, safety, and regulatory requirements (and budgets!)?
- What features might help students to self-manage their sensory or emotional needs?

Managing and developing estates

Essential to growing a provision is the successful management and development of estates, enabling the provision of high-quality education for greater numbers of learners. However, the sites of specialist settings can be large and complex, with specialist equipment such as hoists, lifts, and hydrotherapy pools. As we explored in Chapter 6, enabling environments are crucial, so any site changes must ensure that spaces remain both functional and safe for learners.

However, managing estates is rarely straightforward, particularly when they include older or listed buildings. Surprisingly, new educational buildings can also encounter restrictions, particularly if they need to be sustainable or carbon neutral. Yet, despite a raft of regulations, training opportunities in site management are limited, and leadership qualifications often cover estates only in general terms. Headteacher at Greenside School, Alex Tomkins, explains:

> *Managing estates is not easy. Training is limited and NPQs are often quite generalised. My site is old, with some buildings with leases. My best advice is to think about your site team. In theory, my job should be leading teaching and learning, but I'm often swamped with site problems. Statutory expectations should be advised by your local authority or trust but be sure to understand everything! In practice, it's the Headteacher who is responsible for many things, not the local authority or trust. Checking is wise - use Governors' Health and Safety checks to ensure things are completed right.*

Alex stresses the importance of being aware, and staying on top of, compliance around health and safety and there are online platforms that can support you with this such as Every Compliance (https://www.weareevery.com/compliance_manager/). However, specialist and alternative provisions often require additional considerations, from maintaining specialist equipment to carrying out risk assessments and responding to statutory inspections. Whilst site teams, MAT central teams, and local authorities may advise, accountability usually rests with the Headteacher, making it vital to understand your legal obligations and to ensure robust systems are in place, including:

- Inspections and audits - know when your regular visits take place for areas such as fire safety, legionella testing, and asbestos management, and identify who can support you with these.

- Risk assessments – you may require detailed and bespoke risk assessments for hydrotherapy pools, lifting equipment, minibuses, outdoor learning areas, therapy dogs, and sensory rooms. These should be reviewed annually. An Operations or Site Manager can help oversee these.
- Legal obligations – ensure you are familiar with statutory requirements such as the Health and Safety at Work Act (1974), Equality Act 2010, fire regulations, and data protection.
- Explore whether your Governors have expertise in these areas that can support you.

Getting compliance right ensures your environment is safe, well-managed, and enabling for the young people who use it. Strong systems and staff with expertise in site management will allow your leadership team to focus on strategic school development. Alex highlights the importance of investing in your site team so that they can manage daily operations effectively, enabling leaders to focus on strategic aspects. Leaders need to think intentionally about estates, including:

- Planning for growth in pupil or staff numbers so that the physical environment evolves alongside your organisation's vision. This might involve assessing classroom capacity, parking arrangements, or traffic flow during pick-up and drop-off times (particularly if you have home-to-school transport provided by your local authority).
- Considering what changing learner needs might entail. Leaders we spoke to emphasised that their intake is becoming increasingly complex. As the profile of your cohort shifts, you may need to consider how spaces can be adapted to meet increasing sensory, therapeutic, and learning needs. Around a quarter of learners now start schools in nappies (BBC, 2024), meaning that more intimate care facilities may be required.
- Securing the funding to invest in capital projects. Estate development requires significant financial investment and the ability to make a compelling case for improvements is vital. Building partnerships with the local authority and other stakeholders can open potential funding streams.
- Maximising financial savings e.g. through increasing energy efficiency. Strategic estate management involves identifying potential savings that not only reduce costs but also model environmental responsibility for your community.

When preparing for site development, leaders should consider the learner and staff experience, with thoughtful planning required to reduce anxiety and maintain learning. For example:

- Many neurodivergent individuals experience heightened anxiety when overwhelmed by sensory input. Consider how you'll prepare stakeholders for the disruption of a noisy or dusty building site. This might include regular updates, visual timetables, or virtual walk-throughs to familiarise learners with changes before work begins.
- Identify quiet, safe spaces that learners and staff can use while work is ongoing.
- Work closely with contractors to help them understand the rhythm of your school day and pupil needs. Can deliveries or drilling occur before or after pupils leave?

- Share images of what the completed works will look like so everyone can see the long-term benefits of short-term disruption.

By implementing these strategies, leaders can reduce anxiety and ensure that children continue to learn even during periods of disruption.

Planning beyond the present

When making changes to the environment, it's important to think long term. This is a strategy espoused by Helen Eaton, Neurodiversity and Autism Specialist. Eaton (2025) stresses the importance of planning for the long term and not getting caught up in the now. Your learners may currently be in EYFS (Early Years Foundation Stage), but they won't be forever. Thinking about the resources you'll need to support them in the future is crucial. In education, the urgent often overtakes the important – you set out to achieve something, but then the school minibus breaks down, the fire alarm goes off, or you receive a freedom of information request. It can therefore be hard for leaders to think ahead, but taking time to focus on the future is a hallmark of excellent specialist provision. Regular questions to consider as a leadership team include:

- How will your learner demographic evolve over the next 3–5 years?
- What resources might these learners need that you don't currently have?
- What are the financing and staffing implications of meeting their needs effectively?
- What changes to the environment might be needed – for example, additional therapeutic spaces, more intimate care rooms, extra classrooms, or expanded parking and drop-off/pick-up areas?
- Will alterations need to be made to the timings of the school day, such as staggered starts or lunch times?
- If children are being transported in, how will you (and your local road infrastructure) manage the extra vehicles?
- How sustainable are your estates? Educational provisions are increasingly being asked to consider their environmental impact. Future-proofing estates by embedding sustainability into your planning is pertinent. This might include installing solar panels, improving insulation, harvesting rainwater or introducing electric vehicle charging points. Although these initiatives may involve substantial upfront costs, they often reduce long-term expenditure and can be linked to pupil learning about responsibility and environmental citizenship.
- How might you need to upgrade your digital infrastructure? The pace of technological change is rapid – what works today may be outdated in just a few years. Thinking ahead about the assistive technology needs of your future learners will help you budget and plan your IT networks and equipment appropriately.

Although future-proofing estates and infrastructure is essential, managing growth in your provision isn't only about expanding buildings and facilities. Key to increasing your pupil numbers is thoughtful provision mapping – anticipating not only where learners will be, but also what their future needs are and how you will meet them. Effective provision mapping encourages leaders to see the bigger picture by comparing anticipated needs with current provision to ensure that estate development aligns with curriculum intent and meets the needs of learners.

Space constraints and strategic planning

Leaders we spoke with, such as Headteacher Bridget Young of The Holmewood School, frequently cited the lack of physical space as the biggest barrier to expansion:

> *In order to grow we would need a bigger space. We're based in London so we have no outdoor space. Our rooms are packed to the rafters and they're tiny, but our pupil numbers are still rising.*

This is echoed by Head Teacher Karen Parker of Sir Charles Parsons School:

> *Our Post-16 provision is housed in wooden lodges and they're now full. Our number of students has increased - our PAN (Published Admission Number) is now 210 and it used to be 158 so there's been significant growth. The number of children with SEND in Newcastle continues to grow. All specialist provisions are at capacity. We're having to prepare them earlier for college. Post-16 providers are at capacity - our Post-16 provision is full and that's a problem for September. Our capacity is 40 next year and we're trying to get the number down from 58. We're massively oversubscribed with a Private Finance Initiative (PFI) building which means we lack space as we can't just add on an extra building.*

As Karen highlights, not all provisions have the capacity or ability to drop modular classrooms or extend buildings. This challenge is also compounded by the fact that special schools applying for the Condition Improvement Fund remain the most likely to be denied funding, with only 30 per cent of applications approved in the latest funding round (Dyson, 2025). Leaders of specialist provisions are therefore often left to innovative, and repurpose spaces on their own. However, this can lead to difficult decisions - losing spaces for staff such as staffrooms, etc., can affect staff wellbeing, belonging, and organisational culture. However, there is hope - some approaches that leaders shared with us are:

- Repurposing underused rooms into multipurpose spaces. Modular partitions and flexible seating mean spaces can shift depending on need.
- Consider staggered break or lunch times to maximise use of classrooms and avoid congestion in dining halls or outdoor spaces.
- Develop off-site partnerships (e.g. with leisure centres) to ease pressure on the main site.
- Use outdoor areas creatively for learning and sensory breaks - even small spaces can be transformed with covered outdoor structures or learning pods.
- Tents or canopies can expand usable space without permanent building work.

Even in highly constrained environments, leaders can make site improvements. Creative repurposing and flexible timetabling allow settings to grow sustainably while maintaining high quality provision for learners and staff.

Thinking points

- How can you repurpose existing indoor and outdoor spaces without compromising learner or staff wellbeing?
- Could partnerships with local organisations or off-site facilities relieve pressure?
- How are you using provision mapping to anticipate and respond to emerging learner needs?
- How well do you invest in and develop your site and operations teams so they can manage daily operations effectively?
- What expertise do you have within your team, or governing body, that could strengthen estates and compliance leadership?
- How can you make your estate more energy-efficient or sustainable without compromising the needs of learners?

Leadership scenario

You are the Headteacher of a specialist provision that has seen pupil numbers rise sharply over the past 3 years. Your current estate includes a mix of permanent classrooms, temporary modular buildings, small outdoor spaces, and a large staff/visitor carpark. The next academic year is approaching – your intake is oversubscribed and there is no immediate possibility of expanding the site. What option do you take and why?

- Option 1: Repurpose the staffroom and meeting rooms for additional learning space. This could affect staff morale and wellbeing.
- Option 2: Stagger timetables and breaks to maximise current learning space. This may disrupt established routines and complicate the daily logistics of the school.
- Option 3: Partner with a nearby community centre or leisure facility to host some lessons offsite. This requires transport and has safeguarding implications.
- Option 4: Remove staff and visitor parking and drop four additional modular classrooms. This will tighten budgets for the next few years, including plans to upgrade technology and minibuses. It's likely to be an unpopular decision with staff, families, and visitors.

Of course, there are no right or wrong answers here. The option you're drawn to will likely reflect your values, vision, and your view of organisational culture (just as we discussed in Chapter 1). Knowing yourself as a leader is key and will help you make the right decisions for your provision.

Managing multiple sites

Although it's currently unclear how many specialist provisions span multiple sites, this number is likely to increase as demand for specialist education continues to grow. Managing cross-site provision adds complexity for leaders, requiring careful planning to maintain equity, consistency, and a shared culture. Kimberley Legg, Assistant Headteacher at Addington School, provides some advice on managing cross-site working:

> *It's important that there's a member of senior leadership located at the second site, ensuring that there is regular contact between the two locations. We give staff the option to join meetings or training virtually so that they don't have to travel all the time, but we likewise make sure that there are plenty of opportunities for people to meet face to face and give travel time when we expect them to commute. It's vital that staff working in the satellite centre still feel that they're part of that bigger community. One problem to be aware of is when you have large amounts of sickness absence. You've got to have a pool of staff on the main site who can get to the second site quickly.*

Kimberley highlights several strategies to support cross-site working:

- Rotating senior leaders between sites helps staff and families feel supported and connected to the wider organisation. It also ensures that the leadership team know all sites well and understand that they are accountable for both provisions.
- Using hybrid meetings (a mix of in-person on one site and by means of Teams or Zoom for staff on other sites) allows all staff to participate without excessive travel while still maintaining opportunities for interaction and collaboration.
- Knowing which staff can work across multiple sites ensures continuity of care and learning when unexpected absences occur.
- Leaders must ensure that safeguarding, CPD, and wellbeing initiatives are equally available to staff across all sites.

Managing multiple sites successfully requires leaders to be intentional, visible, and proactive. When this occurs, learners, staff, and families feel supported and everyone remains connected to the organisational vision.

Leadership scenario: Growing your provision

You have been appointed as Executive Headteacher of an alternative provision that is preparing to open two additional satellite centres. One is a 5-minute drive away; the other is a 30-minute commute. Both have their own Head of School and senior leadership teams. You have a strong shared vision, well-established pastoral and curriculum frameworks, and experienced staff at the main site. You have four additional senior leaders, one of whom has just been made Head of School at the main site. You have an established middle leadership team of six. You need to create a balance between giving the new sites the space and freedom to establish their own identities to meet the needs of their learners, and ensuring consistency of standards across the three provisions. How will you achieve this? You should consider:

- How will you communicate and embed your ethos and vision so it is felt and understood at the new sites from day one?
- How will you develop leadership capacity at the new sites to ensure accountability and distributed decision-making?
- Will you look to recruit staff for each new provision or share staff across provisions in which all staff will have elements of multi-site working?
- One new provision takes significantly longer travel time to get to than the other. What opportunities and challenges might occur? How could you overcome these?
- What does your role as Executive Headteacher look like? How does it differentiate from Head of School? How will you navigate your relationship with the Heads of Schools?
- How will you monitor and evaluate outcomes across the three sites, ensuring every learner benefits from personalised, high-quality provision?

Managing risk

As educators, we tend to associate risk with school trips. However, a growing body of research suggests that effective leadership in the public sector is fundamentally about managing risk (National Audit Office, 2023). Good risk management - by taking action before problems arise - helps leaders to be proactive rather than reactive. When assessing risk, we consider the likelihood of the risk and the impact of the risk.

In our organisation, we spend significant time discussing risk because identifying potential issues early allows us to develop solutions before they become problems. Growth and expansion naturally involve risk, but by addressing and managing these risks openly, we shift our mindset so that risks aren't something to fear, but are a manageable part of our growth and progress. Governors with a background in risk management can provide valuable insight and support. The points below encourage you to think about risk management in your setting.

Thinking points

- How confident and effective are you in managing risk?
- How often do you and your leadership team discuss your organisation's risk register?

- How frequently do you monitor and update identified risks?
- How often do you report on risk to your governing body?
- Who can support you in treating and mitigating risks?
- Do staff at all levels feel empowered to identify and reports risks?

Activity: Managing risks alongside growth

Growth works best when risk is anticipated and managed. This activity encourages you to think practically about the challenges growth brings and how you can manage them effectively.

Imagine that your provision is growing, with increased pupil numbers, additional staff, and new classrooms. Identify three potential risks that could arise from this growth. For each risk consider:

- How likely is it to occur?
- What impact could it have on learners, staff, and the wider community?
- What actions could prevent or mitigate it?
- Who could support you to manage this risk?

Organisational design

As well as physical growth, it is important to grow the architecture of your organisation - particularly systems, processes, and staffing - to ensure consistency of standards and pupil experience. As your site develops and the number of learners increases, specialist or additional staffing roles may be needed. However, this has implications for leaders and their ability to form relationships with an increasing number of people. As discussed in Chapter 1, for a Headteacher to meet weekly with 100 staff members would take roughly 8 hours - effectively a full working day. This illustrates the need for effective leadership structures and the distribution of leadership responsibilities as organisations expand. Heikka et al. (2012, p. 34) provide one description of distributed leadership as:

> *the move away from conceptualising leadership as an individual attribute to a collective achievement based on teamwork.*

In practice, this could mean senior leaders taking responsibility for strategically developing areas such as curriculum, personal development, and safeguarding, with middle leaders supporting day-to-day operations and implementation. The Headteacher then takes overall responsibility for the provision, its ethos, strategic growth, and financial stability.

Distributed leadership allows decision-making and expertise to be shared, which in turn develops the next generation of leaders (as explored in Chapter 7).

Distributing leadership is one of the key things we've needed to do as our provision has grown. For us, distributed leadership is about understanding the skills and strengths of your team and using them effectively, ensuring the right person leads each area or task. In practice, distributed leadership can ensure that decision-making is informed by the expertise of those closest to learners.

Moreover, as provisions expand, so too does the need for leadership capacity – whether to support mainstream schools, collaborate across settings, or operate at Executive Head level. A well-structured, distributed leadership model supports leadership development and succession planning alongside meeting operational needs. It also allows leaders to focus on strategic development, while ensuring day-to-day operations run smoothly. Of course, although many people will act as leaders without holding a formally designated role, effective distributed leadership is underpinned by strong positional leadership. It is this formal leadership that creates the context and clarity for distributed leadership to flourish:

> *to be effective, distributed leadership has to be well managed, goal orientated, planned and developed continuously.*
>
> Heikka et al. (2012, p. 37)

As your organisation grows, you are also likely to require increased support from Human Resources (HR), with more staff inevitably generating more requests for flexible working, parental leave, special leave, and reasonable adjustments. Any large-scale restructuring will also need to be compliant with employment laws and involve guidance from HR and consultation with unions. Organisational redesign that impacts workplace structure or individual roles and responsibilities is likely to impact on your staff's personal and professional identities. This can be an emotionally challenging time for leaders as they balance what's best for the organisation with the needs and personal circumstances of individuals.

Growing an organisation inevitably brings tough decisions about people, structures, and resources. These moments can be challenging, but keeping the focus on what's right for children helps guide us through complexity and ensures that every choice supports high-quality outcomes for learners.

Thinking points

- Who will support you as a leader when you need to make difficult decisions?
- How will you involve staff voice in organisational redesign, so that change is co-created rather than imposed?

- How do you ensure that compliance with employment law and unions does not overshadow the focus on learners during times of change?
- In times of organisational change, what strategies can you use to maintain trust, morale, and wellbeing among staff?
- What reflection or feedback mechanisms could help you evaluate whether tough decisions are having the intended impact on learners and staff?
- How do you model values-driven leadership when the right choice for children may be unpopular or challenging for the adults in your organisation?

Navigating change

Large-scale transformations, though often necessary for growth and improvement, can create considerable anxiety for learners, families, and staff. Change brings uncertainty, and this can undermine self-esteem and belonging. Navigating change with empathy and understanding is key to successful implementation. It is important that any changes are in line with your provision's vision and values and that decision-making and day-to-day actions remain purpose-driven. As mentioned in Chapter 1, working in a specialist environment is emotional work, and organisational change can evoke strong reactions. Many staff feel emotionally invested in their learners and, by extension, their organisation. When people resist change, it's often because they care deeply about the way things are and the people involved.

Consistency becomes even more important as a provision grows. For neurodivergent learners, consistent routines and expectations are not only helpful but are also essential. Clear and consistent communication across staff also builds a sense of safety and trust. To support communication and unified messages, simple strategies, such as morning briefings, bring the staff team together, creating a shared sense of purpose and understanding at the start of each day.

If a major part of leadership is problem-solving (Kerns, 2019), then one of the most valuable tasks for leaders during periods of change is to coach others to solve problems, rather than trying to solve everything themselves. This not only empowers others but helps to foster the culture of distributed leadership discussed above.

Most large-scale changes begin as top-down decisions, but successful implementation depends on how well others are involved and how much they believe in the reason for change. Leaders must consider:

- How ready are your stakeholders for change?
- Are we involving the right stakeholder voices (e.g. staff, families, pupils) early enough in the process?

- How will you communicate the vision and rationale for change in a way that both excites and reassures?
- Can all stakeholders see themselves in the future you're building?
- How do you balance the relentless pace of school improvement with the needs of your organisation?
- What predictable structures can you preserve to provide stability to staff and learners during change?
- As changes occur, how will you ensure that your organisation's purpose and the quality of education experience for learners remains uncompromised?

Maintaining relationships through growth

It is widely recognised that the challenges of organisational change lie more in the implementation than the planning. We may wish to be human-centric leaders, but this can become problematic when organisations grow as it can become difficult to sustain meaningful relationships with everyone. The British anthropologist Professor Robin Dunbar suggests that there is a maximum number of meaningful relationships an individual can maintain (Dunbar, 1993). He proposes that humans can maintain around 150 meaningful social connections (including family, friends and colleagues) due to limits imposed by the size of our neocortex, a figure often referred to as Dunbar's Number. Camilleri, Rockey, and Dunbar (2024) suggest that as organisations grow past 150 employees, they are likely to require clearer and more established processes and frameworks - something to consider when planning for sustainable and effective school growth.

Team size is another factor that becomes important as organisations grow. Camilleri, Rockey, and Dunbar (2024) draw on complexity science to suggest that decision-making becomes less effective when more than five people are involved - yet, at Springfields we currently have a senior leadership team of ten. The premise is that, when an issue or topic is contested, five participants balance the need for diversity of thought with the ability to make decisions at speed. For growing organisations, this highlights the importance of considering who is involved in decision-making and how the team is structured. For our leadership team, this might mean identifying a smaller decision-making group that draws upon people's roles, interests, and expertise to the matter at hand, while keeping the wider leadership team involved through briefings or consultative sessions.

An awareness of research from anthropology and social psychology can help leaders plan growth so that it is both relationally and operationally sustainable. For example, smaller decision-making groups or sub-teams with defined remits can preserve relationships and ensure staff feel heard while allowing the organisation to act efficiently.

Thinking points

- How can you and other leaders remain visible, relational, and connected as your staffing group expands?
- Map the relationships you currently hold with staff. Who do you know well? Where are the gaps? What are the implications for future growth?
- How does the size and structure of your leadership team impact the speed and quality of decision making?
- How can an awareness of social psychology and group dynamics help you plan leadership growth in a sustainable way?
- How do you ensure that all voices are heard without slowing down essential strategic decisions?

Growth within the specialist sector is increasingly necessary but challenging. As specialist and alternative provisions expand, leaders face complex decisions about people, structures, and resources. Distributed leadership, strong estate management, and thoughtful HR practices can help leaders navigate these complexities, but what really matters is keeping learners at the centre of every decision. Keeping the focus on what is right for children, what Reach South CEO Tom Leverage (2025) calls 'thinking of the child in the room', ensures that every decision supports high-quality education. No matter how complex growth becomes, staying child-centred ensures that every decision you make strengthens your team, your systems, and, most importantly, the experience and outcomes of the learners in your care.

Chapter summary

Like all organisations, specialist provisions must be responsive to change as the children and families we serve are always evolving.

- As the number of learners with an EHCP rises, specialist and alternative provisions are under growing pressure to increase capacity.
- Two critical elements to sustainable and successful growth include estate management and developing appropriate staffing structures.
- Managing estates can be complex and time-consuming. Developing an operational site team enables leaders to focus on strategic site development.

- Leaders must ensure they remain aware of, and up to date with, all aspects of compliance and health and safety, drawing on external expertise where necessary.
- Using provision mapping strategies helps leaders think long-term about their learners, and the resources, financial, and staffing implications of this.
- Effective risk management enables specialist provisions to identify challenges early and to respond appropriately.
- Dunbar's Number and research into group size suggests that an individual can maintain around 150 meaningful relationships. This has implications for growth and organisational design.
- Growth is not just about increasing the number of pupils but also increasing your impact on pupils. Keeping children at the centre of decision making is essential.

Further reading

- The National Audit Office's 2023 guide, *Overcoming Challenges to Managing Risks in Government*, offers a comprehensive framework aimed at enhancing risk management practices across public sector organisations and can be accessed online at: https://www.nao.org.uk/wp-content/uploads/2023/12/overcoming-challenges-to-managing-risks-in-government.pdf.

References

BBC (2024, 17 August). 'Intervention to help parents with toilet training'. *BBC News*. Available online at: https://www.bbc.co.uk/news/articles/cp3dykw576yo [accessed 27 October 2025].

Camilleri, T., Rockey, S., and Dunbar, R. (2024). *The Social Brain: The Psychology of Successful Groups*. London: Penguin.

Churchill, W. (1925). 'To improve is to change; to be perfect is to change often'. In: *His Complete Speeches, 1897–1963*, edited by Robert Rhodes James, vol. 4, p. 3706. New York: Chelsea House.

Darwin, C. (1859). *On the Origin of Species by Means of Natural Selection*. London: John Murray.

Dunbar, R. I. M. (1993). 'Co-evolution of neocortex size, group size and language in humans'. *Behavioral and Brain Sciences*, *16*(4), 681–694.

Dyson, J. (2025, 30 May). 'More schools miss out as "lottery" repair grants fall again'. *Schools Week*. Available online at: https://schoolsweek.co.uk/more-schools-miss-out-as-lottery-repair-grants-fall-again/?mc_cid=23ef971e67&mc_eid=e31f10d6ee [accessed 19 July 2025].

Eaton, H. (2025). 'The impact and interaction of multiple diagnoses – Autism, ADHD, Dyslexia, Dyspraxia, Dysgraphia and Dyscalculia'. Presented in-person at: A-Fest 2025, Calne, Wiltshire, 25 February.

Health and Safety at Work etc. Act 1974, c. 37. London: The Stationery Office. Available online at: https://www.legislation.gov.uk/ukpga/1974/37/contents [accessed 26 April 2026].

Equality Act 2010, c. 15. Available online at: https://www.legislation.gov.uk/ukpga/2010/15/contents [accessed 26 April 2026].

Heikka, J., Waniganayake, M., and Hujala, E. (2012). 'Contextualizing distributed leadership within early childhood education: Current understandings, research evidence and future challenges'. *Educational Management Administration & Leadership*, *41*(1), 30–44.

Kerns, C. D. (2019). 'Decisive problem solving: A key leadership practice'. *Journal of Management Policy and Practice*, *17*(2). Available online at: https://articlegateway.com/index.php/JMPP/article/view/1813 [accessed 19 July 2025].

Leverage, T. (2025, 2 September). 'CEO welcome address', Reach South Academy Trust, Plymouth.

National Audit Office (2023, December). *Overcoming Challenges to Managing Risks in Government*. Available online at: https://www.nao.org.uk/wp-content/uploads/2023/12/overcoming-challenges-to-managing-risks-in-government.pdf [accessed 19 July 2025].

Roberts, J. (2025, 12 June). 'EHCPs up 11% as DfE mulls their future'. *tes Magazine*. Available online at: https://www.tes.com/magazine/news/specialist-sector/ehcps-dfe-mulls-their-future [accessed 26 April 2026].

Roberts, J. (2026, 19 March). 'Special schools more than 10,000 pupils over capacity'. *tes Magazine*. Available online at: https://www.tes.com/magazine/news/specialist-sector/special-schools-more-10000-pupils-over-capacity [accessed 26 April 2026].

11

Beyond your school gate: Partnerships, community, and SEND system leadership

Understand that there's a need for community. Everything that happens to 'make the magic' in a SEN school is built on relationships at all levels – relationships with our children, with each other, with staff, with the community and stakeholders.

Angela O'Rourke, Headteacher, Southfield SEN School

Chapter overview

Having explored how to create and grow a successful specialist provision, we now invite you to look outward and consider how your organisation can help build a more inclusive educational system – one that ensures every learner, no matter where they go to school, has the support and opportunities they deserve.

This chapter explores how collaborative partnerships can build capacity, share expertise, and strengthen outcomes within your provision and beyond it. We will explore working with local authorities (LAs), building partnerships with universities, growing networks and community links, and establishing an outreach service. Educational leaders have a civic duty to understand the communities they serve and to be active participants within them. Engaging with your community not only strengthens your relationship but also provides valuable insights into local needs, helping you make decisions that can benefit both learners and the wider educational landscape.

From silos to system leadership

Michael Fullan, a leading voice in educational leadership and system change, warns that when leaders lose sight of developing others, they risk not only harming the wider education system but also weakening their own organisation (Fullan, 2002). Building on this, Camilleri, Rockey, and Dunbar (2024) suggest that there are significant benefits to moving beyond our immediate network, including overcoming groupthink, attaining new knowledge, and enabling better decision making. They both provide powerful evidence that if we want our provisions to prosper then we cannot work in silos.

DOI: 10.4324/9781003601388-12

Moreover, there is a growing need for specialist and alternative provisions to contribute to the wider education system. Recent data from Teacher Tapp, a daily survey app capturing insights from more than 10,000 UK educators, show that nearly 90% of teachers feel underprepared to support children identified as having SEND, particularly learners with Social, Emotional and Mental Health needs (Wespieser, 2024). This is echoed by findings from Ofsted (2023), which show that teachers consistently request more training on how best to support learners with additional needs. As diagnostic rates continue to rise, the need for more effective staff training is likely to intensify, given that 56.2% of children with an EHCP are educated in mainstream schools (Department for Education, 2025).

There was consensus among the leaders we spoke with that working beyond our school gates is not an option for specialist provisions, but a moral responsibility. After all, if we really want to help all children with SEND, this means supporting mainstream provisions too. The questions below encourage you to consider how your expertise can have impact across the wider system.

Thinking points

- How outward facing is your organisation? What importance do you place on collaborating and supporting others?
- What role can you play in system leadership - developing other provisions while also developing yourself and your organisation?
- What partnerships can you establish that will create meaningful impact for children, families, and other schools?

Author Anecdote by Nicola B: Collaboration not competition

My previous school was located directly across from a neighbouring secondary school. Each September we'd start the year by comparing our A-Level and GCSE results with theirs and cheering when ours were better. In the years that we did well and they did badly I wondered how those teachers and children felt and the implications for them. Looking back now I feel embarrassed to have cheered. Instead of pitting ourselves in competition with one another, we should have celebrated each other's success. I want all young people to succeed, no matter which school they attend; to paraphrase Arthur Miller (2009/1946): as a teacher, they are all my children. This realisation helped crystalise my motto of 'collaboration not competition', my interest in systemic school improvement, and in building an education system that celebrates when others succeed. Use the moments that make you feel uncomfortable as a catalyst for change. Sit in that discomfort, think, 'what am I going to do about it?', and act.

Working with the local authority

Since local authorities name a child's provision on an EHCP, building a strong relationship with them is crucial. It's likely that your provision will work across multiple LAs that will all have slightly different ways of operating. Here are some of the ways that we work with LAs:

- Providing open mornings to help LA workers understand our provision. This means they can better advise families and professionals on whether we can meet need.
- Providing free training to SENCOs and Resource Base leads.
- Attending Discussion and Decision (DaD panels) to support fair decision making.
- Taking part in joint provision planning - helping anticipate future demand and ensuring the right mix of provision across the county.
- Coordinating closely on admissions and transition arrangements to ensure continuity of support for learners.

As well as working closely with educational teams, you may also need to collaborate with the transport team, particularly if your young people receive home-to-school transport. Building strong relationships with drivers and passenger assistants makes the journey to school more enjoyable for children and the start of the day easier for staff. Aspects to consider include:

- Who is your staff contact for transport and who is their key contact at the LA? This may be a role fulfilled by your Family Liaison Officer or Operations Manager.
- Will you provide training for drivers and assistants? Even brief sessions on understanding your learners' needs, routines, and communication styles can have a huge impact.
- How will you encourage families, teachers, and transport staff to work together? Developing simple routines for sharing updates, observations, and concerns can help everyone feel informed and connected, creating a smoother, safer journey for children.
- Holding monthly check-ins with transport staff to review what's working well, discuss challenges, and identify improvements.
- Invite passenger transport to open evenings for new admissions to help families understand this part of the transition process.

Building partnerships

Partnerships are powerful. In his book *Centennials*, Alex Hill highlights how openness and the inclusion of alternative viewpoints strengthen high-performing teams. Effective organisations value the inclusion of different perspectives. For educational leaders, building partnerships is an effective way to obtain alternative viewpoints.

When building partnerships, it often makes sense to start local - this is because proximity matters when forming relationships. Coburn and Russell (2008) note that networks are more likely to form and thrive when people are physically close. This is why many geographically dispersed MATs tend to form local geographical hubs. On a simple level, being closer together makes it easier to meet, but local networks can often feel more relevant because we tend to be more focused and invested in what's happening nearby.

Another key partner is your local university. Robinson (2017) highlights the value of cross-phase collaboration, particularly between schools and higher education institutions. Education departments are often keen to work with you. Offering placements, experience days, or lectures is typically well received by training providers and those undertaking initial teacher training. Although the immediate return from supporting trainee teachers may be small, the long-term benefits are significant. The quality and quantity of your future job applicants are directly influenced by the experiences of today's trainees - not only whether they complete and pass their course but, more crucially, whether they remain in the profession. Through engaging with course providers and providing an open and welcoming school culture, we can create a positive perception of our profession. In turn, this helps to build a stronger intake of educators who are both equipped and inspired to work in specialist settings.

In time, you may wish to partner with other university departments - for example, by supporting aspiring educational psychologists or therapists. You may find it useful to explore a 'quid pro quo' relationship - that is, requesting that the university support careers visits for your learners in return for providing placements for theirs. Alternatively, you could contribute to research in exchange for training.

Partnerships with mainstream schools are also crucial. If you're part of a mixed MAT, these partnerships may occur naturally, and it is becoming more common for MATs to include both mainstream and specialist settings. Dyson (2025) suggests that the number of MATs with at least one special school is rising, despite a reduction in the number of trusts overall. The number of MATs composed solely of special schools is also falling (Dyson, 2025). Maintaining strong relationships with mainstream settings not only supports smoother transitions for learners (in either direction) but also provides powerful professional learning opportunities for staff. Emma Twell, Safeguarding and SEND Specialist and autistic adult, advocates for job shares between mainstream and specialist provisions, an approach which enables staff to develop specialist expertise while retaining links with mainstream provisions. Flemons and Walker (2024) suggest that pupils could benefit from having both specialist and mainstream settings within the same MAT, as this can enable flexible, personalised timetables that allow learners to access both types of provision. This setup could support learners in specialist or alternative provisions to access GCSEs or other qualifications in mainstream settings, or providing learners who are struggling in mainstream with short-term AP placements.

Part of why we wanted to write this book is our belief in the importance of being leaders who give back to the wider system through sharing and creating collaborative networks and events. As a leadership team, we actively research what other schools do and what works for them - we read other provision's Ofsted reports and browse websites, which is how we found lots of our case study contributors!

It's important that you don't consider other settings as your competition, but as a source of inspiration and positive challenge. Working alongside other educational provisions can encourage us all to do better – a phenomenon social psychologists call social facilitation. In 1898, researcher Norman Triplett observed that cyclists performed better when riding with others than when cycling alone. This phenomenon became known as social facilitation, a principle suggesting that being with others creates a shared energy that enhances performance and increases motivation. Just as Triplett noticed that cyclists ride faster when riding in groups, being around other skilled and committed professionals can elevate our own practice. When we engage with peers and share ideas, it naturally encourages reflection and self-improvement, which benefits our organisational culture and learners. The questions below encourage you to reflect on your own ethos towards collaboration.

Thinking points

- Who inspires you and your leadership team to stretch your thinking or practice?
- How do you model an ethos of 'collaboration not competition'? Do you put as much into the system as you take out?
- What partnerships are you currently proud of? What partnerships would you like to form?
- Are you engaging with networks, CPD, and research in ways that stretch and challenge your thinking?
- How do you ensure your staff continue to grow as specialist practitioners, while also staying connected to developments in mainstream education?

Activity: Partnerships audit

Strong partnerships work best when they are purposeful, mutually beneficial, and aligned with your values. This activity helps you reflect on your current partnerships and their impact.

List all your current partnerships and reflect on the following:

- What is the purpose of each partnership? Does it align with your vision and values?
- How do you know it's an effective partnership? Is it mutually beneficial?
- How does this partnership benefit learners, staff, or the wider organisation?
- How much staff time or resources does this partnership require?
- Are there current partnerships that are over or underutilised?
- Identify one partnership that you'd like to strengthen or deepen. How might you do this?

Establishing an outreach service

Specialist and alternative provisions hold expert knowledge, approaches, and values that can inform and enrich mainstream practice. In the current financial climate, many specialist and alternative provisions are undertaking outreach to support income generation. There's also growing demand for help from mainstream schools, which are increasingly needing to support learners with more complex needs. The likely rise in resource bases and internal alternative provision within mainstream settings will also necessitate specialist and mainstream provisions working more closely together to co-create inclusive education. Engaging with other schools in this way also draws on the social facilitation principle discussed above: being around other skilled professionals can inspire reflection and elevate practice, benefiting learners across the system.

Many LAs are also commissioning specialist provisions to provide an outreach service in their area. Lydia Colios, Assistant Headteacher at Addington School, explains how their outreach service works:

> *Our outreach service is commissioned by Wokingham LA. There's a lead teacher, who has substantial SEND experience, who goes out to work with primary schools. We have a resource library that other schools can use. This means that they're able to try things like wobble stools and bucket time packs. They can try these resources and see if they work for their learners before having to use their own budget.*
>
> *We also run networks and training, for example on annual reviews and pupil voice. We also encourage mainstream schools to come and see our own provision at Addington. There can be a big gap between pupils who can have their needs met in mainstream with reasonable adjustments and pupils that need fulltime specialist provision. Being open and transparent with local schools and letting them see your provision, either helps confirm that pursuing a specialist placement is right or helps them see the adaptations they can make to support learners in their setting.*

Lydia outlines the benefits to sharing beyond your setting. Likewise, Ashley McCormick, SENCO and Senior Leader at Archers Brook, was able to see the benefits of disseminating their Support Square tool across their borough. Having other institutions use the Support Square provided valuable feedback to Archers Brook that the tool worked beyond their setting. Collaboration with a wide range of organisations enabled them to refine and strengthen the Support Square. Ashley exhibits the type of humility we see frequently in education:

> *We're doing this work because we're about making a difference. We're about regulating children, we're not looking to win awards.*

Fulfilling our civic responsibility to all children with SEND was a strong motivator for us to establish an outreach service. Like Ashley, it was about making a difference that resonated beyond our setting.

Case study: Setting up an outreach provision

Since 2020, we have developed our outreach service called Springfields Autism Support. Here's what our experience has taught us:

1. It's about more than money. If your main priority for establishing an outreach service is to make a profit, then you're likely to be disappointed. Although outreach services provide some income generation, it's likely to be less than you think.
2. We believe in a 'participation not profit ethos'. We don't want anyone who needs our support or training not to be able to access it. Our income generation helps us provide free training for families and free places at most of our online training. Any income generated helps us provide more events, making it a virtuous cycle.
3. Be confident about what gives you the credibility to support others. Our Advanced Accreditation with the National Autistic Society (achieved in 2022 and 2025) lets others know they're drawing on acknowledged expertise.
4. Ensure you have the capacity to help. It's important that your organisation has both the skillset and the capacity to support others because your first responsibility is always to deliver your core purpose – educating the young people on roll with you.
5. When starting out, start small. When curating your offer, think of something manageable, something you're good at, passionate about, and that can make a positive difference. What do others tell you you're good at? Start with that.
6. Do a scoping exercise. Gather existing data – what other services are offered locally that you could complement? What gaps are there? Whose voices do you need to listen to and how will you gather these? What's happening nationally? Are there others offering a similar service in other parts of the country? What could you learn from them?
7. Amplify SEND voices. We're keen to give a platform to those with lived experience of SEND. Considering how these individuals can complement or be involved in the coproduction of your training materials is important.
8. As every enquiry for support is different, flexibility and responsiveness are key. Understanding people's needs and contexts helps generate the right package of support. Take time to listen to what they need and don't be afraid to say you're not the right service or to signpost other providers.
9. Identify the right staff – they are your organisation's ambassadors. Make sure your outreach team have the knowledge and skills, as well as the

interest, confidence, and emotional intelligence to work with other organisations. Consider creating a code of conduct that clarifies expectations around response timescales, impartiality, dress code, and remit.

10. Provide in-reach options. Offering visits to your provision, so that others can observe good practice in action, is valuable and cost effective. We offer complimentary in-reach visits as part of any outreach support offer.
11. Provide a mix of costed and free events. We would love to offer everything for free, but we receive no funding to provide training. We must be responsible with our school budget, and this must be spent on our learners. If you are taking resources away from learners during a school day, then there must be a financial charge to the commissioning setting to cover colleague's time. Providing a model that allows for donations enables those who need to attend for free to participate as well as those who can pay.
12. Because it is a two-way process, there are lots of benefits to outreach work. When other organisations seek your support, the exchange is rarely one-sided and you are likely to learn just as much as they are through the process. As well as contributing to a valuable school-led improvement system, you are supporting your own staff to develop new skills, giving them experiences and opportunities that may support retention. Colleagues imparting their expertise get a self-esteem boost alongside professional satisfaction and a sense of moral purpose. Moreover, by enabling your staff to visit and work with other schools, they're likely to bring back a raft of strategies and best practice that will improve and assist your own setting.
13. Be clear on what you're committing to and use a Service Level Agreement (SLA) if necessary. Having a clear agreement will ensure that everyone knows their responsibilities and what they're accountable for. Your school business manager or LA will often have a model template that you can adapt.
14. Consider 'quid pro quo' options. If financial remuneration can't be offered, then explore any quid pro quo opportunities – for example, sharing resources or exchanging training.
15. Marketing. How will you share and advertise your offer? What social media platforms could help you? How will you develop word of mouth? Over time you may need to consider a separate logo and website to provide key information for interested parties.
16. Be clear on how you will measure your impact. Gathering both quantitative and qualitative data can help you understand what's working and show the difference your work is making for learners, schools, and families.

Thinking points

- On a scale of 1 to 10, where 1 means you have no outreach offer in place and 10 means you have a well-established outreach service, where would you place your setting right now? What would help you move one step further along the scale?
- What philosophy underpins your outreach service? Why is this important to you?
- How can you involve staff, families, and mainstream schools in shaping the offer so it reflects local context and priorities?
- What does success look like for your outreach service? How will you measure impact for learners and staff, within and beyond your setting?
- How will you balance capacity between supporting external schools and maintaining high-quality provision within your own setting?
- What professional learning opportunities could arise from outreach work? How might this contribute to staff development and retention?

Leadership scenario

You are the Headteacher of a specialist provision that has recently created an outreach programme to support local schools. Your team has been delivering training and support to three nearby schools and this has been well received.

Your LA asks you to extend your support to a fourth school, which is further away and has a different demographic. You recognise that taking this on could significantly benefit more learners and strengthen community links. However, your leadership team is concerned about capacity, as expanding your outreach work could overload staff and risk compromising the quality of education for your own learners. Some staff are worried about workload and travel time, and a few parents have expressed concerns that your attention is being diverted away from their children.

Do you support the fourth school? You could consider:

- The criteria you will use to decide whether to take on the new outreach work.
- How you can involve your leadership team and other stakeholders in making this decision.
- Whether you could pilot the programme in a manageable way before committing fully.
- How you will balance the moral imperative to support the wider community with the need to maintain high-quality provision for your own learners.
- How you will communicate and negotiate with the LA regarding remuneration for your setting.

There is no right answer here. Your thinking will highlight your leadership values in action - how you evaluate risk, how you balance core purpose with wider moral responsibility, and how you evaluate differing viewpoints. This scenario provides a useful starting point for thinking about the role of schools within their local community, which forms the focus of our next section.

Building community connections

As an English teacher, one of my favourite texts to teach is 'An Inspector Calls' by J.B. Priestley (1992/1945), as I've always enjoyed its themes around social responsibility. A memorable section for me is just before the Inspector's arrival, when factory owner Mr Birling flatly rejects the idea that society should function like a beehive, with everyone working together for the common good. Like the Inspector, I think communal thinking and collective responsibility is a given, particularly since educational provisions are rooted in their communities. However, children in specialist and alternative settings often come from a large geographical area - sometimes living an hour or more away from their provision. This presents unique challenges to our sector in building and sustaining meaningful community links, since we need to support our learners and communities in multiple ways:

- Helping each child feel part of their home community, even if this is several towns away.
- Supporting learners to feel a sense of belonging in their educational setting.
- Fostering connections to your provision's local community, even if your young people won't access this outside of school hours.
- Supporting the local area to see your organisation and its learners as a positive part of their community.

Being understood by the local community is vital to fostering inclusivity, empathy, and understanding around SEND - a sentiment shared by Julliet Doherty, Head of Adult Services at Ascent Autism Specialist College:

> *We're really passionate about giving to the community. We give to the community so that the community understand us better.*

Of course, there may be times, especially when looking to drive school improvement, when a provision needs to redefine itself in the eyes of its community. During our own tenure, we have had to challenge and reshape the longstanding perception of our setting being the 'naughty boys' school' into what it is now - a specialist provision for autism, speech, language, and communication needs. This shift in perception happened over many academic years through sustained dialogue, inclusive practice, and visible impact. We have achieved this by:

- Actively inviting the community into school through events such as Christmas and summer fetes - we put invitations through the letterboxes of our neighbours.
- Building links with local employers and public services by visiting their workplaces and showing interest in what they do.

- Taking our learners out into the local community as part of our Personal Development curriculum.
- Being a force for good by offering free training, events, and networks.
- Getting involved in community events – for example, the town duck race.
- Hosting regular afternoon teas that allow our neighbours to visit and get to know our vision and values.

Thinking points

- What does community mean in the context of your setting? How do you ensure it includes every child and family you serve?
- How does your local community view your provision? How do you know?
- Who are the key people and organisations nearby who share your values and could help you grow or get better?
- How might community partnerships enrich the curriculum, enhance employability pathways, or widen opportunities for your learners?
- What structures or roles in your school could strengthen community engagement?
- How can working with your community help shift perceptions of SEND and promote greater understanding and inclusion?

Author anecdote by Nicola B: Building community networks

This chapter has been one of my favourites to write as I'm passionate about building networks (as I hope you can tell!). I've created lots of networks and events, including: a Women Leading in Education network, a Neurodiversity Network, and a series of events for parents called The Springboard Series. However, the one I'm most proud of, and the one I see as my legacy, is A-Fest – a festival celebrating autism and autistic individuals. At the time of writing, I am planning our ninth A-Fest in February 2027. It is an event that has grown from a one-day internal event to a two-day programme, including a day for external attendees followed by a free online programme for anyone in the world to access. No matter how many events I do, I'm still surprised (and humbled!) w!hen anyone turns up. My top worries are listed below, along with the advice I'd! give to anyone looking to start their own network.

Worry 1: Nobody will come!

When starting a network, aim for quality over quantity. Look for those people whose values and passions align with your own. Starting small is okay. As someone with perfectionist tendencies, I found that when I held my first network event, I needed to adjust the image in my mind of what a 'successful' gathering looked like. I had to remind myself that it wasn't a Buckingham Palace tea party, and that reaching even just one person and making a difference to them would make all the hard work worthwhile. Connecting with those who most share your values and can help you grow the network is invaluable; these are the individuals you should be looking to connect with when starting out.

Worry 2: If not you, then who?

The catalyst for A-Fest was colleagues asking me, as CPD lead, about the training they needed and me not being able to find what they wanted. I decided that I could sit around and wait for the training we needed to magically appear, or I could put it together myself by drawing on internal and external expertise. If the event you want to attend doesn't exist yet, then you need to start it! Because if not you, then who?

Worry 3: There will be no time left for me.

Everyone in education is busy and there's always the worry about adding to your workload. The key is in choosing what resonates most with your values and moral purpose. When it's something you believe in then it doesn't feel like work (yes, really!), it feels like changing the world, even if, initially, it means starting with five teachers in a small corner of Wiltshire. That said, face to face is great but start online if you need to – there are less financial overheads, you can attract attendees from a wider geographical area, and you don't have to worry about refreshments!

Thinking point: Network creation

What networks could you create? Consider:

- What's the network or event you'd like to attend that doesn't currently exist?
- What are the strengths and passions you identified in Chapter 1?
- What are the local needs of your community? When your strengths and passion overlap with local needs, then that's your network.
- What's your first step to putting on an event, and who could support you with it?
- When is it going to happen? Pick a date and stick with it – it'll give you something to work towards. The first event is always the smallest and hardest, but it provides the steepest learning curve – so go for it and (try to) enjoy it!

Consequently, educational leaders need to look and think beyond their school gates. Building strong community links, working closely with LAs, partnering with universities, and starting new networks all make a difference to learners in your provision and beyond. By being reflective, collaborative, and brave enough to step forward, you can strengthen not just your own provision, but the whole community, creating a world where learners, staff, and educational provisions work together for mutual success.

Chapter summary

Educational settings should not operate in isolation. In fact, to truly thrive, we must look outward while creating a culture that welcomes others in.

- Leaders in specialist settings must cultivate meaningful relationships beyond their school gates - with other schools, other professionals, and their local education landscape.
- By engaging with others, educational leaders stay reflective, informed, and responsive to change.
- Collaboration is reciprocal - the more you give, the more you'll gain, and, most importantly, the more children benefit. Share with the sector (and the world) what makes you brilliant, and stay curious about what makes others brilliant too.
- Leaders should see outreach as an extension of their provision - sharing expertise, advocating for inclusion, and helping more children.
- Use other local settings as positive collaborators. Social facilitation theory suggests that the presence of others can encourage you to perform better.
- Developing strong connections with local communities ensures that learners feel included, that your provision is understood and valued, and that opportunities for learning are maximised.
- When establishing networks and partnerships, start small and local and consider quid pro quo relationships if budgets are tight.

Further reading

- Although not focused on specialist provisions, *Towards Selfimproving School Systems: Lessons from a City Challenge*, by Professor Mel Ainscow (2015), presents insights from a decade of research and practice into school collaboration in Manchester.

References

Ainscow, M. (2015). *Towards Self-improving School Systems: Lessons from a City Challenge*. London: Routledge.

Camilleri, T., Rockey, S., and Dunbar, R. (2024). *The Social Brain: The Psychology of Successful Groups*. London: Penguin.

Coburn, C. E., and Russell, J. L. (2008). 'District policy and teachers' social networks'. *Educational Evaluation and Policy Analysis*, *30*, 203–235.

Department for Education (2025). *Special Educational Needs in England: Academic Year 2024/25*. Available online at: https://explore-education-statistics.service.gov.uk/find-statistics/special-educational-needs-in-england/2024-25 [accessed 27 July 2025].

Dyson, J. (2025, 5 August). 'Special trust to join 16-school MAT'. *Schools Week*. Available online at: https://schoolsweek.co.uk/special-trust-joins-16-school-mat/ [accessed 7 August 2025].

Flemons, L., and Walker, M. (2024). *The MAT Factor: Exploring How Multi-academy Trusts are Supporting Pupils with SEND*. Slough: NFER.

Fullan, M. (2002). 'The change leader'. *Educational Leadership*, *59*(8), 16–20.

Miller, A. (2009/1946). *All My Sons*. London: Penguin Classics.

Ofsted (2023). *Independent Review of Teachers' Professional Development in Schools: Phase 1 Findings*. Available online at: https://www.gov.uk/government/publications/teachers-professional-development-in-schools/independent-review-of-teachers-professional-development-in-schools-phase-1-findings [accessed 27 July 2025].

Priestley, J. B. (1992/1945). *An Inspector Calls*. London: Heinemann.

Robinson, D. (2017). 'Effective inclusive teacher education for special educational needs and disabilities: Some more thoughts on the way forward'. *Teaching and Teacher Education*, *61*, 164–178.

Triplett, N. (1898). 'The dynamogenic factors in pacemaking and competition'. *The American Journal of Psychology*, *9*(4), 507–533.

Wespieser, K. (2024, 14 June). 'Evidence summary: SEND – building for an inclusive future'. *Teacher Tapp*. Available online at: https://teachertapp.com/uk/publications/evidence-summary-send/ [accessed 27 July 2025].

Conclusion

If you really want to make an impact on the lives of children, teach in a SEN school.
Angela O'Rourke, Headteacher of Southfield SEN School

Chapter overview

In this final chapter, we build on the outward facing nature of Chapter 11 to explore what may lie ahead for those leading a specialist provision. We reflect on the opportunities and challenges the sector faces and what might be required to meet the needs of children and staff effectively. We also look at the opportunities and career prospects that come after leading in a specialist setting. Finally, we explore the importance of representation and supporting adults with SEND in the workplace.

What lies ahead for specialist provisions?

Camilleri, Rockey, and Dunbar (2024) suggest that leaders should focus on the future, but perhaps the only certainty we have when looking forward is that education will continue to evolve. In 500 BCE, the Greek philosopher Heraclitus stated that, "the only constant in life is change". 2,500 years later, his words remain just as relevant. Although it can be difficult to predict change, two key elements with the potential to transform education are artificial intelligence and flexible working.

Artificial intelligence (AI)

AI has the potential to transform education in the UK significantly, but it poses both opportunities and challenges. The rise of education specialist AI, such as Teachmate AI, has the potential to reduce teacher workload drastically, particularly lesson planning and adaptive teaching. For leaders, it can support with writing policies, communicating with parents, and supporting school development planning. For teachers, it can adapt texts, generate retrieval questions, and make cross-curricular links. Students can also benefit, using it as coach to help them revise and identify gaps in learning.

DOI: 10.4324/9781003601388-13

More broadly, assistive technology shows real benefits for learners with SEND by enabling accessibility, inclusivity, and communication (Lomas and Baker, 2025). Apps such as speech-to-text software and real-time translation offer huge benefits to learners in helping them navigate both education and the world beyond.

AI also looks to have promise in assisting professional development, with instructional coaching companies, such as IRIS Connect, already utilising AI coaching. Lomas and Baker (2025) suggest that AI could be a powerful tool in supporting CPD by providing concise summaries of evidence-based strategies, which will help educators engage more with research.

However, although AI offers many benefits, there are concerns about data privacy (for example, uploading a child's EHCP to an online AI platform may infringe GDPR regulations), the accuracy of AI-generated content, and ensuring that AI tools are used responsibly and ethically. There are also concerns that humans may become over-reliant on AI, diminishing skills such as critical thinking, problem-solving, and creativity. This could lead to a reduction in human involvement and thinking, first described by Lisanne Bainbridge in the 1980s and now known as the automation principle (Bainbridge, 1983). Moreover, not all students and schools have equal access to electronic devices and AI tools, exacerbating a possible digital divide between independent and state-funded institutions (Lucas, 2025). Consequently, as educational leaders it's important to use AI responsibly, considering where and when it adds value and balancing innovation with the duty of care we hold for our learners and staff.

Flexible working

> *We're receiving fewer applications post COVID. People prefer flexible working. For support staff there's also a financial element – in other roles they can receive overtime, so recruitment is difficult.*
>
> Karen Parker, Head Teacher, Sir Charles Parsons School

Since the Covid-19 pandemic, there has been a major change in attitudes towards flexible working in the UK. Significantly, in April 2024 all employees in the UK gained the legal right to request flexible working from their first day of employment. In particular, there has been an increase in the number of individuals working solely from home, rising from around 5% pre-pandemic to 16% by January 2025 (Clark, 2025). More than 4.4 million people (around 13% of the employed population of the UK) now work flexible hours and around 41% of UK workers have the option to work from home regularly, demonstrating a dramatic increase in hybrid working arrangements (Statista, 2026; ONS, 2026; Barber and Boyle, 2026).

Research into the *Working Lives of Teachers and Leaders* by the Department for Education (2025) suggests that an upward trend in flexible working has also occurred in education. It states that by 2025, half of teachers and leaders reported working flexibly, continuing an upward trend from 46% in 2023 and 2024, and 40% in 2022. Even so, education is not yet keeping pace with the wider job market outlined above. As one university careers advisor told me recently, today's graduates see having some opportunity to work from home as their top requirement. To keep teaching an attractive profession, this must be carefully considered, particularly with the current Education Secretary, Bridget Phillipson, advocating for home-based PPA for teachers (Ng, 2024).

Recent Department for Education guidance (2026a) suggests that school leaders generally perceive the benefits of flexible working to outweigh the costs, particularly in relation to staff retention and wellbeing. Department for Education (2026a) guidance on flexible working highlights its role in supporting staff at different stages of their careers, including those with caring responsibilities and those approaching retirement, alongside its wider potential to improve retention in schools.

Research from the Education Endowment Foundation suggests that flexible working can support teacher recruitment and retention by contributing to a healthier work-life balance (Harland et al., 2023). The *Deloitte Gen Z and Millennial Survey* (2025) suggests that flexible and hybrid working opportunities are now a key expectation among Gen Z workers.

In our setting, emphasising that part-time and flexible working options are available has led to an increase in the number of teaching assistant applicants. We have also seen teachers use flexible arrangements to pursue further education – for example, engaging in Masters study alongside work.

Of course, there are challenges to implementing flexible working. As your provision grows, so does your organisation's complexity, which means flexible timetables that enable staff to take PPA from home requires careful planning. It's also worth considering (as we discussed in Chapter 8) when and how flexible workers will access professional development if their contracted hours don't include time to do this.

Although much has been written about the recruitment and retention of teachers, headteacher retention is an equally pressing concern. High levels of accountability, workload, and the emotional demands of the role mean that many headteachers leave the profession earlier than expected (Weale, 2022). This is supported by recent data which suggests around a third of secondary headteachers leave within three years of appointment (Chantler-Hicks, 2025).

At the same time, only 42 percent of deputy and assistant heads aspire to become a head, down from 56 percent before the pandemic (Teacher Tapp and SchoolDash, 2025). One approach to supporting the sustainability of headteachers is a co-headship model, where two leaders share the responsibilities of headship. This model, already adopted successfully in some schools, may offer a way to reduce pressure, provide greater work-life balance, and create a more collaborative form of leadership (Watkins, 2024). It could also be an effective way for a deputy headteacher to try out headship or to support an experienced mainstream leader making the move into specialist or alternative provision.

Kimberley Legg, Assistant Headteacher at Addington School, explains the benefits of their co-head model:

> *We have a co-head model and both Co-Heads were the previous Deputy Heads. It was really great succession planning by the previous Headteacher, who made sure that the team were prepared for them to step away. We were ready and able to take on those different responsibilities and maintain the standards.*
>
> *I think the role of headteacher can be lonely and potentially difficult. I would be more likely to become a headteacher if I could be a Co-Head. It's preferable to be a Co-Head and have somebody to reason and share things with.*

Another recent development to support work-life balance and retention is the 4-day week. Originating in other sectors, there was some initial scepticism that this approach would work within education, driven by concerns that children might miss out on learning. The Education Endowment Foundation (2026) is currently evaluating flexible working approaches designed to explore whether reduced working patterns can improve teacher retention and recruitment. The scoping phase of the study found that the nine-day working fortnight across Dixons Academies Trust was generally well received, with staff reporting improved wellbeing, work-life balance and job satisfaction. Leaders also noted benefits for their own wellbeing.

There is also the growing realisation that staff with additional needs or disabilities may benefit from flexible and home working (Branicki et al., 2024) – a viewpoint also shared by Safeguarding and SEND Specialist and autistic adult, Emma Twell:

> *The education sector is slow-moving in terms of part-time work and working from home, but that means we're missing out on neurodivergent individuals and lots of other people as well. We need to understand that for neurodivergent staff being in the workplace is very tricky and full-time work may be difficult. Full-time work in a high intensity job, like teaching, can lead to emotional burnout.*

The education sector is becoming more open to flexible and hybrid working as a strategic tool to support wellbeing and retain expertise. By providing the opportunity for some hybrid work, leaders can create a more sustainable workforce, respond to individual staff needs, and ensure continuity of high-quality provision for learners.

Leadership journeys – what comes after headship?

If you're reading this book, it's likely you're an existing or aspiring leader, but what comes next after you've led a specialist provision and are looking for your next career opportunity? The academisation of education in England over the past two decades has seen a rapid increase in MATs and with them a myriad of roles on central teams. It is estimated that 80% of trusts now have a dedicated strategic SEND role, underlining the importance of trust-wide leadership in shaping SEND provision (Flemons and Walker, 2024). These leaders help collate and share effective SEND practice across a trust, enabling collaboration and offering guidance and expertise to schools (Flemons and Walker, 2024). England has more than 1,100 MATs (BESA, 2023). If each employs a strategic SEND leader and 10% leave each year, that adds up to around 110 job openings annually, highlighting both the demand and opportunity in this new leadership space. Since most MATs continue to pursue growth strategies (Confederation of School Trusts and Edurio, 2024), it's likely that the number of SEND strategic roles will continue to grow.

Case study: Being a trust strategic SEND lead

One MAT which already has a strategic SEND lead is the Ted Wragg Trust, a trust of 18 schools, consisting of primary, secondary, and all-through provisions. Their Lead for Alternative Provision and Specialism, Matt Bindon, shares his journey to serving in a whole - trust leadership role.

Career history and interview

I spent 15 years in mainstream schools in pastoral and SEND, middle and senior leadership roles. I then spent 5 years as a Headteacher of a multi-site Alternative Provision in the South West and then went onto to lead a 'special measures' all-through SEMH special school.

1. What words of advice or encouragement would you give someone considering working in Alternative Provision?
   For many, the thought of working in AP comes after working in mainstream education and seeking their next challenge. These teachers are often some of the best in the sector because they bring a wealth of experience and are prepared to continue their learning and development in new ways. They celebrate wins from the smallest achievements to lifelong successes in college, work or university.
   I genuinely believe that the greatest impact you can have on changing lives is in the leadership of AP. For many children who arrive at AP, their journey has been hard-fought and full of challenges. To be in a leadership role where you're responsible for succeeding where others haven't, whilst taking on complex challenges with life-changing outcomes, is why many of us enter the profession. Being a leader with the ability to make such a profound difference in AP couldn't be more rewarding. I would say to anyone who wants to stay sharp, feel totally rewarded in their work, and is prepared to put in the legwork, that AP should definitely be something they consider. The impact you can have is profound and the rewards are immeasurable.
2. What makes a good leader of Alternative Provision?
   Great leaders in AP love people. They love students, staff, families, communities, professional, governors - everyone! They are especially good at

loving those in our community who make loving them hard. They see the best in everyone and believe that everyone has potential and that every day is a new day.

Leaders in AP have high standards but are brave in how they apply and flex them to get the best out of people. They are optimists and when this is tested, their ability to move forward and overcome adversity truly shines, and those they lead love this about them. They're also curious. They have their noses in what other people are doing, both in the school and in the sector. They love to stay on the cutting edge of best practices. They read, visit other provisions and connect with other people. Often, this is to find new ideas and ways to shape what they are doing to continue driving improvement. Sometimes, it is to benchmark and sense-check an approach or idea they are working on.

3. What do you wish people knew most about Alternative Provision?

   My passion is to open up the world of AP and special education right at the start of initial teacher training and ensure that everyone who trains to teach spends time in specialist settings. I believe this for two reasons.

   Firstly, everyone who teaches should know what education looks like for every child in their community, whether they attend their school or not. They should understand that special education can be a part of their career at some point, and exposure to it early on is key to informing their decisions as they progress, grow and seek new challenges.

   Secondly, it is crucial for everyone who becomes a teacher to experience special settings (and AP in particular) because if they become leaders they will have to make decisions about permanent exclusions. To live a day in the shoes of children who have been excluded is essential for understanding the gravity of making such difficult decisions.

4. What helps you as a specialist leader?

   I cannot recommend coaching highly enough. I had coaching as a Headteacher for all 5 years of my headship and it benefited me invaluably as a leader but also personally. Finding budget for coaching for all leaders is a must.

5. Can you share an area of best practice?

   Building parental engagement. It was something that we were constantly discussing – moving to a more generationally appropriate way of communicating with families. We issued all staff in the AP I led with mobile phones. The use of a quick text message to families or a voice note, where tone could be applied to a message of praise, or for families where we knew literacy was a challenge. It really overcame barriers in working with families. Constantly writing to families through letters and emails has had its time – now is the time we embrace other mediums. I recorded a video update and posted it on our school's Facebook page and so many families responded to the thread. I do think this is the start of us reaching families in a new way.

6. How does your role support partnership and collaborative working?
   My current role supports mainstream schools using the specialist knowledge I have acquired from special and AP schools and is an important direction of travel. What I have been able to do is work with SEND and inclusion teams and help them think about applying some of the principles and practices that specialist education uses in mainstream settings.
   I really think the next step in developing inclusion in mainstream schools is for special school staff to spend 1–2 days a week in a mainstream school to support lessons, learners and leaders. Additionally, staff from mainstream schools could spend time on small, one-day-a-week secondments, experiencing the special school environment and learning from the sector.
7. What are the opportunities and challenges facing Alternative Provision?
   The biggest opportunity lies in collaboration between special and mainstream schools. Outreach work varies across the country, with some models being more mature than others, but teams working across sectors can have a significant impact.
   The biggest threat is funding and recruitment. Attracting a flow of brilliant people to work in specialist settings continues to be a challenge that both sectors need to jointly solve. Collaboration, secondments and staff-sharing opportunities are essential for recruiting and retaining exceptional staff in the specialist sector.

☆

Matt reminds us that leading any educational setting is a privilege. The thinking points that follow invite you to reflect on your own leadership journey and where it might take you next.

Thinking points

- What aspects of your current role do you find most rewarding and how might these align with a future trust-wide leadership position?
- Does the idea of shaping system-wide SEND provision excite you or feel overwhelming? Why?
- Which skills and experiences would you need to develop to be ready for a trust-wide or strategic leadership role?
- In what ways could coaching or mentoring support your growth and prepare you for your next role?

- Are there opportunities in your current context to trial aspects of trust-wide leadership before committing to a formal role?
- How do you see your career evolving over the next 5 years and where might a trust-wide leadership role fit within that vision?

What challenges do specialist and alternative provisions anticipate?

Specialist provisions are operating against a backdrop of rising demand, more complex cohorts, and ongoing financial pressures. Leaders across the sector consistently highlighted the challenges that affect both their day-to-day practice and longer-term planning.

Early intervention

Many of the leaders we spoke to reflected on the importance of early intervention. Several mentioned that learners had been struggling for years before they received a specialist placement. However, gaining timely support requires a collaborative approach, including working with local authorities and supporting mainstream schools with screening, assessment, and early intervention. This view has been reflected in a recent white paper (Department for Education, 2026b).

Financial pressures

Financial management remains one of the most pressing challenges, as Head Teacher Karen Parker explains:

> *The biggest challenges we currently face are financial. It's important to make sure we're getting the correct top-up funding. We worked with the local authority last year to ensure we were getting the correct level of funding as this affects our budget.*

Many specialist and alternative settings already operate under tight financial constraints, with limited flexibility to respond to rising costs or increasing pupil numbers. Securing adequate top-up funding, managing staffing costs, and maintaining high-quality provision requires careful planning and creative thinking.

Increasingly complex cohorts

There is growing recognition that the number of children with SEND is rising and that many now present with more complex, multiple, or overlapping needs. Leaders reported a noticeable rise not only in the number of children with additional needs or disabilities, but the complexity of their needs. Increasingly, learners have multiple needs which require highly tailored approaches. Leaders must constantly adjust staffing, curriculum, and learning spaces to meet the needs of their cohort effectively. They are increasingly accommodating learners whose developmental level may differ significantly from their chronological age – for example, a greater number of secondary-aged children are working on a primary aged curriculum.

Despite these challenges, it's important as a sector that we remain positive and solution-focused against the often-used narrative that the SEND system is broken or failing. We must also remain patient against a backdrop of never-ending system reviews and a sense of 'too much talk and not enough action' from policymakers. In December 2024, we saw another inquiry opened by Parliament called: 'Solving the SEND Crisis'. Emotive language such as this may discourage people from leading within the specialist sector, so it's important that we act as ambassadors for it and highlight the immense privilege the role entails. As leaders we will continue to find creative ways to meet the needs of our learners. By working closely with mainstream schools, local authorities, and families, we will continue to navigate the pressures ensuring our children get the education they deserve.

What opportunities would specialist provisions like?

Specialist and alternative provisions are keen for opportunities to use their expertise across the sector. Leaders consistently highlighted key areas that could have a transformative impact.

- Dedicated time in specialist or alternative provisions within Initial Teacher Training. Not only would this develop teachers' confidence and skills, but it could grow the future specialist workforce by inspiring more teachers to consider careers in the sector.
- Opportunities to embed collaboration between mainstream and specialist schools. For example, specialist staff could spend time in mainstream settings to support SEND provision, while mainstream teachers could experience specialist contexts through short secondments.
- Specialist Teaching School Hubs or Inclusion Hubs with a specific remit to support mainstream schools with SEND.
- More opportunities to support staff without a degree to become teachers.

Together, these opportunities show that specialist settings can shape the future of inclusive education. By giving trainee teachers time in specialist settings, encouraging collaboration with mainstream schools, and creating new routes into the profession, the sector can build a skilled, confident workforce ready to meet the needs of its learners.

Representation matters: Educators with additional needs in schools

> *It's difficult being neurodivergent and we need more neurodivergent staff. There aren't enough neurodivergent role models in schools and we need to change this. I was working in an autism and SEMH school. I was sitting in Reception and I was talking to a young*

> *person who was struggling that day. The young person told me that I didn't understand their situation because I was normal.*
>
> *I replied: 'What's normal?!'.*
>
> *They said, 'not me because I'm autistic'.*
>
> *I replied, 'I'm autistic'.*
>
> *The young person said that I couldn't be autistic because I was the Headteacher! It's important that there are more role models and that ties into recruitment and retention – we need neurodivergent role models in school.*
>
> Emma Twell, Safeguarding and SEND Specialist and autistic adult

Children with additional needs and disabilities will one day be adults with additional needs and disabilities, so it's essential that workplaces are ready to welcome and support them. We believe that the specialist sector has a responsibility to support and empower SEND adults in the same way we strive to enable our learners. Increasing the number of staff with additional needs and disabilities can have significant benefits for learners. Research by Crompton et al. (2020) found that communication and information sharing within groups of autistic individuals was highly effective, more so than in mixed autistic and neurotypical groups. They also found that autistic individuals may prefer, and benefit from, the company of other autistic individuals over neurotypical individuals. This suggests that autistic teachers teaching autistic children could be a highly effective combination.

Our organisation has seen an increase in applications from neurodivergent staff over the last few years. At interview, many of these candidates said that they wanted to improve opportunities for young people with SEND, having had negative school experiences themselves. Some of these individuals have found it difficult to find or maintain employment due to the reluctance of some employers to make reasonable adjustments. Here are some of things we've learned and implemented as we strive to become a neuro-inclusive employer:

- We have more staff with additional needs and disabilities than we thought, all of whom have different needs requiring understanding and personalisation.
- School environments are busy and can trigger sensory overload – even a staffroom can be too noisy. Consequently, we've established different staff spaces, including a quiet room.
- We've reviewed our school approach to communication, using video briefings more often to reduce tone ambiguous emails.
- We enable staff to join whole – school events virtually or in smaller groups, as a staff body of 150 in one place can be overwhelming.
- We have a short break between the end of the day and the start of afterschool meetings. This allows some time for staff to decompress.
- We have a neurodivergent staff steering group to offer guidance and lived experience.
- We've reviewed our recruitment processes to ensure they are inclusive. For example, by sharing interview questions in advance and providing quiet spaces for breaks.
- We have launched a Neurodiversity Network for Wiltshire as part of our commitment to being ambassadors for the neurodivergent community. This is usually offered completely free to anyone in the community.

What we're going to do next:

- Consider further adjustments to recruitment processes e.g. enabling applicants to record presentations in advance, positioning the panel side-on during interviews, providing guidance on what candidates should wear.
- Reflect more on career progression for staff with additional needs and disabilities and the support they require to be leaders - which may mean rethinking the neurotypical lens through which we currently view leadership.
- Actively ask candidates before interview if we need to make any reasonable adjustments. This is because they might not feel confident disclosing on an application form.
- Explore introducing well being action plans or One Page Profiles that help colleagues understand how an individual might present (particularly during times of crisis or overload) and what would support them.
- Explicitly mention in job adverts that we are open to and encourage applications from candidates with additional needs or disabilities.

Consequently, seeing adults with additional needs and disabilities in our settings matters. Representation shapes culture and shows staff and learners what's possible. When educators with SEND are visible in classrooms, leadership teams, and educational communities, they become role models, inspiring confidence and helping create organisations that value difference. As specialist provisions, we champion our young people with SEND and this shouldn't stop when they leave the school gates. Supporting adults with additional needs and disabilities to flourish in the workplace is a natural continuation of our core purpose and something we're happy to embrace. The questions below encourage you to think about representation in your workplace.

Thinking points

- How well does your setting model inclusive practices for staff?
- What adjustments do you make for staff with additional needs and disabilities and what more could you do to create inclusive spaces?
- In what ways could increasing the number of staff with SEND enrich the experiences and outcomes of your learners?
- How can you use staff networks, steering groups, and peer advocacy to ensure staff with SEND shape your organisation?
- What role can your setting play in influencing others to become more inclusive employers?

From reading to leading

This book has been shaped by the voices, experiences, and generosity of many people, and we're grateful to everyone who has contributed. Collectively, you've helped us to capture what it means to lead specialist and alternative provisions.

Thank you also to our contributors with SEND - your lived experience is paramount. It reminds us to see education through the eyes of our learners and to make the world a better place for them.

And to you, our reader. Writing a book is a humbling experience - you never know if your words will resonate or if anyone will take the time to read them, so if you've reached this final page then well done too! The pace of education is relentless and making time to read is an achievement in itself - thank you for spending some of your valuable time with us. We hope you leave with increased knowledge and confidence, but more importantly a renewed commitment to championing the children, families, and staff within our sector. The future of specialist and alternative education depends on leaders like you who are ready to step forward; and, remember, you're not alone - there's a whole community of specialist leaders alongside you.

We hope this book has made you think differently about the specialist and alternative sector and inspired you to go from reading to leading. So, lead well, lead wisely and go and lead a sensational SEND provision.

Chapter summary

The conclusion considers the key issues shaping the future of the specialist sector. It reflects on both the opportunities and challenges facing specialist provision, and what is required to effectively meet the needs of children and staff.

- The rise of Artificial Intelligence has the potential to reduce teacher and leader workload.
- Artificial Intelligence can support educators' professional development through personalised coaching and making research more accessible.
- Assistive technology can support learners with SEND both in the classroom and beyond it.
- Employees have the legal right to request flexible working and this is becoming increasingly popular amongst young workers.
- Flexible working can support the recruitment and retention of your staff team.
- Co-headship models may encourage more Deputy and Assistant Headteachers to aspire for headship.
- Strategic SEND leadership roles are becoming more common in Multi-academy Trusts, providing further career progression for experienced SEND leaders.
- Supporting adults with additional needs and disabilities into the workplace can have significant benefits for learners.

Further reading

- If you're interested in the rise of AI, then Lomas and Baker (2025) look specifically at how AI could support autistic learners, and Anna Chatwin (2025) explores how generative AI can support inclusive and adaptive teaching.
- If you're interested in becoming a neuro-inclusive employer, then you might like to explore the Autistic School Staff Project led by Dr Rebecca Wood (https://autisticschoolstaffproject.com/). You can also read their book, *Learning from Autistic Teachers: How to be a Neurodiversity Inclusive School* (2022).

References

Bainbridge, L. (1983). 'Ironies of automation'. *Automatica, 19*(6), 775–779.

Barber, S., and Boyle, M. (2026, 10 April). 'Working from home statistics: How many people work from home?' Finder.com. Available online at: https://www.finder.com/uk/savings-accounts/working-from-home-statistics [accessed 2 May 2026].

British Educational Suppliers Association (BESA) (2023). *Key UK Education Statistics*. Available online at: https://www.besa.org.uk/insights/education-statistics/ [accessed 28 July 2025].

Branicki, L., Brammer, S., Brosnan, M., Garcia-Lazaro, A., Lattanzio, S., and Newnes, L. (2024). 'Factors shaping the employment outcomes of neurodivergent and neurotypical people: Exploring the role of flexible and homeworking practices'. *Human Resource Management, 63*(6), 1001–1023.

Camilleri, T., Rockey, S., and Dunbar, R. (2024). *The Social Brain: The Psychology of Successful Groups*. London: Penguin.

Chantler-Hicks, L. (2025, 2 October). '1 in 3 secondary heads leave within three years'. *Schools Week*. Available online at: https://schoolsweek.co.uk/retention-1-in-3-secondary-heads-leave-within-three-years/ [accessed 26 April 2026].

Chatwin, A. (2025). 'Inclusive education in the age of AI: Adaptive teaching strategies using ChatGPT'. *Impact*. Part of My College, Chartered College of Teaching. Available online at: https://my.chartered.college/impact_article/inclusive-education-in-the-age-of-ai-adaptive-teaching-strategies-using-chatgpt/ [accessed 12 August 2025].

Clark, D. (2025). 'Share of people working remotely, hybrid working, or at work in the UK 2020–2025'. *Statista*. Available online at: https://www.statista.com/statistics/1207746/coronavirus-working-location-trends-britain/ [accessed 27 April 2025].

Confederation of School Trusts and Edurio (2024). *National School Trust Report: September 2024*. [online] CST and Edurio. Available online at: https://my.cstuk.org.uk/resources/national-school-trust-report-2024 [accessed 28 July 2025].

Crompton, C. J., Ropar, D., Evans-Williams, C. V., Flynn, E.G., and Fletcher-Watson, S. (2020). 'Autistic peer-to-peer information transfer is highly effective'. *Autism, 24*(7), 1704–1712.

Department for Education (2025). *Working Lives of Teachers and Leaders: Wave 4 Summary Report*. London: Department for Education. Available online at: https://assets.publishing.service.gov.uk/media/693bdc426a12691d48491e9b/Working_lives_of_teachers_and_leaders_wave_4_summary_report.pdf [accessed 18 May 2026].

Department for Education (2026a). *Flexible Working in Schools*. Guidance. Available online at: https://www.gov.uk/government/publications/flexible-working-in-schools/flexible-working-in-schools-2 [accessed 2 May 2026].

Department for Education (2026b). *Every child achieving and thriving* (CP 1508-I; ISBN 978-1-5286-6032-7). GOV.UK. Available online at: https://www.gov.uk/government/publications/every-child-achieving-and-thriving/every-child-achieving-and-thriving-html-version [accessed 2 May 2026].

Deloitte (2025). *Gen Z and Millennial Survey, 2025*. Available online at: https://www.deloitte.com/content/dam/assets-shared/docs/campaigns/2025/2025-genz-millennial-survey.pdf [accessed 22 April 2026].

Education Endowment Foundation (EEF) (2026). *Teacher Choices: Nine-Day Working Fortnight*. Available online at: https://educationendowmentfoundation.org.uk/projects-and-evaluation/projects/teacher-choices-ndwf [accessed 26 April 2026].

Flemons, L., and Walker, M. (2024). *The MAT Factor: Exploring How Multi-academy Trusts are Supporting Pupils with SEND*. Slough: NFER.

Harland, J., Bradley, E., and Worth, J. (2023). *Understanding the Factors That Support the Recruitment and Retention of Teachers – Review of Flexible Working Approaches'*. Available online at: https://d2tic4wvo1iusb.cloudfront.net/production/documents/projects/Review-of-flexible-working-approaches.pdf?v=1745772088 [accessed 27 April 2025].

Heraclitus (c. 500 BCE). Fragment DK 22B12, quoted in Plato's *Cratylus* (401d) (C. D. C. Reeve, Trans.). In Plato, *Cratylus* (pp. xx). Hackett Publishing. Paraphrase of: 'All things move, and nothing remains'.

Lomas, C., and Baker, G. (2025). 'Utilising AI and emerging technologies to support learners with autism'. *Impact*. Part of My College, Chartered College of Teaching. Available online at: https://my.chartered.college/impact_article/utilising-ai-and-emerging-technologies-to-support-learners-with-autism/ [accessed 12 August 2025].

Lucas, R. (2025, 16 July). 'New "digital divide" emerges as private schools "forge ahead" on AI'. *Schools Week*. Available online at: https://schoolsweek.co.uk/new-digital-divide-emerges-as-private-schools-forge-ahead-on-ai/ [accessed 14 August 2025].

Ng, E. (2024, 21 December). 'Teachers in the UK should be permitted to work from home – Education Secretary'. *The Independent*. Available online at: https://www.independent.co.uk/news/uk/teachers-bridget-phillipson-education-secretary-government-english-b2668463.html [accessed 28 October 2025].

Office for National Statistics (2026). 'Number of people in employment (aged 16 and over, seasonally adjusted): 000s'. Series ID: MGRZ. ONS. Available online at: https://www.ons.gov.uk/employmentandlabourmarket/peopleinwork/employmentandemployeetypes/timeseries/mgrz/lms [accessed 2 May 2026].

Statista (2026). 'Number of employees in flexible working contracts in the United Kingdom in 2025, by type of contract'. *Statista*. Available online at: https://www.statista.com/statistics/415888/number-of-employees-flexible-working-contracts-uk-by-type/ [accessed 2 May 2026].

Teacher Tapp, and SchoolDash (2025). *Teacher Recruitment and Retention in 2025* (Gatsby Foundation). Available online at: https://teachertapp.com/content/uploads/2025/04/RELEASED_Teacher-Recruitment-and-Retention-in-2025.pdf [accessed 2 May 2026].

UK Parliament (2024, 20 December). 'Solving the SEND crisis – Education Committee launches major Inquiry'. Available online at: https://committees.parliament.uk/committee/203/education-committee/news/204487/solving-the-send-crisis-education-committee-launches-major-inquiry/ [accessed 2 May 2026].

Watkins, C. (2024, 15 May). 'Are two heads better than one? Co-headship and sharing the load'. *Twinkl Leader's Digest*. Available online at: https://www.twinkl.co.in/news/are-two-heads-better-than-one-co-headship-and-sharing-the-load [accessed 28 August 2025].

Weale, S. (2022, 26 April). ' School leader retention rates in England declining, DfE data shows'. *The Guardian*. Available online at: https://www.theguardian.com/education/2022/apr/26/school-leader-retention-rates-in-england-declining-dfe-data-shows [accessed 28 August 2025].

Wood, R. et al. (2019). *Autistic School Staff Project*. [online] Autistic School Staff Project. Available at: https://autisticschoolstaffproject.com/ [accessed 28 July 2025].

Wood, R. (ed.). (2022). *Learning from Autistic Teachers: Neurodiversity in the Inclusive School*. London: Routledge.

INDEX

D

E

For Product Safety Concerns and Information please contact our EU
representative GPSR@taylorandfrancis.com
Taylor & Francis Verlag GmbH, Kaufingerstraße 24, 80331 München, Germany

www.ingramcontent.com/pod-product-compliance
Lightning Source LLC
LaVergne TN
LVHW081115160826
845780LV00029B/245

* 9 7 8 1 0 3 2 9 8 9 1 7 4 *